P9-DBJ-727

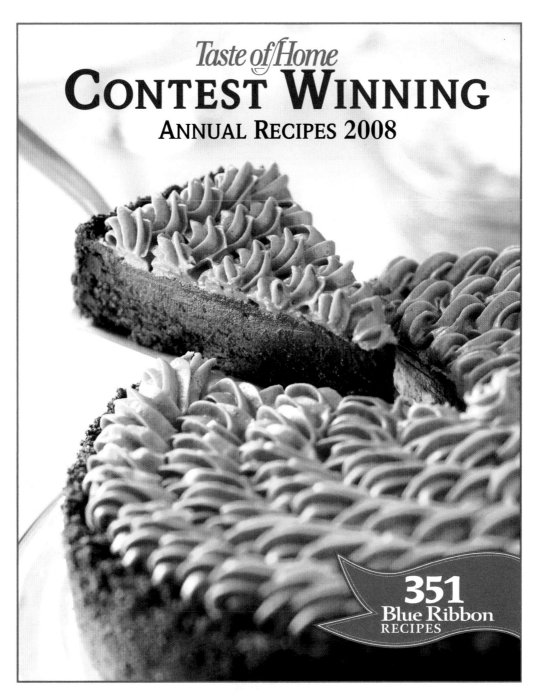

Taste of Home

CONTEST WINNING
ANNUAL RECIPES 2008

351
Blue Ribbon
RECIPES

Taste of Home
B O O K S

Taste of Home
CONTEST WINNING
ANNUAL RECIPES 2008

THE READER'S DIGEST ASSOCIATION, INC.
President and Chief Executive Officer: Mary G. Berner
President, RDA Food & Entertaining: Suzanne M. Grimes

CONTEST WINNING ANNUAL RECIPES 2008
Senior Vice President, Editor in Chief: Catherine Cassidy
Vice President, Executive Editor/Books: Heidi Reuter Lloyd
Creative Director: Ardyth Cope
Editor: Michelle Bretl
Art Director: Gretchen Trautman
Senior Editor/Books: Mark Hagen
Content Production Supervisor: Julie Wagner
Layout Designers: Kathy Crawford, Catherine Fletcher, Kathleen Bump
Proofreader: Linne Bruskewitz
Editorial Assistant: Barb Czysz

Food Director: Diane Werner RD
Test Kitchen Manager: Karen Scales
Recipe Editors: Sue A. Jurack (Senior), Mary King, Christine Rukavena
Recipe Asset System Manager: Coleen Martin
Photographers: Rob Hagen (Senior), Dan Roberts, Jim Wieland, Lori Foy
Food Stylists: Sarah Thompson (Senior), Tamara Kaufman, Julie Herzfeldt
Assistant Food Stylists: Kaitlyn Besasie, Alynna Malson, Shannon Roum, Leah Rekau
Set Stylists: Jenny Bradley Vent (Senior), Stephanie Marchese (Senior), Melissa Haberman, Dee Dee Jacq
Photo Studio Coordinator: Kathy Swaney

Chief Marketing Officer: Lisa Karpinski
Vice President/Book Marketing: Robert Graham Botta
Creative Director/Creative Marketing: James Palmen

Taste of Home Books
© 2008 Reiman Media Group, Inc.
5400 S. 60th St., Greendale WI 53129
International Standard Book Number (10): 0-89821-686-9
International Standard Book Number (13): 978-0-89821-686-8
International Standard Serial Number: 1548-4157

PICTURED ON FRONT COVER:
Chocolate Velvet Dessert (p. 211). Photography by Jim Wieland. Food styled by Julie Herzfeldt. Set styled by Jenny Bradley Vent.

For other *Taste of Home* books and products, visit **www.ShopTasteofHome.com**.

Table of Contents

Italian Red Pepper Bruschetta, p. 8

Vegetable Oven Pancake, p. 72

Cranberry Sweet Potato Bake, p. 143

Orange-Hazelnut Spiral Rolls, p. 156

Strawberry Cheesecake Torte, p. 191

351 Winners from National Recipe Contests— All Here in One Convenient Cookbook!

WHEN all of the recipes in a cookbook have been honored in a national contest, you can rest assured that every single one is exceptional. That's why the first four editions of *Contest Winning Annual Recipes* have proven so popular with cooks from across the country...and why they asked for a fifth!

Contest Winning Annual Recipes 2008 is jam-packed with 351 delicious, reader-submitted specialties that stood out from the culinary crowd. Each memorable dish was a prize winner in either *Taste of Home* magazine or one of its sister publications—*Quick Cooking, Light & Tasty, Country* and *Country Woman*. That's the best from five different publications in one big cookbook!

These 351 sensational recipes, all tested by experts, include an entire year's worth of winners. It's a can't-miss collection that's truly the "cream of the crop."

Wondering how a recipe becomes a prize winner? First, home cooks read our request for contest entries and send in their all-time best—the must-have dishes family and friends ask for again and again.

Then our expert home economists sort through the many recipes we receive and test the most promising ones. They prepare the top choices for our judging panel, which includes experienced food editors and home economists. After much sampling (yum!), the judges pick a grand prize winner and runners-up.

Winners from Dozens of Contests

The contests spotlighted in this cookbook cover a wide range of recipes—snacks and beverages; special salads; soups and stews; main courses; side dishes and condiments; breads and rolls; cookies, bars and candy; cakes and pies; and delectable desserts. No matter what type of recipe you're looking for, you're sure to find it in this one-of-a-kind collection.

For a complete list of chapters, please see the Table of Contents on page 3. Here's a quick summary of the year's worth of contests in this book and the top prize winner of each category:

- **Bountiful Buffet:** Guests will line up in a hurry when the Grand Prize winner, luscious Chocolate Velvet Dessert (p. 211), is on your buffet table.
- **Great Coffee Cakes:** Wake up the whole gang with yummy Raspberry Streusel Coffee Cake (p. 73) for breakfast...and enjoy the extras as a snack later!
- **Cherry Best:** With a steaming mug of coffee, tea or hot chocolate, buttery Cherry Chip Scones (p. 157) taste like a special indulgence.
- **Picnics and Potlucks:** Your family and friends are sure to snatch up every finger-licking piece of cheesy, oven-fried Parmesan Chicken (p. 109).
- **Onions and Garlic:** Dip into first-place Onion Beef Au Jus (p. 115)—hot open-faced sandwiches served with plenty of tangy broth on the side.
- **Wings and Drums:** A lip-smacking sauce makes sweet-and-sour Tempura Chicken Wings (p. 13) perfect for sports events, birthday parties...anytime!
- **Speedy Soups:** In less than half an hour, you can simmer up a big pot of meaty Italian Peasant Soup (p. 53) and warm your family heart and soul.

Hearty Chili Mac, p. 66

Pork with Pineapple Salsa, p. 105

- **Crunched-for-Time Casseroles:** Cheese-topped Taco Lasagna (p. 93) puts popular taco ingredients in the oven for a crowd-pleasing meal every time.

- **Glorious Grilling:** Fire up for spectacular fresh-air fare—individual Chicken Pizza Packets (p. 101) loaded with mozzarella, pepperoni and veggies.

- **Timely Trimmed-Down Dishes:** For fantastic flavor without all of the fat and calories, dig into succulent Pork with Pineapple Salsa (p. 105).

- **Time-Saving Sandwiches:** If you're a fan of sandwiches, you won't want to miss oven-baked Pizza Loaf (p. 133), the delicious Grand Prize winner.

- **Fast Freezer Desserts:** Feeling too rushed to make a sweet treat? Keep your cool by preparing Macadamia Berry Dessert (p. 223) ahead of time.

- **Crazy About Cupcakes:** With a unique topping, Cream-Filled Pumpkin Cupcakes (p. 205) look too special to eat...but you won't be able to resist!

- **Extraordinary Eggs:** Roll out hearty Italian Sausage Strata (p. 81) for your next breakfast and start the day in a mouth-watering way.

- **Going Bananas:** You'll get bunches of recipe requests when you serve the delectable first-place finisher, Chocolate Chip Banana Cream Pie (p. 201).

- **Cornucopia of Corn:** The pick of this contest crop was Corn Medley Salad (p. 33), chock-full of red pepper, onion and other garden-fresh veggies.

- **Great Ground Beef:** This ever-popular ingredient can easily turn into a family-pleasing entree—tangy Picante Cranberry Meatballs (p. 119).

- **Presents from the Pantry:** Need a great Christmas gift? Simply pack a batch of Chunky Peanut Brittle (p. 175) in a festive holiday tin.

- **Trim and Tasty Appetizers:** Served in a fun bread bowl, oven-baked Beef 'n' Cheese Dip (p. 9) is sure to tide over your guests before dinner.

- **Classic Light Cakes:** Strawberry Cheesecake Torte (p. 191) will amaze everyone who samples it. They'll have a hard time believing it's light!

- **Pasta Pleasers:** Combine oodles of noodles with Southwestern spices in Taco Twist Soup (p. 67) for a can't-miss main course.

- **Superb Herb Recipes:** When you're ready for a change of pace at dinnertime, liven things up with the top recipe, Honey Rosemary Chicken (p. 129).

- **Spinach Sensations:** Kids and adults alike will grab a second slice of Four-Cheese Spinach Pizza (p. 17), a taste-tempting meatless pie.

- **Pared-Down Pork:** Try delicious Pork Loin with Currant Sauce (p. 125) as the main course for a holiday dinner or other special occasion.

Starting to work up an appetite? Just pick any of the celebrated dishes you see showcased in *Contest Winning Annual Recipes 2008*. No matter which one you choose, you're guaranteed to have a winner!

Cream Cheese Swirl Brownies, p. 179

Raspberry Mint Cooler, p. 18

Crab-Filled Veggie Bites, p. 16

Italian Red Pepper Bruschetta, p. 8

Snacks & Beverages

Looking for special hors d'oeurves to serve at a party? Want after-school munchies to tide over the kids before dinner? No matter what kind of appetizer or thirst-quencher you need, you'll find a wide variety here.

Deviled Ham Stuffed Eggs, p. 8

1 loaf (1 pound) unsliced Italian bread
3 garlic cloves, minced, *divided*
3 tablespoons olive oil, *divided*
2 large sweet red peppers, chopped
1 medium onion, chopped
1-1/2 teaspoons Italian seasoning
2 tablespoons plus 1/4 cup coarsely chopped fresh basil, *divided*
2 tablespoons minced fresh parsley
1 tablespoon minced fresh oregano
6 plum tomatoes, sliced
3/4 cup shredded part-skim mozzarella cheese
3 slices reduced-fat provolone cheese, julienned
1/4 cup shredded Parmesan cheese

1. Cut bread in half lengthwise; place on a baking sheet. In a nonstick skillet, saute 2 garlic cloves in 2 tablespoons oil until tender. Brush over cut side of bread.

2. In the same skillet, saute the red peppers, onion, Italian seasoning and remaining garlic in remaining oil until vegetables are tender; remove from the heat. Add 2 tablespoons basil, parsley and oregano; cool slightly. Place in a blender or food processor; cover and process until pureed. Spread over bread.

3. Top with tomato slices and cheese. Sprinkle with remaining basil. Bake at 400° for 10-13 minutes or until cheese is melted and edges are golden brown. **Yield:** 12 servings.

🎗🎗🎗

Italian Red Pepper Bruschetta

(Also pictured on page 6)
Prep/Total Time: 30 min.

Josephine Devereaux Piro, Easton, Pennsylvania

To make this easy appetizer, I top Italian bread with fresh basil, oregano and garlic, plus red peppers, tomatoes and cheeses.

🎗🎗🎗

Deviled Ham Stuffed Eggs

(Also pictured on page 7)
Prep: 15 min. + chilling

Margaret Walker, Pace, Florida

I make these stuffed eggs once a month for a fellowship meal at church, and I've yet to bring one back home!

8 hard-cooked eggs
1/4 cup deviled ham spread
1/4 cup finely chopped green onions
1/4 cup sweet pickle relish
1/3 cup finely chopped celery
1/3 cup mayonnaise
1 teaspoon prepared mustard
1/8 teaspoon salt
1/8 teaspoon pepper
Paprika

Slice eggs in half lengthwise; remove yolks and set whites aside. In a small bowl, mash yolks with a fork. Add the next eight ingredients; mix well. Stuff or pipe into egg whites. Refrigerate until serving. Sprinkle with paprika. **Yield:** 8 servings.

Beef 'n' Cheese Dip

Prep: 10 min. **Bake:** 1 hour

Heather Melnick, Macedon, New York

I combined two of my favorite recipes to create a hearty dip baked in a bread shell. Reduced-fat and fat-free ingredients lighten up this snack a bit.

- 1 package (8 ounces) reduced-fat cream cheese
- 1-1/2 cups (6 ounces) shredded reduced-fat cheddar cheese
- 1/2 cup fat-free sour cream
- 2 packages (2-1/2 ounces *each*) thinly sliced dried beef
- 1/2 cup chopped green onions
- 1/2 cup mild pepper rings, drained and chopped
- 2 teaspoons Worcestershire sauce
- 1 loaf (1 pound) unsliced round rye bread
- Assorted fresh vegetables

1. For the dip, in a mixing bowl, combine the cream cheese, cheddar cheese and sour cream. Stir in the dried beef, green onions, peppers and Worcestershire sauce.

2. Cut the top fourth off the loaf of bread; carefully hollow out the bottom, leaving a 1-in. shell. Cube removed bread and top of loaf; set aside. Fill bread shell with beef mixture. Wrap in foil; place on a baking sheet.

3. Bake at 350° for 60-70 minutes or until heated through. Serve with vegetables and reserved bread cubes. **Yield:** 3 cups.

Editor's Note: Mild pepper rings come in jars and can be found in the pickle and olive aisle of most grocery stores.

3 tablespoons finely chopped onion
1 to 2 jalapeno peppers, seeded and finely
   chopped
2 teaspoons minced garlic, *divided*
2 teaspoons Liquid Smoke, optional, *divided*
1/4 teaspoon salt
15 whole chicken wings (about 3 pounds)
1 small onion, sliced
1 cup water

1. In a small bowl, combine the barbecue sauce, jam, chopped onion, peppers, 1 teaspoon garlic, 1 teaspoon Liquid Smoke if desired and salt; mix well. Cover and refrigerate for at least 2 hours.

2. Cut wings into three sections; discard wing tip section. Place the wings in a greased 15-in. x 10-in. x 1-in. baking pan. Top with sliced onion and remaining garlic. Combine the water and remaining Liquid Smoke if desired; pour over wings. Cover and bake at 350° for 30 minutes or until chicken juices run clear.

3. Transfer wings to a greased broiler pan; brush with sauce. Broil 4-6 in. from the heat for 20-25 minutes, turning and basting every 5 minutes or until wings are well coated. **Yield:** 2-1/2 dozen.

Editor's Note: 3 pounds of uncooked chicken wing sections (wingettes) may be substituted for the whole chicken wings. Omit cutting wings and discarding tips. When cutting or seeding hot peppers, use rubber or plastic gloves to protect your hands. Avoid touching your face.

Raspberry Barbecue Wings

Prep: 15 min. + chilling **Bake:** 50 min.

Sandra Fisher, Missoula, Montana

I came up with this recipe when I got tired of the same old wings. These are baked with onion and garlic, then broiled and basted with a mixture of jam, barbecue sauce and jalapenos. The sauce is excellent on pork and is great for dipping, too.

2/3 cup barbecue sauce
2/3 cup seedless raspberry jam

Southern Spiced Pecans

Prep: 10 min. **Bake:** 25 min.

Carol Feaver, Marion, Ohio

Pop a few of these tasty pecans in your mouth, and you'll immediately want more! A mix of salty and sweet, the nuts are seasoned with cumin, cayenne, sugar and salt. They make a great hostess gift, too.

1/2 cup butter, cubed
1-1/2 teaspoons ground cumin
1/4 teaspoon cayenne pepper
3 cups pecan halves
2 tablespoons sugar
1 teaspoon salt

1. In a large skillet, melt butter. Add cumin and cayenne; cook and stir for 1 minute. Remove from the heat; stir in pecans, sugar and salt; toss to coat.

2. Spread in a single layer in a greased 15-in. x 10-in. x 1-in. baking pan. Bake at 300° for 25-30 minutes or until lightly browned, stirring occasionally. Cool. Store in an airtight container. **Yield:** 3 cups.

🎗🎗🎗
Creamy Fruit Dip
Prep: 15 min. + chilling

Judith Reed, Kingsford, Michigan

After one taste of this delightful dip, your fruit tray won't seem complete without it. My family enjoys this lightened-up recipe just as much as full-fat varieties.

✓ Uses less fat, sugar or salt. Includes Nutrition Facts and Diabetic Exchange.

   1 package (8 ounces) fat-free cream cheese
3/4 cup packed brown sugar
   1 cup (8 ounces) reduced-fat sour cream
   2 teaspoons vanilla extract
   1 teaspoon lemon extract
1/2 teaspoon ground cinnamon
   1 cup cold 2% milk
   1 package (3.4 ounces) instant vanilla pudding mix
Assorted fresh fruit

1. In a small mixing bowl, beat the cream cheese and brown sugar until smooth. Beat in the sour cream, vanilla extract, lemon extract and cinnamon until smooth. Add milk; mix well.

2. Add pudding mix; beat on low speed for 2 minutes. Cover and refrigerate for at least 1 hour. Serve with fruit. **Yield:** about 3-1/2 cups.

Nutrition Facts: 1/4 cup equals 118 calories, 2 g fat (2 g saturated fat), 8 mg cholesterol, 211 mg sodium, 21 g carbohydrate, trace fiber, 4 g protein. **Diabetic Exchange:** 1-1/2 starch.

🎗🎗🎗
Jalapeno Chicken Wraps
Prep: 15 min. **Grill:** 20 min.

Leslie Buenz, Tinley Park, Illinois

These easy appetizers are always a hit at parties. Zesty strips of chicken and bits of onion sit in jalapeno halves that are wrapped in bacon and grilled. Serve them with blue cheese or ranch salad dressing for dipping.

   1 pound boneless skinless chicken breasts
   1 tablespoon garlic powder
   1 tablespoon onion powder
   1 tablespoon pepper
   2 teaspoons seasoned salt
   1 teaspoon paprika
   1 small onion, cut into strips
15 jalapeno peppers, halved and seeded
   1 pound sliced bacon, halved widthwise
Blue cheese salad dressing

1. Cut chicken into 2-in. x 1-1/2-in. strips. In a large resealable plastic bag, combine the garlic powder, onion powder, pepper, seasoned salt and paprika; add chicken and shake to coat. Place a chicken and onion strip in each jalapeno half. Wrap each with a piece of bacon and secure with toothpicks.

2. Grill, uncovered, over indirect medium heat for 18-20 minutes or until chicken juices run clear and bacon

is crisp, turning once. Serve with blue cheese dressing. **Yield:** 2-1/2 dozen.

Editor's Note: When cutting or seeding hot peppers, use rubber or plastic gloves to protect your hands. Avoid touching your face.

🎀🎀🎀
Honey-Glazed Wings
Prep: 20 min. + marinating **Bake:** 50 min.

Marlene Wahl, Baldwin, Wisconsin

My family prefers chicken wings that are mildly seasoned with honey, ginger, soy sauce and chili sauce. Tasty and tender, these crowd-pleasers are sure to be a hit at your next Super Bowl party, birthday bash or other get-together.

- 15 **whole chicken wings (about 3 pounds)**
- 1/2 **cup honey**
- 1/3 **cup soy sauce**
- 2 **tablespoons vegetable oil**
- 2 **tablespoons chili sauce**
- 2 **teaspoons salt**
- 1 **teaspoon garlic powder**
- 1 **teaspoon Worcestershire sauce**
- 1/2 **teaspoon ground ginger**

1. Cut chicken wings into three sections; discard wing tip section. Set wings aside. In a small saucepan, combine the honey, soy sauce, oil, chili sauce, salt, garlic powder, Worcestershire sauce and ginger. Cook and stir until blended and heated through. Cool to room temperature.

2. Place the chicken wings in a large resealable plastic bag; add honey mixture. Seal bag and turn to coat. Refrigerate for at least 8 hours or overnight.

3. Drain and discard marinade. Place wings in a well greased 15-in. x 10-in. x 1-in. baking pan. Bake, uncovered, at 375° for 30 minutes. Drain; turn wings. Bake 20-25 minutes longer or until chicken juices run clear and glaze is set. **Yield:** 2-1/2 dozen.

Editor's Note: 3 pounds of uncooked chicken wing sections (wingettes) may be substituted for the whole wings. Omit cutting wings and discarding tips.

🎀🎀🎀
Cheesy Beef Taco Dip
Prep/Total Time: 20 min.

Carol Smith, Sanford, North Carolina

For a warm, hearty snack with a bit of a kick, try this recipe. It's a hit with my family, and guests rave about it, too. Just add a basket of your favorite tortilla chips.

- 2 **pounds ground beef**
- 1 **large onion, finely chopped**
- 1 **medium green pepper, finely chopped**
- 1 **pound process cheese (Velveeta), cubed**
- 1 **pound pepper Jack cheese, cubed**
- 1 **jar (16 ounces) taco sauce**
- 1 **can (10 ounces) diced tomatoes and green chilies, drained**
- 1 **can (4 ounces) mushroom stems and pieces, drained and chopped**
- 1 **can (2-1/4 ounces) sliced ripe olives, drained**

Tortilla chips

In a large skillet, cook beef, onion and green pepper over medium heat until meat is no longer pink; drain. Stir in process cheese, pepper Jack cheese, taco sauce, tomatoes, mushrooms and olives. Cook and stir over low heat until cheese is melted. Serve warm with chips. **Yield:** 10 cups.

Warm for a While

Want to make sure your Cheesy Beef Taco Dip stays warm on the table during a party or other get-together? Just transfer the dip to a slow cooker and turn the heat setting to low.

Tempura Chicken Wings

Prep: 40 min. **Bake:** 25 min.

Susan Wuckowitsch, Lenexa, Kansas

When I moved to Kansas from Texas, I brought many of my mom's best-loved recipes with me...including these saucy sweet-and-sour wings everyone loves.

> 15 **whole chicken wings (about 3 pounds)**
> 1 **cup cornstarch**
> 3 **eggs, lightly beaten**
> **Oil for deep-fat frying**
> 1/2 **cup sugar**
> 1/2 **cup white vinegar**
> 1/2 **cup currant jelly**
> 1/4 **cup soy sauce**
> 3 **tablespoons ketchup**
> 2 **tablespoons lemon juice**

1. Cut the chicken wings into three sections; discard the wing tip section. Place cornstarch in a large resealable plastic bag; add chicken wings, a few at a time, and shake to coat evenly. Dip wings in eggs.

2. In an electric skillet or deep-fat fryer, heat oil to 375°. Fry wings for 8 minutes or until golden brown and juices run clear, turning occasionally. Drain on paper towels.

3. In a small saucepan, combine the sugar, vinegar, jelly, soy sauce, ketchup and lemon juice. Bring to a boil. Reduce heat; simmer, uncovered, for 10 minutes.

4. Place chicken wings in a greased 15-in. x 10-in. x 1-in. baking pan. Pour half of the sauce over wings. Bake, uncovered, at 350° for 15 minutes. Turn wings; top with remaining sauce. Bake 10-15 minutes longer or until chicken juices run clear and coating is set. **Yield:** 2-1/2 dozen.

Editor's Note: 3 pounds of uncooked chicken wing sections (wingettes) may be substituted for the whole chicken wings. Omit cutting wings and discarding tips.

Grand Prize Winner

Warm Bacon Cheese Spread

Prep: 15 min. **Bake:** 1 hour

Nicole Marcotte, Smithers, British Columbia

My friends threaten not to come by unless this dip is on the menu! The rich spread bakes right in a bread bowl.

> 1 round loaf (1 pound) sourdough bread
> 1 package (8 ounces) cream cheese, softened
> 1-1/2 cups (12 ounces) sour cream
> 2 cups (8 ounces) shredded cheddar cheese
> 1-1/2 teaspoons Worcestershire sauce
> 3/4 pound sliced bacon, cooked and crumbled
> 1/2 cup chopped green onions

Assorted crackers

1. Cut the top fourth off the loaf of bread; carefully hollow out the bottom, leaving a 1-in. shell. Cut the removed bread and top of loaf into cubes; set aside.

2. In a mixing bowl, beat the cream cheese. Add the sour cream, cheddar cheese and Worcestershire sauce until combined; stir in bacon and onions. Spoon into bread shell. Wrap in a piece of heavy-duty foil (about 24 in. x 17 in.). Bake at 325° for 1 hour or until heated through. Serve with crackers and reserved bread cubes. **Yield:** 4 cups.

Mediterranean Salsa

Prep: 15 min. **Cook:** 15 min. + chilling

Margaret Potempa, Oshkosh, Wisconsin

When entertaining, I rely on this make-ahead salsa that's full of peppers, eggplant and zucchini. Low in sodium, it gets its delicious flair from garlic, basil and thyme.

✓ Uses less fat, sugar or salt. Includes Nutrition Facts and Diabetic Exchanges.

> 2 cups cubed peeled eggplant (1/2-inch cubes)
> 1 cup cubed sweet red pepper (1/2-inch cubes)
> 1 cup cubed green pepper (1/2-inch cubes)
> 1 cup cubed zucchini (1/2-inch cubes)
> 3 garlic cloves, minced
> 2 tablespoons olive oil
> 1 large tomato, cut into 1/2-inch cubes
> 2 tablespoons cider vinegar
> 1 tablespoon dried basil
> 1 teaspoon dried thyme
> 1/2 teaspoon sugar
> 1/2 teaspoon salt
> 1/4 to 1/2 teaspoon coarsely ground pepper

Toasted bread rounds

In a large nonstick skillet, saute the eggplant, peppers, zucchini and garlic in oil for 8 minutes. Add the tomato, vinegar, basil, thyme, sugar, salt and pepper. Cook 4-5 minutes longer or until vegetables are tender. Cover and refrigerate for at least 4 hours. Serve with toasted bread. **Yield:** about 2-1/2 cups.

Nutrition Facts: 1/4 cup equals 45 calories, 3 g fat (trace saturated fat), 0 cholesterol, 121 mg sodium, 5 g carbohydrate, 1 g fiber, 1 g protein. **Diabetic Exchanges:** 1 vegetable, 1/2 fat.

🎖🎖🎖
Sesame Chicken Bites

Prep/Total Time: 30 min.

Kathy Green, Layton, New Jersey

So tender and tasty, these chicken appetizers are enhanced by a honey-mustard dipping sauce. I used to spend several days creating hors d'oeuvres for our holiday open house, and these bites were among the favorites.

- 1/2 cup dry bread crumbs
- 1/4 cup sesame seeds
- 2 teaspoons minced fresh parsley
- 1/2 cup mayonnaise
- 1 teaspoon onion powder
- 1 teaspoon ground mustard
- 1/4 teaspoon pepper
- 1 pound boneless skinless chicken breasts, cut into 1-inch cubes
- 2 to 4 tablespoons vegetable oil

HONEY-MUSTARD SAUCE:
- 3/4 cup mayonnaise
- 4-1/2 teaspoons honey
- 1-1/2 teaspoons Dijon mustard

1. In a large resealable plastic bag, combine crumbs, sesame seeds and parsley; set aside. In a small bowl, combine mayonnaise, onion powder, mustard and pepper. Coat chicken in mayonnaise mixture, then add to crumb mixture, a few pieces at a time; shake to coat.

2. In a large skillet, saute chicken in oil in batches until juices run clear, adding additional oil as needed. In a small bowl, combine sauce ingredients. Serve with the chicken. **Yield:** 8-10 servings.

🎖🎖🎖
Grilled Wing Zingers

Prep: 35 min. **Grill:** 35 min.

Angela Roster, Greenbackville, Virginia

My husband fine-tuned this recipe, and the results were spectacular! These spicy-hot chicken wings are true party pleasers.

- 40 whole chicken wings (about 8 pounds)
- 2 cups packed brown sugar
- 2 cups hot sauce
- 1/2 cup butter, cubed
- 2 tablespoons cider vinegar
- 1/3 cup sugar
- 1/2 cup Italian seasoning
- 1/4 cup dried rosemary, crushed
- 1/4 cup paprika
- 1/4 cup chili powder
- 1/4 cup pepper
- 2 tablespoons cayenne pepper
- 1 cup blue cheese salad dressing
- 1/2 cup ranch salad dressing

Celery sticks

1. Cut wings into three sections; discard wing tip section. Set wings aside. In a saucepan, bring brown sugar, hot sauce, butter and vinegar to a boil. Reduce heat; simmer, uncovered, for 6-8 minutes or until butter is melted and sauce is heated through. Cool.

2. In a gallon-size resealable plastic bag, combine the sugar, seasonings and 1 cup sauce. Add chicken wings in batches; seal bag and toss to coat evenly.

3. Cover and grill wings over indirect medium heat for 35-45 minutes or until juices run clear, turning and basting occasionally with remaining sauce.

4. In a small bowl, combine blue cheese and ranch salad dressing; serve with chicken wings and celery sticks. **Yield:** about 6-1/2 dozen.

Editor's Note: 8 pounds of uncooked chicken wing sections (wingettes) may be substituted for the whole wings. Omit cutting wings and discarding tips.

Crab-Filled Veggie Bites

(Also pictured on page 6)

Prep: 20 min. + chilling

Debbie Bloomer, Omaha, Nebraska

Whenever I'm invited to a party, people ask me to bring these. The crab filling is also good as a cracker spread.

12 **cherry tomatoes**
12 **fresh snow peas**
1 **can (6 ounces) crabmeat, drained, flaked and cartilage removed *or* 1 cup finely chopped imitation crabmeat**
2 **tablespoons reduced-fat spreadable cream cheese**
1 **tablespoon finely chopped green onion**
2 **teaspoons reduced-fat sour cream**
2 **teaspoons chili sauce**
1 **teaspoon lemon juice**
1/2 **teaspoon prepared horseradish**

1. Cut a thin slice off the top of each tomato. Scoop out and discard pulp; invert tomatoes onto paper towels to drain.

2. Meanwhile, place snow peas in a small saucepan; add 1 in. of water. Bring to a boil. Reduce heat; cover and simmer for 1-2 minutes or until crisp-tender. Drain and immediately place peas in ice water. Drain and pat dry. With a sharp knife, split each pea pod along the curved edge.

3. In a small bowl, combine the remaining ingredients. Fill tomatoes and peas with crab mixture; arrange on a serving platter. Cover and refrigerate for at least 30 minutes before serving. **Yield:** 2 dozen.

Nutrition Facts: 1 appetizer equals 14 calories, trace fat (trace saturated fat), 7 mg cholesterol, 38 mg sodium, 1 g carbohydrate, trace fiber, 2 g protein.

Mexican Corn Dip

Prep: 15 min. + chilling

Laura Cameron, Delaware, Ohio

For a tasty dip you can make the day before, try this rave-winning recipe. Mildly spicy, it's easy to alter if you want it to have more of a kick. Make sure your corn chips are large enough to scoop up a hearty helping!

2 **cups (8 ounces) shredded cheddar cheese**
1 **can (11 ounces) yellow and white whole kernel corn, drained**
1 **can (11 ounces) Mexicorn, drained**
4 **ounces pepper Jack cheese, shredded**
1/4 **cup chopped green onions**
1 **can (4 ounces) chopped green chilies**
1 **jalapeno pepper, seeded and chopped**
3/4 **cup mayonnaise**
3/4 **cup sour cream**
1/8 **teaspoon sugar**
Additional chopped green onions, optional
Tortilla *or* corn chips

In a large bowl, combine the first seven ingredients. In a small bowl, combine the mayonnaise, sour cream and sugar; stir into corn mixture. Cover and refrigerate overnight. Sprinkle with additional green onions if desired. Serve with chips. **Yield:** 8-10 servings.

Editor's Note: When cutting or seeding hot peppers, use rubber or plastic gloves to protect your hands. Avoid touching your face.

Four-Cheese Spinach Pizza

Prep/Total Time: 30 min.

Barbara Robinson, Hamburg, Pennsylvania

I adapted this recipe from one given to me by my aunt. I especially like to make this unusual pizza in summer, when fresh spinach and basil are plentiful. They are key to the wonderful taste.

- **2 packages (10 ounces** *each***) fresh spinach**
- **3/4 cup shredded part-skim mozzarella cheese,** *divided*
- **1/2 cup fat-free cottage cheese**
- **1/3 cup grated Parmesan cheese**
- **1/4 teaspoon salt**
- **1/8 teaspoon pepper**
- **1 prebaked Italian bread shell crust (10 ounces)**
- **1 medium tomato, chopped**
- **1/4 cup chopped green onions**
- **1/4 cup sliced ripe olives**
- **1 teaspoon minced fresh basil**
- **1 teaspoon olive oil**
- **1 teaspoon balsamic vinegar**
- **1 garlic clove, minced**
- **1/2 cup crumbled feta cheese**

1. In a large nonstick skillet coated with cooking spray, saute the spinach for 2-3 minutes or until wilted; remove spinach from the skillet. Cool slightly; chop.

2. In a large bowl, combine 1/4 cup mozzarella cheese, cottage cheese and Parmesan cheese. Stir in the spinach, salt and pepper. Spread over crust to within 1/2 in. of edge.

3. In a large bowl, combine the tomato, onions, olives, basil, oil, vinegar and garlic; sprinkle over spinach mixture. Top with the feta cheese and remaining mozzarella cheese. Bake at 400° for 12-14 minutes or until cheese softens and is lightly browned. **Yield:** 6 servings.

🎗🎗🎗 Raspberry Mint Cooler

(Also pictured on page 6)

Prep: 15 min. + chilling Cook: 10 min.

Patty Kile, Greentown, Pennsylvania

This is a delightful punch to serve guests in the summer, when mint and raspberries are fresh.

> 9 cups water, *divided*
> 1 to 1-1/2 cups coarsely chopped fresh mint
> 1/2 cup sugar
> 3 packages (10 ounces *each*) frozen sweetened raspberries
> 2-1/4 cups lemonade concentrate, undiluted (18 ounces)
> Ice cubes

1. In a large saucepan, bring 3 cups water, mint and sugar to a boil. Reduce heat; simmer, uncovered, for 10-15 minutes. Stir in the raspberries, lemonade concentrate and remaining water. Refrigerate overnight.

2. Strain raspberry mixture, reserving the liquid. Press berries and mint through a sieve; discard seeds and mint. Combine raspberry juice with the reserved liquid. Serve over ice. **Yield:** 11 servings.

🎗🎗🎗 Party Cheese Balls

Prep: 20 min. + chilling

Shirley Hoerman, Nekoosa, Wisconsin

These tangy cheese balls are guaranteed to spread cheer. The ingredients create a colorful presentation and savory flavor.

> 1 package (8 ounces) cream cheese, softened
> 2 cups (8 ounces) shredded cheddar cheese
> 1 jar (5 ounces) sharp American cheese spread
> 1 jar (5 ounces) pimiento cheese spread
> 3 tablespoons finely chopped onion
> 1 tablespoon lemon juice
> 1 teaspoon Worcestershire sauce
> Dash garlic salt
> 1/2 cup chopped pecans, toasted
> 1/2 cup minced fresh parsley
> Assorted crackers

1. In a mixing bowl, combine the first eight ingredients; beat until blended. Cover and refrigerate for 15 minutes or until easy to handle.

2. Shape into two balls; roll one ball in pecans and one in parsley. Cover and refrigerate. Remove from the refrigerator 15 minutes before serving with crackers. **Yield:** 2 cheese balls (1-3/4 cups each).

Salmon Mousse Cups

Prep: 25 min. + chilling **Bake:** 10 min. + cooling

Fran Rowland, Phoenix, Arizona

I make these tempting tarts for parties. They disappear at an astonishing speed, so I usually double or triple the recipe. The salmon-cheese filling and flaky crust melt in your mouth.

1 package (3 ounces) cream cheese, softened
1/2 cup butter, softened
1 cup all-purpose flour
FILLING:
1 package (8 ounces) cream cheese, softened
1 cup fully cooked salmon chunks *or* 1 can (7-1/2 ounces) salmon, drained, bones and skin removed
2 tablespoons chicken broth
2 tablespoons sour cream
1 tablespoon finely chopped onion
1 teaspoon lemon juice
1/2 teaspoon salt
2 tablespoons minced fresh dill

1. In a small mixing bowl, beat the cream cheese and butter until smooth. Add flour; mix well. Shape into 24 balls; press onto the bottom and up the sides of greased miniature muffin cups. Bake at 350° for 10-15 minutes or until golden brown. Cool for 5 minutes before removing from the pans to wire racks to cool completely.

2. For filling, in a mixing bowl, beat the cream cheese until smooth. Add the salmon, broth, sour cream, onion, lemon juice and salt; mix well. Spoon into the shells. Refrigerate for at least 2 hours. Sprinkle with dill. **Yield:** 2 dozen.

Crispy Onion Wings

Prep: 15 min. **Bake:** 30 min.

Jonathan Hershey, Akron, Ohio

My wife, daughters and I often enjoy these buttery wings while watching TV. The crisp coating is also great on the chicken tenders I make from cut-up boneless chicken breasts.

12 whole chicken wings (about 2-1/2 pounds)
2-1/2 cups crushed potato chips
1 can (2.8 ounces) french-fried onions, crushed
1/2 cup cornmeal
2 teaspoons dried oregano
1 teaspoon onion salt
1 teaspoon garlic powder
1 teaspoon paprika
2 eggs, beaten
1/4 cup butter, melted

1. Line a 15-in. x 10-in. x 1-in. baking pan with foil and grease the foil; set aside. Cut chicken wings into three sections; discard wing tip section.

2. In a large resealable plastic bag, combine the chips, onions, cornmeal and seasonings; mix well. Dip the wings in eggs. Place in the bag, a few at a time; shake to coat and press crumb mixture into chicken.

3. Place wings in prepared pan; drizzle with butter. Bake, uncovered, at 375° for 30-35 minutes or until the chicken juices run clear and the coating is crisp. **Yield:** 2 dozen.

Editor's Note: 2-1/2 pounds of uncooked chicken wing sections (wingettes) may be substituted for the whole chicken wings. Omit cutting wings and discarding tips.

🎗🎗🎗 Garlic-Cheese Chicken Wings

Prep: 20 min. **Bake:** 1 hour 20 min. + cooling

Donna Pierce, Lady Lake, Florida

I developed this recipe several years ago using chicken breasts, then decided to try it on wings as an appetizer. It was a hit! If you like garlic, you're sure to enjoy these zesty bites.

- 2 large whole garlic bulbs
- 1 tablespoon plus 1/2 cup olive oil, *divided*
- 1/2 cup butter, melted
- 1 teaspoon hot pepper sauce
- 1-1/2 cups seasoned bread crumbs
- 3/4 cup grated Parmesan cheese
- 3/4 cup grated Romano cheese
- 1/2 teaspoon pepper
- 15 whole chicken wings (about 3 pounds)

1. Remove papery outer skin from garlic (do not peel or separate cloves). Cut top off garlic bulbs. Brush with 1 tablespoon oil. Wrap each bulb in heavy-duty foil. Bake at 425° for 30-35 minutes or until softened. Cool for 10-15 minutes.

2. Squeeze the softened garlic into a blender or food processor. Add butter, hot pepper sauce and remaining oil; cover and process until smooth. Pour into a shallow bowl. In another shallow bowl, combine the bread crumbs, cheeses and pepper.

3. Cut chicken wings into three sections; discard wing tip section. Dip chicken wings into the garlic mixture, then coat with crumb mixture. Place on a greased rack in a 15-in. x 10-in. x 1-in. baking pan; drizzle with any remaining garlic mixture. Bake, uncovered, at 350° for 50-55 minutes or until chicken juices run clear. **Yield:** 2-1/2 dozen.

Editor's Note: 3 pounds of uncooked chicken wing sections (wingettes) may be substituted for the whole chicken wings. Omit cutting wings and discarding tips.

🎗🎗🎗 Artichoke Mushroom Caps

Prep: 30 min. **Grill:** 10 min.

Ruth Lewis, West Newton, Pennsylvania

These crumb-topped appetizers are warm from the grill and never last long at our get-togethers. The rich filling of cream cheese, artichoke hearts, Parmesan cheese and green onion is terrific. If you prefer, you can broil the stuffed mushroom caps in your oven instead.

- 1 package (3 ounces) cream cheese, softened
- 1/4 cup mayonnaise
- 1 jar (6-1/2 ounces) marinated artichoke hearts, drained and finely chopped
- 1/4 cup grated Parmesan cheese
- 2 tablespoons finely chopped green onion
- 20 to 25 large fresh mushrooms, stems removed
- 1/4 cup seasoned bread crumbs
- 2 teaspoons olive oil

1. In a mixing bowl, beat the cream cheese and mayonnaise until smooth. Beat in the artichoke hearts, Parmesan cheese and green onion. Lightly spray the tops of the mushrooms with cooking spray. Spoon the cream cheese mixture into the mushroom caps. Combine the seasoned bread crumbs and oil; sprinkle over the stuffed mushroom caps.

2. Grill mushrooms, covered, over indirect medium heat for 8-10 minutes or until mushrooms are tender. **Yield:** about 2 dozen.

Bacon Ranch Dip

Prep: 5 min. + chilling

Pam Garwood, Lakeville, Minnesota

I used reduced-fat ingredients to lighten up this scrumptious Parmesan and bacon dip a bit. The proportions can easily be adjusted for smaller or larger groups.

- 1/2 cup reduced-fat mayonnaise
- 1/2 cup reduced-fat ranch salad dressing
- 1/2 cup fat-free sour cream
- 1/2 cup shredded Parmesan cheese
- 1/4 cup crumbled cooked bacon

Assorted fresh vegetables

In a bowl, combine the first five ingredients; mix well. Cover and refrigerate for at least 1 hour before serving. Serve with vegetables. **Yield:** 1-1/2 cups.

Honey Banana Punch

Prep: 15 min. + freezing

Patricia Stephens, Monticello, Kentucky

Here's a great punch recipe I got from a beekeeper's association. The mix of banana and citrus creates a light, sunny flavor.

- 2 cups frozen orange juice concentrate
- 5 ripe bananas, cut into chunks
- 1 can (46 ounces) pineapple juice
- 2 cups water
- 3/4 cup honey
- 1/2 cup sugar
- 1/3 cup sugar sweetened lemonade soft drink mix
- 4 liters lemon-lime soda, chilled

1. In a blender, combine juice concentrate and bananas; cover and process until smooth. Pour into a large bowl; add pineapple juice, water, honey, sugar and drink mix. Stir until sugar is dissolved. Pour into two 2-qt. freezer containers. Cover; freeze until slushy.

2. To serve, transfer each portion of fruit slush to a large pitcher. Add 2 liters of soda to each pitcher; stir to blend. **Yield:** 7-1/2 gallons (30 servings).

Nice Ice Cubes

To prevent punch from becoming watered down when you add ice cubes, just fill ice cube trays with extra punch instead of water.

🎀🎀🎀
Garlic-Onion Tomato Pizza

Prep: 30 min. + rising **Bake:** 15 min.

Tammy Thomas, Sheboygan, Wisconsin

You won't miss the traditional tomato sauce when you bite into a slice of this pizza—it is absolutely delicious! We like it hot or at room temperature. It makes a wonderful appetizer cut into small pieces...or you can use the same topping for bruschetta.

- 2 teaspoons cornmeal
- 2 packages (1/4 ounce *each*) active dry yeast
- 2 cups warm water (110° to 115°)
- 5 to 6 cups all-purpose flour
- 4 teaspoons plus 1 tablespoon olive oil, *divided*
- 1 teaspoon salt
- 2 medium sweet onions, thinly sliced
- 8 large garlic cloves, halved
- 6 to 8 plum tomatoes, cut lengthwise into eighths and seeded
- 2 tablespoons dried oregano
- 2 tablespoons dried parsley flakes

Pepper to taste

- 1-1/2 cups (6 ounces) shredded part-skim mozzarella cheese
- 1/4 cup grated Romano cheese

1. Sprinkle cornmeal evenly over two greased 14-in. pizza pans; set aside. In a bowl, dissolve yeast in water; add 4-1/2 cups flour, 4 teaspoons oil and salt; beat until smooth. Add enough remaining flour to form a soft dough.

2. Turn onto a floured surface; knead until smooth and elastic, about 6-8 minutes. Place in a greased bowl, turning once to grease top. Cover and let rise in a warm place until doubled, about 1 hour.

3. Punch dough down; divide in half. Press each portion into prepared pans. Prick dough with a fork. Bake at 450° for 4-5 minutes.

4. Broil onions and garlic in batches 3-4 in. from the heat until softened and lightly browned. Broil tomato slices for 2 minutes on each side. Finely chop garlic.

5. Arrange onions, garlic and tomatoes over crust. Sprinkle with oregano, parsley, pepper and cheeses; drizzle with remaining oil. Bake at 450° for 8-9 minutes or until cheese is melted. **Yield:** 2 pizzas (8 slices each).

🎖🎖🎖 Tangy Barbecue Wings

Prep: 1-1/2 hours **Cook:** 3 hours

Sherry Pitzer, Troy, Missouri

When I took these slow-cooked wings to work, they were gone before I got even a bite! The sauce is lip-smacking good.

      25 whole chicken wings (about 5 pounds)
2-1/2 cups hot and spicy ketchup
    2/3 cup white vinegar
    1/2 cup plus 2 tablespoons honey
    1/2 cup molasses
        1 teaspoon salt
        1 teaspoon Worcestershire sauce
    1/2 teaspoon onion powder
    1/2 teaspoon chili powder
    1/2 to 1 teaspoon Liquid Smoke, optional

1. Cut chicken wings into three sections; discard wing tip sections. Place chicken wings in two greased 15-in. x 10-in. x 1-in. baking pans. Bake, uncovered, at 375° for 30 minutes; drain. Turn wings; bake 20-25 minutes longer or until chicken juices run clear.

2. Meanwhile, in a large saucepan, combine the ketchup, vinegar, honey, molasses, salt, Worcestershire sauce, onion powder and chili powder. Add Liquid

Smoke if desired. Bring to a boil. Reduce heat; simmer, uncovered, for 25-30 minutes.

3. Drain wings; place a third of them in a 5-qt. slow cooker. Top with about 1 cup sauce. Repeat layers twice. Cover and cook on low for 3-4 hours. Stir before serving. **Yield:** about 4 dozen.

Editor's Note: 5 pounds of uncooked chicken wing sections (wingettes) may be substituted for the whole wings. Omit cutting wings and discarding tips.

🎖🎖🎖 Mint Cocoa Mix

Prep/Total Time: 5 min.

LaVonne Hegland, St. Michael, Minnesota

I've made this beverage mix many times as a Christmas gift for neighbors and our three sons' teachers. The mint flavor makes the warm drink wonderfully refreshing.

        1 package (30 ounces) instant chocolate drink mix
        1 package (25.6 ounces) nonfat dry milk powder
2-1/2 cups confectioners' sugar
        1 cup powdered nondairy creamer
      25 peppermint candies, crushed
ADDITIONAL INGREDIENT (for each serving):
        1 cup milk

In a large bowl, combine the first five ingredients; mix well. Store the cocoa mix in an airtight container in a cool dry place for up to 6 months. **Yield:** 53 servings (17-2/3 cups total).

To prepare hot drink: Warm milk; stir in 1/3 cup mix until dissolved. **Yield:** 1 serving.

Gift of Good Cheer

For a heartwarming Christmas gift, wrap up some of the cocoa mix in a decorated bag or jar and add the preparation directions. Pair the mix with a fun holiday mug or marshmallows.

⚜ ⚜ ⚜
Phyllo Turkey Egg Rolls

Prep: 30 min. **Bake:** 25 min.

Kara de la Vega, Suisun City, California

Here's a light twist on traditional egg rolls. Your guests will never guess that these tasty bites feature healthy ingredients.

✓ Uses less fat, sugar or salt. Includes Nutrition Facts and Diabetic Exchanges.

  1 pound ground turkey breast
  4 cups coleslaw mix (about 8 ounces)
1/4 cup chopped green onions
  3 tablespoons reduced-sodium soy sauce
  2 garlic cloves, minced
1/2 teaspoon Chinese five-spice powder
  1 teaspoon grated fresh gingerroot

24 sheets phyllo dough (14 inches x 9 inches)
Refrigerated butter-flavored spray
Sweet-and-sour sauce *and/or* hot mustard, optional

1. Crumble the ground turkey into a large nonstick skillet. Cook over medium heat until no longer pink; drain. Add the coleslaw mix, onions, soy sauce, garlic, five-spice powder and ginger. Cook for 2-3 minutes or until coleslaw is wilted. Remove from the heat.

2. Place one sheet of phyllo dough on a work surface with a long side facing you; spritz with butter spray and brush to evenly distribute. Repeat with two more sheets of phyllo, spritzing and brushing each layer. (Keep remaining phyllo dough covered with waxed paper to avoid drying out.)

3. Cut the stack widthwise into two 14-in. x 4-1/2-in. strips. Place 1/4 cup of turkey mixture along one short side of each rectangle. Fold in long sides; starting at the filling edge, roll up tightly. Place seam side down on ungreased baking sheets. Spritz top with butter spray. Repeat with remaining phyllo and filling.

4. Bake at 350° for 25-30 minutes, then broil 6 in. from the heat for 5 minutes or until golden brown. Serve warm with sweet-and-sour sauce and/or mustard if desired. **Yield:** 16 egg rolls.

Nutrition Facts: 1 eggroll equals 108 calories, 4 g fat (1 g saturated fat), 22 mg cholesterol, 236 mg sodium, 12 g carbohydrate, 1 g fiber, 7 g protein. **Diabetic Exchanges:** 1 starch, 1 lean meat.

Editor's Note: This recipe was tested with I Can't Believe It's Not Butter Spray.

⚜ ⚜ ⚜
Cappuccino Punch

Prep: 10 min. + chilling

Rose Reich, Nampa, Idaho

When I tried this punch at a friend's wedding shower, I had to have the recipe. Your own guests will eagerly gather around the punch bowl when you ladle out this frothy ice cream drink.

1/2 cup sugar
1/4 cup instant coffee granules
  1 cup boiling water
  8 cups milk
  1 quart vanilla ice cream, softened
  1 quart chocolate ice cream, softened

1. In a small bowl, combine the sugar and coffee; stir in boiling water until dissolved. Cover and refrigerate until chilled.

2. Just before serving, pour coffee mixture into a 1-gal. punch bowl. Stir in milk. Add scoops of ice cream; stir until melted. **Yield:** about 1 gallon.

15 whole chicken wings (about 3 pounds)
1/2 cup cornstarch
1/4 cup all-purpose flour
1/4 cup sugar
2 teaspoons sesame seeds
1-1/2 teaspoons salt
2 eggs
1/4 cup vegetable oil
5 teaspoons soy sauce
2 green onions, finely chopped
Oil for deep-fat frying

1. Cut the chicken wings into three sections; discard the wing tip section. In a large bowl, combine the cornstarch, flour, sugar, sesame seeds and salt. Combine the eggs, oil and soy sauce; gradually whisk into the dry ingredients until blended. Stir in the onions. Add the chicken wings and stir to coat. Cover and refrigerate for at least 3 hours.

2. Remove wings and discard the batter. In an electric skillet or deep-fat fryer, heat 1-1/2 in. of oil to 375°. Fry wings, 8-10 at a time, for 5-6 minutes on each side or until chicken juices run clear. Drain on paper towels. **Yield:** 2-1/2 dozen.

Editor's Note: 3 pounds of uncooked chicken wing sections (wingettes) may be substituted for the whole wings. Omit cutting wings and discarding tips.

Deep-Fried Chicken Wings

Prep: 15 min. + marinating **Cook:** 20 min.

Tami McLean, Brampton, Ontario

A soy sauce mixture with sesame seeds and green onion adds flavor to these deep-fried chicken wings. My husband just loves wings, and these are by far his favorite!

Cereal Crunchies

Prep/Total Time: 20 min.

Juanita Carlsen, North Bend, Oregon

Folks can't get enough of this irresistible snack mix. A slightly sweet vanilla coating is the perfect match for the blend of miniature pretzels, crispy cereal and salted nuts.

2 cups Multi-Bran Chex
2 cups Corn Chex
2 cups Cheerios
2 cups miniature pretzels
1 cup salted mixed nuts
1/3 cup reduced-fat margarine
1/3 cup packed brown sugar
1/4 cup light corn syrup
2 to 3 teaspoons butter flavoring
1-1/2 teaspoons salt
2 tablespoons vanilla extract
1/4 teaspoon baking soda

1. In a large microwave-safe bowl, combine the cereals, pretzels and nuts; set aside. In a large saucepan, combine the margarine, brown sugar, corn syrup, butter flavoring and salt. Bring to a boil. Boil, uncovered, for 5 minutes. In a small bowl, combine vanilla and baking soda. Remove brown sugar syrup from the heat; stir in vanilla mixture (syrup will foam). Pour over cereal mixture and toss to coat.

2. Microwave, uncovered, on high for 2 minutes; stir. Microwave 2-3 minutes longer; stir. Microwave at 50% power for 2-3 minutes, stirring after 2 minutes. Cool for 3 minutes, stirring well several times. Spread onto waxed paper to cool. **Yield:** 8-1/2 cups.

Editor's Note: This recipe was tested in a 1,100-watt microwave.

❧❧❧
Onion Brie Appetizers

Prep: 25 min. + chilling **Bake:** 15 min.

Carole Resnick, Cleveland, Ohio

Guests will think you spent hours preparing these special-looking appetizers, but they're really easy to assemble using purchased puff pastry. The tasty combination of Brie, caramelized onions and caraway is terrific.

- 2 medium onions, thinly sliced
- 3 tablespoons butter
- 2 tablespoons brown sugar
- 1/2 teaspoon white wine vinegar
- 1 sheet frozen puff pastry, thawed
- 4 ounces Brie or Camembert, rind removed, softened
- 1 to 2 teaspoons caraway seeds
- 1 egg
- 2 teaspoons water

1. In a large skillet, cook the onions, butter, brown sugar and vinegar over medium-low heat until onions are golden brown, stirring frequently. Remove with a slotted spoon; cool to room temperature.

2. On a lightly floured surface, roll puff pastry into an 11-in. x 8-in. rectangle. Spread Brie over pastry. Cover with the onions; sprinkle with caraway seeds.

3. Roll up one long side to the middle of the dough; roll up the other side so the two rolls meet in the center. Using a serrated knife, cut into 1/2-in. slices. Place on parchment paper-lined baking sheets; flatten to 1/4-in. thickness. Refrigerate for 15 minutes.

4. In a small bowl, beat egg and water; brush over slices. Bake at 375° for 12-14 minutes or until puffed and golden brown. Serve warm. **Yield:** 1-1/2 dozen.

❧❧❧
Cheesy Pita Crisps

Prep/Total Time: 25 min.

Christine Mattiko, Dallastown, Pennsylvania

I first made these golden wedges when my college roommates and I wanted garlic bread but had only pitas on hand.

✓ Uses less fat, sugar or salt. Includes Nutrition Facts and Diabetic Exchanges.

- 2 whole wheat pita breads (6 inches)
- 1/4 cup reduced-fat margarine, melted
- 1/2 teaspoon garlic powder
- 1/2 teaspoon onion powder
- 1/4 teaspoon salt
- 1/4 teaspoon pepper
- 3 tablespoons grated Parmesan cheese
- 1/2 cup shredded part-skim mozzarella cheese

1. Split each pita bread into two rounds. Cut each round into four triangles; place with the inner side up on a baking sheet coated with cooking spray.

2. In a bowl, combine the melted margarine, garlic powder, onion powder, salt and pepper; stir in the Parmesan cheese. Spread mixture over the pita bread triangles. Sprinkle with the mozzarella cheese. Bake at 400° for 12-15 minutes or until golden brown. **Yield:** 8 servings.

Nutrition Facts: 2 triangles equals 95 calories, 5 g fat (2 g saturated fat), 6 mg cholesterol, 264 mg sodium, 9 g carbohydrate, 1 g fiber, 4 g protein. **Diabetic Exchanges:** 1 fat, 1/2 starch.

Hot Spinach Artichoke Dip

Prep/Total Time: 15 min.

Michelle Wentz, Fort Polk, Louisiana

No one will ever suspect that this creamy party classic is lower in fat than the much-loved original. The combination of artichoke hearts, spinach and Parmesan cheese gives it great flavor.

✓ Uses less fat, sugar or salt. Includes Nutrition Facts and Diabetic Exchanges.

- 1 small onion, finely chopped
- 2 packages (10 ounces *each*) frozen chopped spinach, thawed and squeezed dry
- 1 package (8 ounces) fat-free cream cheese, cubed
- 1 cup (8 ounces) reduced-fat sour cream
- 1 can (14 ounces) water-packed artichoke hearts, rinsed, drained and chopped
- 3/4 cup grated Parmesan cheese
- 1/4 teaspoon salt
- 1/8 teaspoon pepper
- 1/8 to 1/4 teaspoon crushed red pepper flakes
- 1/4 cup shredded reduced-fat cheddar cheese

Assorted reduced-fat melba toast *or* pita chips

1. In a large nonstick skillet coated with cooking spray, cook and stir onion until tender. Add spinach; cook and stir over medium heat until heated through. Reduce heat to low; stir in cream cheese and sour cream. Add artichoke hearts, Parmesan cheese, salt, pepper and red pepper flakes; cook for 1-2 minutes or until heated through.

2. Transfer to an ungreased 1-1/2-qt. microwave-safe dish; sprinkle with cheddar cheese. Cover and microwave on high for 2-3 minutes or until cheese is melted. Serve warm with melba toast or pita chips. **Yield:** 18 servings.

Nutrition Facts: 1/4 cup equals 71 calories, 3 g fat (2 g saturated fat), 9 mg cholesterol, 342 mg sodium, 6 g carbohydrate, 2 g fiber, 6 g protein. **Diabetic Exchanges:** 1 lean meat, 1 vegetable.

Ginger-Orange Wings

Prep: 45 min. **Cook:** 10 min.

Lora Fletcher, Lyons, Oregon

The sweet-and-sour sauce in this recipe was originally for pork spareribs, but my family has always enjoyed it this way. The tangy wings can be served warm or cold.

- 25 whole chicken wings (about 5 pounds)
- 2 cups all-purpose flour
- 3 teaspoons seasoned salt
- 2 teaspoons garlic salt
- 1/3 cup vegetable oil
- 2 cups orange marmalade
- 1 cup ketchup
- 1/2 cup soy sauce
- 3/4 teaspoon ground ginger

1. Cut chicken wings into three sections; discard wing tip section. In a large resealable plastic bag, combine the flour, seasoned salt and garlic salt. Add chicken wings, a few at a time, and shake to coat. In a large skillet, fry wings in oil, a few at a time, for 3-4 minutes on each side or until golden and crispy.

2. Drain pan drippings; return all chicken to the pan. Combine the marmalade, ketchup, soy sauce and ginger; pour over chicken and stir to coat. Cover and cook over medium-low heat for 10-15 minutes or until wings are well coated. **Yield:** about 4 dozen.

Editor's Note: 5 pounds of uncooked chicken wing sections (wingettes) may be substituted for the whole wings. Omit cutting wings and discarding tips.

Creamy Herb Appetizer Pockets

Prep: 25 min. + chilling

Tina Scarpaci, Chandler, Arizona

I combined a creamy cheese sauce and an artichoke dip to come up with these bite-size, no-mess morsels. The filling is tucked into triangles made from crescent roll dough.

 Uses less fat, sugar or salt. Includes Nutrition Facts and Diabetic Exchanges.

- 1 **carton (4.4 ounces) reduced-fat garlic-herb cheese spread**
- 4 **ounces reduced-fat cream cheese**
- 2 **tablespoons half-and-half cream**
- 1 **garlic clove, minced**
- 1 **tablespoon dried basil**
- 1 **teaspoon dried thyme**
- 1/2 **teaspoon celery salt**
- 1/4 **teaspoon dill weed**
- 1/4 **teaspoon salt**
- 1/4 **teaspoon pepper**
- 3 **to 4 drops hot pepper sauce**
- 1/2 **cup chopped canned water-packed artichoke hearts**
- 1/4 **cup chopped roasted red peppers**
- 2 **tubes (8 ounces *each*) refrigerated reduced-fat crescent rolls**

1. In a small mixing bowl, beat the cheese spread, cream cheese, half-and-half and garlic until blended. Beat in the herbs, salt, pepper and hot pepper sauce. Fold in artichokes and red peppers. Cover and refrigerate for at least 1 hour.

2. Unroll both tubes of crescent roll dough. On a lightly floured surface, form each tube of dough into a long rectangle; seal the seams and perforations. Roll each into a 16-in. x 12-in. rectangle. Cut length-wise into four strips and width-wise into three strips; separate the squares.

3. Place 1 rounded tablespoon of filling in the center of each square. Fold in half, forming triangles. Crimp edges to seal; trim if necessary. Place on ungreased baking sheets. Bake at 375° for 10-15 minutes or until golden brown. Serve warm. **Yield:** 2 dozen.

Nutrition Facts: 2 pockets equals 96 calories, 5 g fat (2 g saturated fat), 7 mg cholesterol, 302 mg sodium, 10 g carbohydrate, trace fiber, 3 g protein. **Diabetic Exchanges:** 1 starch, 1 fat.

Editor's Note: This recipe was tested with Boursin Light Cheese Spread with garlic and fine herbs. One carton contains about 7 tablespoons of cheese spread.

🎀🎀🎀
Mexican Chicken Wings
Prep: 15 min. **Bake:** 50 min.

Barbara McConaughey, Houlton, Wisconsin

When I make these spicy appetizers for parties, I never have leftovers. The hot wings go so well with the cool, zippy dip.

- 12 **whole chicken wings (about 2-1/2 pounds)**
- 1/3 **cup all-purpose flour**
- 1/3 **cup cornmeal**
- 1 **tablespoon ground cumin**
- 1-1/2 **teaspoons salt**
- 1-1/2 **teaspoons pepper**
- 3/4 **teaspoon cayenne pepper**

JALAPENO CILANTRO DIP:
- 2-1/2 **cups (20 ounces) sour cream**
- 3 **cups fresh cilantro leaves**
- 6 **green onions, cut into 3-inch pieces**
- 4 **jalapeno peppers, seeded**
- 3 **teaspoons salt**

1. Cut wings into three sections; discard wing tip section. In a large resealable plastic bag, combine flour, cornmeal, cumin, salt, pepper and cayenne. Add the wings, a few at a time. Seal bag and shake to coat.

2. Transfer to a greased 13-in. x 9-in. x 2-in. baking pan. Bake, uncovered, at 375° for 25-27 minutes on each side or until chicken juices run clear and coating is set.

3. Meanwhile, in a blender, combine dip ingredients. Cover; process until blended. Refrigerate until serving. Serve with wings. **Yield:** 2 dozen (3-2/3 cups dip).

Editor's Note: 2-1/2 pounds of uncooked chicken wing sections (wingettes) may be substituted for the whole chicken wings. Omit cutting wings and discarding tips. When cutting or seeding hot peppers, use rubber or plastic gloves to protect your hands. Avoid touching your face.

🎀🎀🎀
Caramel Crunch
Prep: 15 min. **Bake:** 45 min.

Mary Koogler, Mitchellville, Iowa

Everyone in our family has a sweet tooth, so this drizzled mix of popcorn, almonds and cereal always goes quickly. My "off-limits" batches are divided into plastic bags, tied with ribbon and shared with all of the snackers on my Christmas list.

- 9 **cups popped popcorn**
- 9 **cups Crispix cereal**
- 1 **cup slivered almonds**
- 1 **cup butter, cubed**
- 1/2 **cup light corn syrup**
- 2 **cups packed brown sugar**
- 1/2 **teaspoon baking soda**

1. In a very large heatproof bowl, combine the popcorn, cereal and almonds; set aside. In a large heavy-duty saucepan, melt the butter; stir in corn syrup and brown sugar. Cook and stir over medium heat until mixture comes to a boil. Reduce heat to medium-low. Cook 5 minutes longer, stirring occasionally.

2. Remove from the heat. Stir in baking soda (mixture will foam up and get lighter in color). Carefully pour over the popcorn mixture; stir to coat evenly.

3. Transfer to two 15-in. x 10-in. x 1-in. baking pans coated with cooking spray. Bake at 250° for 45 minutes, stirring every 15 minutes. Spread on waxed paper to cool. Store the mix in airtight containers. **Yield:** about 4-1/2 quarts.

Spinach Berry Salad, p. 36

Chicken and Black Bean Salad, p. 41

Pita Pocket Chicken Salad, p. 32

Special Salads

From tender pasta and garden veggies to cool gelatin and fresh fruit, the mouth-watering medleys in this chapter will toss plenty of extra flavor into your menu on weekdays, holidays…any day at all!

Rosy Rhubarb Mold, p. 46

✿✿✿ Rainbow Pasta Salad

Prep/Total Time: 30 min.

Julie Wilson, Chetek, Wisconsin

I like to serve this colorful salad over a bed of leafy green lettuce for a pretty presentation. With its rich sour cream and dill dressing, it makes a great change-of-pace pasta salad for picnics. No one even guesses I lightened up the recipe a bit.

> 2 cups uncooked tricolor spiral pasta
> 1 cup (8 ounces) fat-free sour cream
> 1/2 cup reduced-fat mayonnaise
> 1 tablespoon dill weed
> 1/2 teaspoon garlic salt
> 1/2 teaspoon ground mustard
> **Dash pepper**
> 1/2 pound fresh asparagus, trimmed
> 1 tablespoon water
> 1 cup cubed fully cooked lean ham
> 1 small onion, chopped
> 1 small sweet red pepper, chopped
> 1/2 cup cubed reduced-fat cheddar cheese
> **Leaf lettuce, optional**

1. Cook the pasta according to package directions. Meanwhile, for the dressing, combine the sour cream, mayonnaise, dill, garlic salt, mustard and pepper in a bowl; set aside. Rinse the pasta in cold water and drain well; set aside.

2. Cut the tips off six asparagus spears; chop the remaining asparagus. Place chopped asparagus and tips and water in a microwave-safe dish. Cover and microwave on high for 1-2 minutes or until crisp-tender. Rinse with cold water; pat dry. Set aside asparagus tips for garnish.

3. In a large bowl, combine the pasta, chopped asparagus, ham, onion, red pepper and cheese. Add dressing and toss to coat. Refrigerate until serving. Serve in a lettuce-lined bowl if desired; garnish with asparagus tips. **Yield:** 6 servings.

✿✿✿ Pita Pocket Chicken Salad

(Also pictured on page 30)

Prep/Total Time: 15 min.

Natasha Randall, Austin, Texas

We wanted something cool for lunch one summer day, so I tossed together whatever I had in the refrigerator. The result was this wonderful salad, which is stuffed into pitas.

> 2 cups cubed cooked chicken
> 1-1/2 cups seedless red grapes, halved
> 1 cup chopped cucumber
> 3/4 cup sliced almonds
> 3/4 cup shredded part-skim mozzarella cheese
> 1/2 cup poppy seed salad dressing
> 6 pita breads (6 inches), halved
> **Leaf lettuce, optional**

In a large bowl, combine the chicken, grapes, cucumber, almonds and mozzarella cheese. Drizzle with dressing and toss to coat. Line pita breads with lettuce if desired; fill with chicken salad. **Yield:** 6 servings.

Corn Medley Salad

Prep: 15 min.
Cook: 10 min. + chilling

Judy Meckstroth, New Bremen, Ohio

Whenever I need a dish to pass that's guaranteed to please, I put together this easy corn salad. Whether you serve it from a crystal dish, a ceramic crock or a plastic bowl, it will stand out as a mealtime highlight.

- 2/3 cup sugar
- 2/3 cup cider vinegar
- 2/3 cup vegetable oil
- 1 can (15-1/4 ounces) whole kernel corn, drained
- 1 can (15 ounces) whole baby corn, rinsed and drained, halved
- 1 can (11 ounces) yellow and white whole kernel corn, drained
- 1 can (11 ounces) white *or* shoepeg corn, drained
- 1 large sweet red pepper, chopped
- 1 medium red onion, chopped
- 4 to 5 celery ribs, sliced

Leaf lettuce, optional

1. In a small saucepan, combine the sugar, cider vinegar and oil. Cook over medium heat for 5 minutes, stirring until the sugar is dissolved. Cool completely.

2. In a bowl, combine the corn, red pepper, onion and celery. Add dressing and toss to coat. Cover and refrigerate overnight. Stir well. Serve with a slotted spoon in a lettuce-lined bowl if desired. **Yield:** 10-12 servings.

🎀🎀🎀
Sesame Chicken Couscous Salad

Prep: 20 min. + chilling

Tari Ambler, Shorewood, Illinois

I grow many of the ingredients for this recipe. Fresh-tasting and crunchy, it's a perfect summer salad. Try leaving out the chicken and just mix the veggies with couscous for a fun side dish.

1-1/2 cups reduced-sodium chicken broth
   3 teaspoons reduced-sodium soy sauce, *divided*
   2 teaspoons sesame oil, *divided*

   1 cup uncooked couscous
   2 green onions, sliced
1-1/2 cups fresh or frozen sugar snap peas
  3/4 cup fresh broccoli florets
1-1/2 cups cubed cooked chicken
   1 large sweet red pepper, chopped
  3/4 cup diced zucchini
   2 tablespoons cider vinegar
   1 tablespoon apple juice concentrate
   1 tablespoon water
   2 teaspoons canola oil
 1/2 teaspoon ground ginger
 1/4 teaspoon pepper
   2 tablespoons slivered almonds, toasted
   2 teaspoons sesame seeds, toasted
Leaf lettuce, optional

1. In a saucepan, combine the broth, 1 teaspoon soy sauce and 1 teaspoon sesame oil; bring to a boil. Stir in couscous. Cover and remove from the heat. Let stand for 5 minutes. Fluff with a fork. Stir in green onions. Cover and refrigerate until chilled.

2. Place the peas in a steamer basket in a saucepan over 1 in. of water; bring to a boil. Cover and steam for 1 minute. Add the broccoli; cover and steam 2 minutes longer or until crisp-tender. Rinse in cold water; drain. Transfer to a serving bowl; add the chicken, red pepper and zucchini.

3. In a jar with a tight-fitting lid, combine the vinegar, apple juice concentrate, water, canola oil, ginger, pepper and remaining soy sauce and sesame oil. Shake well. Pour over chicken mixture and toss to coat. Cover and refrigerate for 30 minutes or until chilled. Serve over couscous in a lettuce-lined bowl if desired. Sprinkle with almonds and sesame seeds. **Yield:** 4 servings.

🎀🎀🎀
Cran-Apple Salad

Prep/Total Time: 5 min.

Lucille Foster, Grant, Nebraska

This tart and tasty salad goes wonderfully with so many different types of meals. Folks will think you slaved over it, but with just four ingredients, preparation takes only minutes. Adding crunchy walnuts, celery and apples is a special way to dress up the canned cranberry sauce.

   1 can (16 ounces) whole-berry cranberry sauce
   1 medium unpeeled tart apple, diced
   1 celery rib, thinly sliced
 1/2 cup chopped walnuts

In a large salad bowl, combine the cranberry sauce, apple and celery. Cover and refrigerate until serving. Just before serving, stir in walnuts. **Yield:** 4-6 servings.

🎗🎗🎗
Polish Potato Salad

Prep/Total Time: 30 min.

Odette Dallaire, Los Alamos, New Mexico

When my in-laws from Poland visited, I made this meaty salad for them because they're fond of sausage and potatoes. They liked it enough to request the recipe!

- 8 to 10 small red potatoes
- 2 uncooked bratwurst
- 1 fresh kielbasa *or* Polish sausage link

- 5 teaspoons sugar
- 4 teaspoons all-purpose flour
- 1 teaspoon salt
- 1 teaspoon ground mustard
- 1/2 teaspoon celery seed
- 2 tablespoons butter
- 3/4 cup reduced-sodium chicken broth
- 1/3 cup white wine vinegar
- 1 small red onion, sliced
- 1/2 cup sliced celery
- 1/4 cup minced fresh parsley

1. Place potatoes in a large saucepan and cover with water. Bring to a boil. Reduce heat; cover and cook for 15-20 minutes or until tender but firm. Meanwhile, in a large skillet, cook sausage over medium heat until no longer pink. Remove and cut into 1/4-in. slices; set aside.

2. In the same skillet, combine the sugar, flour, salt, mustard and celery seed. Cook and stir over medium heat in butter until mixture is hot and bubbly. Gradually add broth and vinegar; bring to a boil. Cook and stir until thickened. Stir in the onion, celery, parsley and sausage.

3. Drain the potatoes; peel and slice into skillet. Gently stir into the sausage mixture. Heat through. **Yield:** 6-8 servings.

🎗🎗🎗
Artichoke Spinach Salad

Prep/Total Time: 15 min.

Nancy Lee Jennings, Fairfax, Virginia

The fresh spinach gives this medley bright green color, and the tangy dressing adds just the right flavor.

- 12 cups torn fresh spinach
- 8 green onions, chopped
- 6 hard-cooked eggs, sliced
- 1/2 pound fresh mushrooms, sliced
- 1 can (8 ounces) sliced water chestnuts, drained
- 1 jar (6-1/2 ounces) marinated artichoke hearts, drained and quartered
- 8 bacon strips, cooked and crumbled

DRESSING:
- 1/2 cup cider vinegar
- 1/2 cup sugar
- 1/2 teaspoon salt
- 1/2 teaspoon ground mustard
- 1 teaspoon grated onion
- 1 cup vegetable oil

In a large bowl, combine the first seven ingredients. For dressing, combine the vinegar, sugar, salt, mustard and onion in a blender; cover and process until

smooth. While processing, gradually add oil in a steady stream. Drizzle over salad; gently toss to coat. Refrigerate any leftover dressing. **Yield:** 10-12 servings.

🎀🎀🎀
Spinach Berry Salad

(Also pictured on page 30)

Prep/Total Time: 10 min.

Lisa Lorenzo, Willoughby, Ohio

Knowing my passion for light recipes, my mother shared this salad idea with me. Colorful and topped with a homemade dressing, it's as pleasing to the eye as it is to the palate.

> ✓ Uses less fat, sugar or salt. Includes Nutrition Facts and Diabetic Exchanges.

- **4 cups packed torn fresh spinach**
- **1 cup sliced fresh strawberries**
- **1 cup fresh or frozen blueberries**
- **1 small sweet onion, sliced**
- **1/4 cup chopped pecans, toasted**

CURRY SALAD DRESSING:
- **2 tablespoons white wine vinegar**
- **2 tablespoons balsamic vinegar**
- **2 tablespoons honey**
- **2 teaspoons Dijon mustard**
- **1 teaspoon curry powder**
- **1/4 teaspoon salt**
- **1/8 teaspoon pepper**

In a large salad bowl, toss together the spinach, strawberries, blueberries, onion and pecans. In a jar with a tight-fitting lid, combine the dressing ingredients; shake well. Pour over salad and toss to coat. Serve immediately. **Yield:** 4 servings.

Nutrition Facts: 1-1/2 cups equals 141 calories, 6 g fat (1 g saturated fat), 0 cholesterol, 250 mg sodium, 22 g carbohydrate, 4 g fiber, 3 g protein. **Diabetic Exchanges:** 1 vegetable, 1 fruit, 1 fat.

🏵🏵🏵
Zesty Potato Salad

Prep: 25 min. + chilling

Raquel Haggard, Edmond, Oklahoma

I adjusted the original recipe for this cold, creamy salad to better suit my tastes. The cilantro comes through nicely, while green chilies and chili powder provide a little kick.

✓ Uses less fat, sugar or salt. Includes Nutrition Facts and Diabetic Exchange.

- **2 pounds red potatoes, cubed**
- **3/4 cup fat-free mayonnaise**
- **1/3 cup reduced-fat sour cream**
- **1/3 cup minced fresh cilantro**
- **1 can (4 ounces) chopped green chilies**
- **3 green onions, finely chopped**
- **1 tablespoon lemon juice**
- **1 teaspoon chili powder**
- **1/2 teaspoon salt**
- **1/4 teaspoon pepper**
- **Dash garlic powder**

1. Place potatoes in a saucepan and cover with water. Bring to a boil. Reduce heat; cover and cook for 15 minutes or just until tender. Drain and rinse with cold water.

2. In a small bowl, combine the remaining ingredients. Place potatoes in a large bowl. Add dressing and toss to coat. Cover and refrigerate for 2 hours or until chilled. **Yield:** 6 servings.

Nutrition Facts: 3/4 cup equals 162 calories, 2 g fat (1 g saturated fat), 7 mg cholesterol, 693 mg sodium, 32 g carbohydrate, 4 g fiber, 4 g protein. **Diabetic Exchange:** 2 starch.

🏵🏵🏵
Cashew Turkey Pasta Salad

Prep: 20 min. + chilling **Grill:** 25 min. + cooling

Karen Wyffels, Lino Lakes, Minnesota

Cashews add a nice crunch to this grilled turkey and spiral pasta combo. I first tasted this delightfully different salad at a baby shower and asked the hostess for her recipe. Since then, I've served it for many occasions.

- **2 bone-in turkey breast halves, skin removed**
- **3 cups uncooked tricolor spiral pasta**
- **2 celery ribs, diced**
- **6 green onions, chopped**
- **1/2 cup diced green pepper**
- **1-1/2 cups mayonnaise**
- **3/4 cup packed brown sugar**
- **1 tablespoon cider vinegar**
- **1-1/2 teaspoons salt**
- **1-1/2 teaspoons lemon juice**
- **2 cups salted cashew halves**

1. Grill turkey, covered, over medium heat for 25-30 minutes on each side or until juices run clear. Cool slightly. Cover and refrigerate until cool. Meanwhile, cook pasta according to package directions; drain and rinse in cold water.

2. Chop turkey; place in a large bowl. Add the pasta, celery, onions and green pepper. In a small bowl, combine the mayonnaise, brown sugar, vinegar, salt and lemon juice; pour over pasta mixture and toss to coat. Cover and refrigerate for at least 2 hours. Just before serving, stir in the cashews. **Yield:** 12 servings.

🎗🎗🎗
Corn and Black Bean Salad
Prep: 20 min. + chilling

Carrie Palmquist, Canova, South Dakota

I'm often asked to create new recipes for parties. This corn medley, cooked up for a barbecue, is one dish that went over big. Filled with multicolored vegetables and plenty of seasonings, the salad has great eye appeal and loads of flavor.

- 1 can (15-1/4 ounces) whole kernel corn, drained
- 1 can (15 ounces) black beans, rinsed and drained
- 1 medium sweet red pepper, chopped
- 1 medium tomato, seeded and chopped
- 6 green onions, chopped
- 1/2 cup chopped red onion
- 1 jalapeno pepper, seeded and finely chopped
- 1 garlic clove, minced
- 3/4 cup Italian salad dressing
- 1 tablespoon minced fresh cilantro
- 1 tablespoon lime *or* lemon juice
- 3/4 teaspoon hot pepper sauce
- 1/2 teaspoon chili powder

In a large bowl, combine the first eight ingredients. In a small bowl, combine the salad dressing, cilantro, lime juice, hot pepper sauce and chili powder. Pour over corn mixture and toss to coat. Cover and refrigerate for at least 6 hours or overnight. Serve with a slotted spoon. **Yield:** 6-8 servings.

Editor's Note: When cutting or seeding hot peppers, use rubber or plastic gloves to protect your hands. Avoid touching your face.

🎗🎗🎗
Festive Potato Salad
Prep/Total Time: 35 min.

Gloria Warczak, Cedarburg, Wisconsin

My family likes creamy-type potato salads, so I fix this often. It's usually partially eaten before I can even say, "It's ready!"

- 8 medium red potatoes, cooked and cubed
- 2 celery ribs with leaves, thinly sliced
- 2 green onions with tops, chopped
- 4 hard-cooked eggs, chopped
- 1/2 cup chopped peeled cucumber
- 1/4 cup chopped sweet red pepper
- 1/4 cup chopped green pepper
- 1-1/4 cups mayonnaise
- 1/4 cup sour cream
- 1/4 cup plain yogurt
- 1 tablespoon *each* minced fresh basil, marjoram and dill *or* 1 teaspoon *each* dried basil, marjoram and dill weed
- 1 teaspoon sugar
- 1/2 teaspoon salt
- 1/2 teaspoon pepper
- 4 plum tomatoes, coarsely chopped
- 1 cup frozen peas, thawed
- 1 cup (4 ounces) shredded cheddar cheese

Leaf lettuce, optional

In a large bowl, combine the first seven ingredients. In another bowl, combine the mayonnaise, sour cream, yogurt and seasonings. Pour over potato mixture; toss to coat. Gently stir in tomatoes, peas and cheese. Cover and refrigerate until serving. **Yield:** 14 servings.

Tossed Salad with Artichokes

Prep/Total Time: 10 min.

Karen Kay Brondel, Centertown, Missouri

This is a wonderful salad recipe I received from a friend. It's quick and easy to prepare, and it's always a hit with guests.

- 1 medium head iceberg lettuce, torn
- 1 bunch romaine, torn
- 1 cup thinly sliced red onion
- 1 jar (6-1/2 ounces) marinated artichoke hearts, drained
- 1/2 cup shredded Parmesan cheese
- 1/2 cup olive oil
- 1/3 cup red wine vinegar

In a large bowl, combine the lettuce, romaine, onion, artichoke hearts and Parmesan cheese. In a small bowl, whisk the oil and vinegar; drizzle over salad and toss to coat. **Yield:** 8-10 servings.

Summer Fruit Salad

Prep: 25 min. + chilling

James Korzenowski, Dearborn, Michigan

A tangy cream cheese dressing makes this refreshing medley extra special. I've presented it both as a salad and as dessert.

PINEAPPLE CREAM CHEESE DRESSING:
- 1/3 cup sugar
- 4 teaspoons cornstarch
- 1/4 teaspoon salt
- 1 cup pineapple juice
- 1/4 cup orange juice
- 2 tablespoons lemon juice
- 2 eggs, lightly beaten
- 2 packages (3 ounces *each*) cream cheese, softened

SALAD:
- 2 cups sliced fresh strawberries
- 2 cups pineapple tidbits
- 1-1/2 cups seedless green *or* red grapes, halved
- 1-1/2 cups diced peaches *or* nectarines
- 1 cup fresh blueberries *or* raspberries
- 1/4 cup sugar

Leaf lettuce, optional

1. In a small saucepan, combine the sugar, cornstarch and salt. Stir in the juices until smooth. Bring to a boil; cook and stir for 2 minutes or until thickened. Remove from the heat.

2. Stir a small amount into the eggs; return all to the pan, stirring constantly. Cook and stir until mixture reaches 160° and is thickened. Remove from the heat; cool slightly. In a small mixing bowl, beat cream cheese until smooth. Add juice mixture; mix well. Cover and refrigerate overnight.

3. In a large bowl, combine the fruit. Sprinkle with sugar; toss to coat. Cover and refrigerate overnight. Serve in a lettuce-lined bowl if desired with the dressing. **Yield:** 8 servings.

✿✿✿ Black Bean Bow Tie Salad

Prep/Total Time: 15 min.

Teresa Smith, Huron, South Dakota

Even people who don't like beans will compliment me on this delicious salad. It's a favorite at family events and other get-togethers. The dressing gets a kick from cilantro and lime.

☑ Uses less fat, sugar or salt. Includes Nutrition Facts and Diabetic Exchanges.

- **8 ounces uncooked bow tie pasta**
- **2/3 cup reduced-sodium chicken broth *or* vegetable broth**
- **3 garlic cloves, sliced**
- **1 can (15 ounces) black beans, rinsed and drained, *divided***
- **1/2 cup fresh cilantro leaves**
- **3 tablespoons lime juice**
- **2 tablespoons olive oil**
- **1 tablespoon tomato paste**
- **1-1/2 teaspoons dried oregano**
- **3/4 teaspoon salt**
- **1 medium zucchini, cut in half lengthwise and sliced**
- **1 medium sweet red pepper, chopped**
- **1 medium green pepper, chopped**
- **1/3 cup chopped red onion**

1. Cook pasta according to package directions. Rinse with cold water and drain; set aside. In a small saucepan, bring broth and garlic to a boil. Reduce heat; simmer, uncovered, for 5 minutes or until garlic is tender. Cool slightly.

2. Transfer to a food processor. Add 1/4 cup black beans, cilantro, lime juice, oil, tomato paste, oregano and salt; cover and process until smooth. Transfer to a large serving bowl. Add the pasta, zucchini, peppers, onion and remaining beans; toss gently to coat. Refrigerate until serving. **Yield:** 10 servings.

Nutrition Facts: 1 cup equals 159 calories, 4 g fat (1 g saturated fat), 0 cholesterol, 352 mg sodium, 26 g carbohydrate, 4 g fiber, 6 g protein. **Diabetic Exchanges:** 1-1/2 starch, 1 vegetable, 1/2 fat.

✿✿✿ Apple Luncheon Salad

Prep: 10 min. + chilling

Audrey Marsh, Arva, Ontario

Served with fresh-baked bread, this meaty salad makes a nice light meal. I've also used this recipe for entertaining, and it has always been a success at potluck dinners.

- **3 cups diced red apples**
- **1 cup julienned cooked roast beef**
- **1 cup thinly sliced celery**
- **4 green onions, thinly sliced**
- **1/4 cup minced fresh parsley**
- **1/3 cup vegetable oil**
- **2 tablespoons cider vinegar**
- **1 garlic clove, minced**
- **1/2 teaspoon salt**
- **1/4 teaspoon pepper**
- **Lettuce leaves, optional**

In a bowl, combine the first five ingredients. In a small bowl, combine oil, vinegar, garlic, salt and pepper; mix

well. Pour over apple mixture; toss to coat. Cover and refrigerate for at least 1 hour. Serve on lettuce if desired. **Yield:** 4-6 servings.

🎖️🎖️🎖️

Chicken and Black Bean Salad

(Also pictured on page 30)

Prep/Total Time: 20 min.

Cindie Ekstrand, Duarte, California

Here in California, we cook out year-round. I often grill extra chicken specifically with this quick salad in mind. It's so colorful and fresh-tasting, even our kids love it.

1/3 cup olive oil
2 tablespoons lime juice
2 tablespoons chopped fresh cilantro
1-1/2 teaspoons sugar
1 garlic clove, minced
1/2 teaspoon chili powder
1/2 teaspoon salt
1/4 teaspoon pepper
1 can (15 ounces) black beans, rinsed and drained
1 can (11 ounces) Mexicorn, drained
1 medium sweet red pepper, julienned
1/3 cup sliced green onions
6 cups torn romaine
1-1/2 cups cooked chicken strips
Additional cilantro, optional

1. In a jar with a tight-fitting lid, combine the first eight ingredients; shake well and set aside.

2. In a bowl, toss beans, corn, red pepper and onions; set aside. Arrange romaine on individual plates; top with bean mixture and chicken. Drizzle with dressing; garnish with cilantro if desired. **Yield:** 6 servings.

Great Greens

For your green salads, select the freshest greens and make sure they are dry before assembling the salad. Wet greens can make the salad soggy. Allow greens to stand at room temperature no longer than 15 minutes before serving.

🎗🎗🎗
Crazy Quilt Salad
Prep: 15 min. + chilling

Roseanne Martyniuk, Red Deer, Alberta

This sensational bean salad started out with my mother's recipe, which I changed a bit to suit our tastes. The thyme and ground mustard give it such zest.

1 can (16 ounces) kidney beans, rinsed and drained
1 can (15-1/4 ounces) lima beans, rinsed and drained
1 can (14-1/2 ounces) cut green beans, drained
1 can (14-1/2 ounces) cut wax beans, drained
1 cup thinly sliced celery
1 large green pepper, chopped
1/2 cup thinly sliced onion

DRESSING:
1/3 cup cider vinegar
1/4 cup vegetable oil
1-1/2 teaspoons ground mustard
1 teaspoon dried thyme
1/2 teaspoon salt
1/4 teaspoon pepper
1/4 teaspoon garlic powder

Place the first seven ingredients in a large bowl. Combine the dressing ingredients; mix well. Pour over the bean mixture; toss gently. Cover and refrigerate salad for 6 hours or overnight, stirring occasionally. **Yield:** 10-12 servings.

🎗🎗🎗
Apple Mallow Salad
Prep: 25 min. + chilling

Paula Marchesi, Rocky Point, Long Island, New York

I enjoy picking fresh apples at local orchards. Using both red and green apples makes this salad especially festive-looking for a Christmas brunch or dinner. And everyone likes the fluffy marshmallows and crunchy peanuts.

1 can (20 ounces) crushed pineapple
1/2 cup sugar
1 tablespoon all-purpose flour
1 to 2 tablespoons white vinegar
1 egg, beaten
1 carton (12 ounces) frozen whipped topping, thawed
2 medium red apples, diced
2 medium green apples, diced
4 cups miniature marshmallows
1 cup honey-roasted peanuts

1. Drain pineapple, reserving juice; set pineapple aside. In a saucepan, combine sugar, flour, vinegar and reserved juice until smooth. Bring to a boil; cook and stir for 2 minutes or until thickened. Remove from the heat. Stir a small amount of hot mixture into egg; return all to the pan, stirring constantly. Bring to a gentle boil; cook and stir for 2 minutes. Remove from the heat; cool.

2. Fold in whipped topping. Fold in the apples, marshmallows and reserved pineapple. Cover and refrigerate for 1 hour. Just before serving, fold in the peanuts. **Yield:** 16-20 servings.

2 cups water
3/4 cup sugar
3/4 cup orange juice concentrate
3/4 cup lemonade concentrate
1 can (20 ounces) pineapple tidbits, drained
2 medium firm bananas, cut into 1/2-inch slices
1-1/2 cups watermelon chunks
1-1/2 cups green grapes
1-1/2 cups quartered strawberries
1-1/2 cups cubed peaches
2 kiwifruit, peeled, quartered and sliced

1. In a small saucepan, bring water and sugar to a boil, stirring constantly. Remove from the heat; stir in orange juice and lemonade concentrates. In a large bowl, combine the pineapple, bananas, watermelon, grapes, strawberries and peaches. Add juice mixture and mix well.

2. Place about 1/2 cup fruit mixture in 5-oz. disposable plastic wine glasses with removable bottoms or 5-oz. disposable cups. Top each with four kiwi pieces. Cover and freeze until firm. May be frozen for up to 1 month. Remove from the freezer about 1-3/4 hours before serving. **Yield:** 18 servings.

Nutrition Facts: 1/2 cup equals 124 calories, 1 g fat (1 g saturated fat), 0 cholesterol, 2 mg sodium, 31 g carbohydrate, 2 g fiber, 1 g protein. **Diabetic Exchange:** 2 fruit.

Fancy Frozen Fruit Cups

Prep: 20 min. **Cook:** 20 min. + freezing

Alynce Wyman, Pembina, North Dakota

In the summer, I make a big batch of these delicious, slushy fruit cups and store them in the freezer. We also like them with blueberries, raspberries, muskmelon and cherries.

 Uses less fat, sugar or salt. Includes Nutrition Facts and Diabetic Exchange.

Loaded Baked Potato Salad

Prep: 20 min. **Bake:** 40 min. + cooling

Jackie Deckard, Solsberry, Indiana

I revamped my mother's potato salad recipe to taste more like baked potatoes with all the fixin's, which I love. It's now the most-requested dish at our family gatherings. Even my mother asked for a copy of the recipe!

5 pounds small unpeeled red potatoes, cubed
1 teaspoon salt
1/2 teaspoon pepper
8 hard-cooked eggs, chopped
1 pound sliced bacon, cooked and crumbled
2 cups (8 ounces) shredded cheddar cheese
1 sweet onion, chopped
3 dill pickles, chopped
1-1/2 cups (12 ounces) sour cream
1 cup mayonnaise
2 to 3 teaspoons prepared mustard

1. Place the potatoes in a greased 15-in. x 10-in. x 1-in. baking pan; sprinkle with salt and pepper. Bake, uncovered, at 425° for 40-45 minutes or until tender. Cool in pan on a wire rack.

2. In a large bowl, combine the potatoes, eggs, bacon, cheese, onion and pickles. In a small bowl, combine the sour cream, mayonnaise and mustard; pour over the potato mixture and toss to coat. Serve immediately. **Yield:** 20 servings.

★★★
Black-Eyed Pea Salad

Prep: 15 min. + chilling

Ruth Hunter, Newton, Pennsylvania

This is a wonderful recipe to serve any time of the year, but I think the salad is especially good with ripe cherry tomatoes picked fresh from the garden.

- 1 package (16 ounces) frozen black-eyed peas
- 1 package (10 ounces) frozen peas, thawed
- 4 green onions, sliced
- 2 celery ribs, chopped
- 1 medium sweet yellow pepper, diced
- 2 medium carrots, coarsely chopped
- 1/3 cup chopped fresh mint
- 1/2 cup olive oil
- 1/3 cup white wine vinegar
- 2 garlic cloves, minced
- 1 teaspoon salt
- 1/4 teaspoon pepper
- 1 cup halved cherry tomatoes
- 1/4 pound sliced bacon, cooked and crumbled

1. Cook the black-eyed peas according to package directions; drain and place in a large bowl. Stir in the peas, onions, celery, yellow pepper, carrots and mint.

2. In a jar with a tight-fitting lid, combine the oil, vinegar, garlic, salt and pepper; shake well. Drizzle over salad; toss to coat. Cover and refrigerate overnight. Top with tomatoes and bacon. **Yield:** 10-12 servings.

★★★
Christmas Fruit Salad

Prep: 10 min. + chilling **Cook:** 10 min.

Ina Vickers, Dumas, Arkansas

It was at the first Thanksgiving I spent with my husband's family that I tasted this salad. My mother-in-law shared the recipe. Now I serve it for special occasions, and it's become a mainstay at the potlucks we have at work.

- 3 egg yolks, beaten
- 3 tablespoons water
- 3 tablespoons white vinegar
- 1/2 teaspoon salt
- 2 cups heavy whipping cream, whipped
- 3 cups miniature marshmallows
- 2 cups halved green grapes
- 1 can (20 ounces) pineapple tidbits, drained
- 1 can (11 ounces) mandarin oranges, drained
- 1 jar (10 ounces) red maraschino cherries, drained and sliced
- 1 cup chopped pecans
- 3 tablespoons lemon juice

1. In a large saucepan, combine egg yolks, water, vinegar and salt. Cook over medium heat, stirring constantly, until mixture thickens and reaches 160°. Remove from the heat and cool; fold in whipped cream.

2. In a large bowl, combine remaining ingredients. Add dressing; toss to coat. Cover and refrigerate for 24 hours before serving. **Yield:** 12-14 servings.

Flank Steak Spinach Salad

Prep: 15 min. + marinating Grill: 15 min. + standing

Freddie Johnson, San Antonio, Texas

Moist marinated steak, wild rice, almonds and veggies blend together nicely in this colorful main-dish salad.

- 4 beef flank steaks (about 1 pound *each*)
- 1 bottle (16 ounces) Italian salad dressing, *divided*
- 1-1/4 cups uncooked wild rice
- 2 packages (6 ounces *each*) fresh baby spinach
- 1/2 pound fresh mushrooms, sliced
- 1 large red onion, thinly sliced
- 1 pint grape tomatoes, halved
- 1 package (2-1/2 ounces) slivered almonds, toasted

1. Place steaks in a gallon-size resealable plastic bag; add 3/4 cup salad dressing. Seal bag and turn to coat. Refrigerate overnight. Prepare the rice according to package directions. In a bowl, combine rice with 1/2 cup salad dressing. Cover and refrigerate overnight.

2. Drain and discard marinade from steaks. Grill steaks, uncovered, over medium heat for 6-8 minutes on each side or until meat reaches desired doneness (for medium-rare, a meat thermometer should read

145°; medium, 160°; well-done, 170°). Let stand for 10 minutes. Thinly slice against the grain; cool to room temperature.

3. To serve, arrange spinach on a large platter. Top with the rice, mushrooms, onion, tomatoes and steak. Sprinkle with almonds; drizzle with remaining salad dressing. **Yield:** 16 servings.

Shrimp Shell Salad

Prep/Total Time: 20 min.

Adrienne Barbe, Litchfield, Connecticut

My mother came up with this lovely medley, which I modified to make it lower in fat. Instead of buying small shrimp and chopping them, I often use salad shrimp.

- 1 cup fat-free mayonnaise
- 1/2 cup seafood cocktail sauce
- 1 teaspoon prepared horseradish
- 1/2 teaspoon dried tarragon
- 1/2 teaspoon dried basil
- 1/4 teaspoon celery seed
- 1/8 teaspoon pepper
- 2 hard-cooked eggs
- 2 cups cooked small shrimp, *divided*
- 2 cups cooked small pasta shells
- 3 celery ribs with leaves, chopped
- 3 green onions, thinly sliced
- 5 lettuce leaves

1. For dressing, in a bowl, whisk the first seven ingredients. Cover and refrigerate until chilled. Cut eggs in half; discard yolks or save for another use. Chop egg whites. Set aside 10 shrimp for garnish; chop remaining shrimp.

2. In a bowl, combine the chopped shrimp, pasta, celery, egg whites and green onions. Add dressing and toss to coat. Serve on lettuce. Garnish with reserved shrimp. **Yield:** 5 servings.

Rosy Rhubarb Mold

(Also pictured on page 31)

Prep: 25 min. + chilling

Regina Albright, Southhaven, Mississippi

Any meal benefits from this ruby-colored salad. The combination of sweet, tangy and crunchy ingredients is irresistible.

✓ Uses less fat, sugar or salt. Includes Nutrition Facts and Diabetic Exchange.

- **4 cups chopped fresh *or* frozen rhubarb**
- **1 cup water**
- **2/3 cup sugar**
- **1/4 teaspoon salt**
- **1 package (6 ounces) strawberry gelatin**
- **1-1/2 cups cold water**
- **1/4 cup lemon juice**
- **2 cans (11 ounces *each*) mandarin oranges, drained**
- **1 cup chopped celery**

Optional garnishes: lettuce leaves, sliced strawberries, green grapes, sour cream and ground nutmeg

1. In a saucepan, combine rhubarb, water, sugar and salt; bring to a boil over medium heat. Boil for 1-2 minutes or until the rhubarb is tender; remove from the heat. Stir in gelatin until dissolved. Stir in cold water and lemon juice. Chill until partially set.

2. Fold in oranges and celery. Pour into a 6-cup mold or an 8-in. square dish coated with cooking spray. Chill until set. Unmold onto lettuce leaves or cut into squares. If desired, garnish with fruit and serve with sour cream sprinkled with nutmeg. **Yield:** 12 servings.

Nutrition Facts: 1/2 cup equals 79 calories, trace fat (0 saturated fat), 0 cholesterol, 98 mg sodium, 19 g carbohydrate, 0 fiber, 2 g protein. **Diabetic Exchange:** 1 fruit.

Picnic Pasta Salad

Prep/Total Time: 25 min.

Felicia Fiocchi, Vineland, New Jersey

My family's not big on pasta salads made with mayonnaise. This version that uses Italian dressing instead was a hit.

- 1 package (12 ounces) tricolor spiral pasta
- 1 package (10 ounces) refrigerated tricolor tortellini
- 1 jar (7-1/2 ounces) marinated artichoke hearts, undrained
- 1/2 pound fresh broccoli florets (about 1-3/4 cups)
- 12 ounces provolone cheese, cubed
- 12 ounces hard salami, cubed
- 1 medium sweet red pepper, chopped
- 1 medium green pepper, chopped
- 1 can (15 ounces) garbanzo beans *or* chickpeas, rinsed and drained
- 2 cans (2-1/4 ounces *each*) sliced ripe olives, drained
- 1 medium red onion, chopped
- 4 garlic cloves, minced
- 2 envelopes Italian salad dressing mix

1. Cook the spiral pasta and tortellini according to the package directions. Drain and rinse in cold water. Place in a large bowl; add the artichokes, broccoli,

provolone cheese, salami, peppers, beans, ripe olives, onion and garlic.

2. Prepare salad dressing according to package directions; pour over salad and toss to coat. Serve immediately or cover and refrigerate until serving. **Yield:** 14-16 servings.

Shrimp Potato Salad

Prep/Total Time: 25 min.

Gladys Wolff, Coventry, Rhode Island

Because Rhode Island is known as the Ocean State, I think this recipe represents my state well. The shrimp adds a delicious new twist to traditional potato salad. Plus, leftovers make a terrific lunch the next day.

- 1 pound fresh *or* frozen cooked shrimp, peeled and deveined
- 2 tablespoons lemon juice
- 4 cups cubed peeled potatoes, cooked and cooled
- 1/4 cup sliced green onions
- 1/4 cup minced fresh parsley
- 1 cup (8 ounces) sour cream
- 1 teaspoon salt
- 1/4 teaspoon white pepper
- 1/4 teaspoon dried tarragon
- 1/4 teaspoon ground mustard
- 1/8 teaspoon celery seed
- 1 garlic clove, minced, optional

In a large bowl, toss the shrimp with lemon juice; add the potatoes, onions and parsley. In a small bowl, combine the sour cream, salt, pepper, tarragon, mustard, celery seed and garlic if desired; pour over the potato mixture and toss. Cover and refrigerate until serving. **Yield:** 4-6 servings.

DRESSING:
- 1 cup cider vinegar
- 1/2 cup sugar
- 1/4 cup olive oil
- 1 teaspoon ground mustard
- 1-1/2 teaspoons poppy seeds

SALAD:
- 2 tablespoons butter
- 3/4 cup sliced almonds
- 3 tablespoons sugar
- 8 cups torn romaine
- 8 ounces Brie *or* Camembert, rind removed, cubed
- 1 package (6 ounces) dried cherries

1. For the dressing, in a jar with a tight-fitting lid, combine the dressing ingredients; shake until the sugar is dissolved.

2. For the salad, in a heavy skillet, melt butter over medium heat. Add almonds; cook and stir until nuts are toasted, about 4 minutes. Sprinkle with sugar; cook and stir until sugar is melted, about 3 minutes. Spread on foil to cool; break apart.

3. In a large salad bowl, combine the romaine, cheese and dried cherries. Shake dressing; drizzle over salad. Sprinkle with sugared almonds and toss to coat. **Yield:** 10 servings.

🎗 🎗 🎗
Cherry Brie Tossed Salad

Prep/Total Time: 20 min.

Toni Borden, Wellington, Florida

Draped in a light dressing and sprinkled with almonds, this pretty salad is a variation of a recipe that's been passed around at school events, church activities and birthday parties.

🎗 🎗 🎗
Hot German Rice Salad

Prep/Total Time: 20 min.

Lyn Rhein, Stuttgart, Arkansas

This area has a long rice-growing history, and I use rice in many recipes. With plenty of bacon, this hearty and satisfying salad is practically a meal in itself.

- 8 bacon strips
- 1/3 cup sugar
- 1/3 cup cider vinegar
- 3/4 teaspoon celery seed
- 1/8 teaspoon pepper
- 1/4 cup chopped pimientos
- 1/4 cup chopped green pepper
- 1 tablespoon chopped onion
- 3-1/2 cups hot cooked rice
- 1 hard-cooked egg, sliced

In a skillet over medium heat, cook the bacon until crisp. Drain, reserving 1/3 cup drippings. Crumble the bacon and set aside. Add the sugar, vinegar, celery seed and pepper to drippings. Bring to a boil; cook and stir for 1 minute. Stir in pimientos, green pepper, onion, rice and bacon. Garnish with egg. Serve warm. **Yield:** 4-6 servings.

1/2 cup vegetable oil
1/3 cup sugar
1/4 cup cider vinegar
1 garlic clove, minced
1/4 teaspoon salt
1/4 teaspoon paprika
Pinch white pepper
8 cups torn romaine
4 cups torn Bibb *or* Boston lettuce
2-1/2 cups sliced fresh strawberries
1 cup (4 ounces) shredded Monterey Jack cheese
1/2 cup chopped walnuts, toasted

Combine the first seven ingredients in a jar with a tight-fitting lid; shake well. Just before serving, toss the salad greens, strawberries, cheese and walnuts in a large salad bowl. Drizzle with the salad dressing and toss. **Yield:** 6-8 servings.

Strawberry Tossed Salad

Prep/Total Time: 15 min.

Patricia McNamara, Kansas City, Missouri

One thing I particularly like about this recipe is that it's so versatile. I've served the salad with poultry, ham and pork all throughout the year...and have even used it to add festive green and red color to the table at Christmas.

Toasting Technique

Toasting nuts before using them in a recipe intensifies their flavor. To toast nuts for Strawberry Tossed Salad, spread them on a baking sheet and bake them at 350° for 5 to 10 minutes or until they are lightly toasted. Be sure to watch them carefully so they don't burn.

Hot Five-Bean Salad

Prep/Total Time: 25 min.

Angela Leinenbach, Mechanicsville, Virginia

This crowd-pleaser is like a German potato salad made with colorful beans. My mom's been preparing this dish for years. It's so simple to create and great for church suppers.

8 bacon strips, diced
2/3 cup sugar
2 tablespoons cornstarch
1-1/2 teaspoons salt
Pinch pepper
3/4 cup white vinegar
1/2 cup water
1 can (16 ounces) kidney beans, rinsed and drained
1 can (15-1/4 ounces) lima beans, rinsed and drained
1 can (15 ounces) garbanzo beans *or* chickpeas, rinsed and drained
1 can (14-1/2 ounces) cut green beans, drained
1 can (14-1/2 ounces) cut wax beans, drained

1. In a skillet, cook bacon over medium heat until crisp. Remove to paper towels to drain, reserving 1/4 cup drippings. Add sugar, cornstarch, salt and pepper to drippings. Stir in vinegar and water; bring to a boil, stirring constantly. Cook and stir for 2 minutes.

2. Add the beans; reduce heat. Cover and simmer for 15 minutes or until beans are heated through. Place in a serving bowl; top with bacon. **Yield:** 10-12 servings.

Hearty Chili Mac, p. 66

Spinach Lentil Stew, p. 54

Barley Chicken Chili, p. 60

Soups & Stews

When it comes to comfort food, it's hard to beat a piping-hot bowl of soup or stew. Warm up inside and out with the creamy chowders, meaty chili, hearty bisques and more in this chapter.

Three-Bean Soup, p. 63

3 to 4 medium baking potatoes, baked
5 bacon strips, diced
2 cans (10-3/4 ounces *each*) condensed cream of potato soup, undiluted
1 can (10-3/4 ounces) condensed cheddar cheese soup, undiluted
3-1/2 cups milk
2 teaspoons garlic powder
2 teaspoons Worcestershire sauce
1/2 teaspoon onion powder
1/4 teaspoon pepper
Dash Liquid Smoke, optional
1 cup (8 ounces) sour cream
Shredded cheddar cheese

🎗🎗🎗

Easy Baked Potato Soup

Prep/Total Time: 30 min.

Julie Smithouser, Colorado Springs, Colorado

I came up with this comforting soup when I was crunched for time and wanted to use up leftover baked potatoes. Since then, it has become a mealtime staple. Its wonderful aroma always gets cheers from my husband when he arrives home from work.

1. Peel and dice the baked potatoes; set aside. In a Dutch oven or soup kettle, cook the bacon over medium heat until crisp. Using a slotted spoon, remove bacon to paper towels. Drain, reserving 1-1/2 teaspoons drippings.

2. Add the soups, milk, garlic powder, Worcestershire sauce, onion powder, pepper, Liquid Smoke if desired and reserved potatoes to the drippings. Cook, uncovered, for 10 minutes or until heated through, stirring occasionally.

3. Stir in sour cream; cook for 1-2 minutes or until heated through (do not boil). Garnish with cheddar cheese and bacon. **Yield:** 10 servings (2-1/2 quarts).

🎗🎗🎗

Chilled Berry Soup

Prep: 10 min. + chilling

Lisa Watson, Sparta, Michigan

While on vacation, I had a cool strawberry soup at a restaurant. I enjoyed my bowlful so much that the chef gave me the recipe, but I eventually found this version, which I like even better. The ginger ale adds a special zing.

✓ Uses less fat, sugar or salt. Includes Nutrition Facts and Diabetic Exchanges.

1 quart fresh strawberries, hulled
1/3 cup ginger ale
1/4 cup milk
1/3 cup sugar
1 tablespoon lemon juice
1 teaspoon vanilla extract
1 cup (8 ounces) sour cream

Place strawberries in a food processor or blender; cover and process until smooth. Add ginger ale, milk, sugar, lemon juice and vanilla; cover and process until blended. Pour into a large bowl; whisk in sour cream until smooth. Cover and refrigerate until thoroughly chilled, about 2 hours. **Yield:** 4 servings.

Nutrition Facts: 1 cup equals 189 calories, 5 g fat (4 g saturated fat), 19 mg cholesterol, 55 mg sodium, 32 g carbohydrate, 3 g fiber, 5 g protein. **Diabetic Exchanges:** 1-1/2 fruit, 1 fat-free milk.

Italian Peasant Soup

Prep/Total Time: 25 min.

Kim Knight, Hamburg, Pennsylvania

My father shared this recipe with me, and I use it when I need a hearty, healthy meal. The quick soup is loaded with sausage, chicken, beans and spinach.

- 1 pound Italian sausage links, casings removed and cut into 1-inch slices
- 2 medium onions, chopped
- 6 garlic cloves, chopped
- 1 pound boneless skinless chicken breasts, cut into 1-inch cubes
- 2 cans (15 ounces *each*) cannellini *or* white kidney beans, rinsed and drained
- 2 cans (14-1/2 ounces *each*) chicken broth
- 2 cans (14-1/2 ounces *each*) diced tomatoes
- 1 teaspoon dried basil
- 1 teaspoon dried oregano
- 6 cups fresh spinach leaves, chopped

Shredded Parmesan cheese, optional

1. In a Dutch oven or soup kettle, cook sausage over medium heat until no longer pink; drain. Add onions and garlic; saute until tender. Add chicken; cook and stir until no longer pink.

2. Stir in the beans, broth, tomatoes, basil and oregano. Cook, uncovered, for 10 minutes. Add the spinach and heat just until wilted. Serve with Parmesan cheese if desired. **Yield:** 11 servings (2-3/4 quarts).

Grand Prize Winner

1/2 cup chopped onion
2 garlic cloves, minced
1 tablespoon vegetable oil
5 cups water
1 cup dried lentils, rinsed
4 teaspoons vegetable *or* chicken bouillon granules
3 teaspoons Worcestershire sauce
1/2 teaspoon salt
1/2 teaspoon dried thyme
1/4 teaspoon pepper
1 bay leaf
1 cup chopped carrots
1 can (14-1/2 ounces) diced tomatoes, undrained
1 package (10 ounces) frozen chopped spinach, thawed and squeezed dry
1 tablespoon red wine vinegar

🎀🎀🎀

Spinach Lentil Stew

(Also pictured on page 50)

Prep: 10 min. **Cook:** 40 min.

Alice McEachern, Surrey, British Columbia

When my kids requested more vegetarian dishes, this chunky stew became a favorite. Sometimes we ladle it over rice.

1. In a large saucepan, saute onion and garlic in oil until tender. Add the water, lentils, bouillon, Worcestershire sauce, salt, thyme, pepper and bay leaf; bring to a boil. Reduce heat; cover and simmer for 20 minutes.

2. Add the carrots, tomatoes and spinach; return to a boil. Reduce heat; cover and simmer 15-20 minutes longer or until lentils are tender. Stir in vinegar. Discard bay leaf. **Yield:** 6 servings.

🎀🎀🎀

Chicken 'n' Dumpling Soup

Prep: 35 min. **Cook:** 1 hour 45 min.

Rachel Hinz, St. James, Minnesota

This is a recipe I had to learn…if I wanted to marry into my husband's family! It's their traditional Christmas Eve meal.

1 broiler/fryer chicken (3 to 3-1/2 pounds)
3 quarts water
1/4 cup chicken bouillon granules
1 bay leaf
1 teaspoon whole peppercorns
1/8 teaspoon ground allspice
6 cups uncooked wide noodles
4 cups sliced carrots
1 package (10 ounces) frozen mixed vegetables
3/4 cup sliced celery
1/2 cup chopped onion
1/4 cup uncooked long grain rice
2 tablespoons minced fresh parsley

DUMPLINGS:
1-1/3 cups all-purpose flour
2 teaspoons baking powder
1 teaspoon dried thyme
1/2 teaspoon salt
2/3 cup milk
2 tablespoons vegetable oil

1. In a Dutch oven or soup kettle, combine the first six ingredients; bring to a boil. Reduce heat; cover and simmer for 1-1/2 hours. Remove chicken; allow to cool. Strain broth; discard bay leaf and peppercorns. Skim fat. Debone chicken and cut into chunks; return chicken and broth to pan. Add noodles, vegetables, rice and parsley; bring to a simmer.

2. For dumplings, combine flour, baking powder, thyme and salt in a bowl. Combine milk and oil; stir into dry ingredients. Drop by teaspoonfuls onto simmering soup. Reduce heat; cover and simmer for 15 minutes (do not lift the cover). **Yield:** 20 servings (5 quarts).

Sausage Cabbage Soup

Prep: 20 min. **Cook:** 20 min.

Stella Garrett, Orlando, Florida

I've prepared this satisfying soup for lunch and as a Sunday supper. It's really good with a green salad and bread.

- 1 medium onion, chopped
- 1 tablespoon vegetable oil
- 1 tablespoon butter
- 2 medium carrots, thinly sliced and halved
- 1 celery rib, thinly sliced
- 1 teaspoon caraway seeds
- 2 cups water
- 2 cups chopped cabbage
- 1/2 pound fully cooked smoked kielbasa *or* Polish sausage, halved and cut into 1/4-inch slices
- 1 can (14-1/2 ounces) diced tomatoes, undrained
- 1 tablespoon brown sugar
- 1 can (15 ounces) white kidney beans, rinsed and drained
- 1 tablespoon white vinegar
- 1 teaspoon salt
- 1/4 teaspoon pepper
- Minced fresh parsley

1. In a 3-qt. saucepan, saute onion in oil and butter until tender. Add carrots and celery; saute for 3 minutes. Add caraway; cook and stir 1 minute longer. Add water, cabbage, sausage, tomatoes and brown sugar; bring to a boil.

2. Reduce the heat; cover and simmer for 15-20 minutes or until the vegetables are tender. Add the beans, vinegar, salt and pepper. Simmer, uncovered, for 5-10 minutes or until heated through. Sprinkle with parsley. **Yield:** 6 servings.

Cauliflower Soup

Prep/Total Time: 30 min.

Debbie Ohlhausen, Chilliwack, British Columbia

Cauliflower and shredded carrot share center stage in this creamy, cheesy soup that's sure to warm you up on the chilliest nights. We like it with hot pepper sauce, but that ingredient can be omitted with equally tasty results.

- 1 medium head cauliflower, broken into florets
- 1 medium carrot, shredded
- 1/4 cup chopped celery
- 2-1/2 cups water
- 2 teaspoons chicken *or* vegetable bouillon granules
- 3 tablespoons butter
- 3 tablespoons all-purpose flour
- 3/4 teaspoon salt
- 1/8 teaspoon pepper
- 2 cups milk
- 1 cup (4 ounces) shredded cheddar cheese
- 1/2 to 1 teaspoon hot pepper sauce, optional

1. In a large bowl, combine the cauliflower, carrot, celery, water and bouillon. Bring to a boil. Reduce heat; cover and simmer for 12-15 minutes or until vegetables are tender (do not drain).

2. In another large saucepan, melt butter. Stir in the flour, salt and pepper until smooth. Gradually add milk. Bring to a boil over medium heat; cook and stir for 2 minutes or until thickened. Reduce heat. Stir in the cheese until melted. Add hot pepper sauce if desired. Stir into the cauliflower mixture. **Yield:** 8 servings (about 2 quarts).

🎗🎗🎗
Pizza Soup

Prep: 5 min. Cook: 40 min.

Jackie Brossard, Kitchener, Ontario

This tomato-based soup is a family favorite, and it's been a big hit with my canasta group as well. I like to top each robust bowlful with a slice of toasted French bread and mozzarella cheese, but you can have fun incorporating other popular pizza toppings such as cooked sausage.

- 2 cans (14-1/2 ounces *each*) diced tomatoes
- 2 cans (10-3/4 ounces *each*) condensed tomato soup, undiluted
- 2-1/2 cups water
- 1 package (3-1/2 ounces) sliced pepperoni, quartered
- 1 medium sweet red pepper, chopped
- 1 medium green pepper, chopped
- 1 cup sliced fresh mushrooms
- 2 garlic cloves, minced
- 1/2 teaspoon rubbed sage
- 1/2 teaspoon dried basil
- 1/2 teaspoon dried oregano
- Salt and pepper to taste
- 10 slices French bread, toasted
- 1-1/2 cups (6 ounces) shredded part-skim mozzarella cheese

1. In a Dutch oven or soup kettle, bring the tomatoes, soup and water to a boil. Reduce heat; cover and simmer for 15 minutes. Mash with a potato masher. Add the pepperoni, red and green peppers, mushrooms, garlic, sage, basil, oregano, salt and pepper. Cover and simmer for 10 minutes or until vegetables are tender.

2. Ladle into ovenproof bowls. Top each with a slice of bread and sprinkle with cheese. Broil 4 in. from the heat until the cheese is melted and bubbly. **Yield:** 10 servings (about 2-1/2 quarts).

✿✿✿ Creamy Corn Crab Soup

Prep/Total Time: 30 min.

Carol Ropchan, Willingdon, Alberta

Corn really stars in this fast, easy and tasty soup...and I think the crabmeat makes it a little more special. It gets high marks from both busy cooks and those who love homemade food. Plus, the recipe takes just 30 minutes to prepare.

- 1 medium onion, chopped
- 2 tablespoons butter
- 3 cups chicken broth
- 3 cups frozen corn
- 3 medium potatoes, peeled and diced
- 1 can (6 ounces) crabmeat, drained, flaked and cartilage removed *or* 1 cup flaked imitation crabmeat
- 1 cup milk
- 1/2 teaspoon salt
- 1/4 teaspoon pepper

1. In a large saucepan, saute onion in butter until tender. Add the broth, corn and potatoes; bring to a boil. Reduce heat; cover and simmer for 15 minutes. Remove from the heat; cool slightly.

2. In a blender or food processor, puree half of the corn mixture. Return to the pan. Stir in the crab, milk salt and pepper; cook over low heat until heated through (do not boil). **Yield:** 7 servings.

✿✿✿ Ham and Corn Chowder

Prep/Total Time: 25 min.

Sharon Price, Caldwell, Idaho

I'm always on the lookout for soup recipes because my husband and I love them, particularly in the winter months. This chowder gets a little kick from cayenne and jalapeno pepper.

- 2 celery ribs, chopped
- 1/4 cup chopped onion
- 1 jalapeno pepper, seeded and chopped
- 2 tablespoons butter
- 2 tablespoons all-purpose flour
- 3 cups milk
- 2 cups cubed fully cooked ham
- 2 cups cubed cooked potatoes
- 1-1/2 cups fresh *or* frozen corn
- 1 can (14-3/4 ounces) cream-style corn
- 3/4 teaspoon minced fresh thyme *or* 1/4 teaspoon dried thyme
- 1/8 to 1/4 teaspoon cayenne pepper
- 1/8 teaspoon salt

In a large saucepan, saute the celery, onion and jalapeno in butter until tender. Stir in the flour until blended. Gradually add milk. Bring to a boil; cook and stir for 2 minutes or until thickened. Stir in the remaining ingredients. Bring to a boil. Reduce heat; cover and simmer for 10 minutes or until heated through. **Yield:** 8 servings (2 quarts).

Editor's Note: When cutting or seeding hot peppers, use rubber or plastic gloves to protect your hands. Avoid touching your face.

🎗🎗🎗
Tortellini Vegetable Soup

Prep/Total Time: 30 min.

Deborah Hutchinson, Enfield, Connecticut

Tomatoes, carrots, green beans, potatoes, corn and celery are the perfect complements to convenient frozen tortellini in this heartwarming soup. Add a crusty loaf of bread and a green salad, and dinner is ready in no time.

- 1 **large onion, chopped**
- 2 **celery ribs, chopped**
- 2 **tablespoons vegetable oil**
- 2 **cans (14-1/2 ounces *each*) beef broth**
- 1 **cup *each* frozen corn, sliced carrots and cut green beans**
- 1 **cup diced uncooked potatoes**
- 1 **teaspoon dried basil**
- 1 **teaspoon dried thyme**
- 1/2 **teaspoon minced chives**
- 2 **cans (14-1/2 ounces *each*) diced tomatoes, undrained**
- 2 **cups frozen beef *or* cheese tortellini**

In a Dutch oven or soup kettle, saute the onion and celery in oil. Add the broth, corn, carrots, beans, po-

tatoes, basil, thyme and chives; bring to a boil. Reduce heat; cover and simmer for 10-15 minutes or until potatoes are tender. Add the tomatoes and tortellini. Simmer, uncovered, for 4-5 minutes or until tortellini is heated through. **Yield:** 10 servings (2-1/2 quarts).

🎗 🎗 🎗
Harvest Soup

Prep: 10 min. Cook: 25 min.

Janice Mitchell, Aurora, Colorado

Loaded with ground beef, squash, tomatoes and two kinds of potatoes, this hearty soup makes a great family meal.

> ✓ Uses less fat, sugar or salt. Includes Nutrition Facts and Diabetic Exchanges.

- 1 **pound lean ground beef**
- 3/4 **cup chopped onion**
- 2 **garlic cloves, minced**
- 3-1/2 **cups water**
- 2-1/4 **cups chopped peeled sweet potatoes**
- 1 **cup chopped red potatoes**
- 1 **cup chopped peeled acorn squash**
- 2 **teaspoons beef bouillon granules**
- 2 **bay leaves**
- 1/2 **teaspoon chili powder**
- 1/2 **teaspoon pepper**
- 1/8 **teaspoon ground allspice**
- 1/8 **teaspoon ground cloves**
- 1 **can (14-1/2 ounces) diced tomatoes, undrained**

In a large saucepan, cook the beef, onion and garlic over medium heat until meat is no longer pink; drain. Add the water, potatoes, squash, bouillon, bay leaves, chili powder, pepper, allspice and cloves. Bring to a boil. Reduce heat; cover and simmer for 15-20 minutes or until vegetable are tender. Add the tomatoes. Cook and stir until heated through. Discard bay leaves. **Yield:** 6 servings.

Nutrition Facts: 1-1/2 cups equals 241 calories, 7 g fat (3 g saturated fat), 28 mg cholesterol, 493 mg sodium, 26 g carbohydrate, 4 g fiber, 18 g protein. **Diabetic Exchanges:** 2 lean meat, 2 vegetable, 1 starch.

Savory Tomato Beef Soup

Prep: 30 min. **Cook:** 4 hours

Edna Tilley, Morganton, North Carolina

This soup's one my mother taught me to make. It's good all year but especially when the weather's cold. In winter, I serve big bowlfuls with grilled cheese sandwiches.

- 1 pound beef stew meat, cut into 1/2-inch cubes
- 1 small meaty beef soup bone (beef shanks *or* short ribs)
- 2 tablespoons vegetable oil
- 4 cups water
- 1 can (28 ounces) diced tomatoes, undrained
- 1 cup chopped carrots
- 1 cup chopped celery
- 1/4 cup chopped celery leaves
- 1 tablespoon salt
- 1/2 teaspoon dried marjoram
- 1/2 teaspoon dried basil
- 1/4 teaspoon dried savory
- 1/4 teaspoon dried thyme
- 1/8 teaspoon ground mace
- 1/8 teaspoon hot pepper sauce

In a Dutch oven or soup kettle, brown the stew meat and soup bone in oil. Add the remaining ingredients; bring to a boil. Reduce heat; cover and simmer for 4-5 hours or until meat is tender. Skim fat. Remove meat from bone; cut into 1/2-in. cubes. Return to soup; heat through. **Yield:** 6-8 servings (about 2 quarts).

Cream of Cabbage Soup

Prep/Total Time: 30 min.

Helen Riesterer, Kiel, Wisconsin

People love this soup's flavor and creamy cheese consistency. I've given the recipe to friends, who've varied it a little. One substituted summer squash and zucchini for the rutabaga.

- 4 cups water
- 2 tablespoons chicken bouillon granules
- 3 cups diced peeled potatoes
- 1 cup finely chopped onion
- 1 cup diced peeled rutabaga
- 1/2 cup diced carrots
- 6 cups chopped cabbage
- 1 cup chopped celery
- 1/2 cup chopped green pepper
- 1 garlic clove, minced
- 1 teaspoon salt
- 1 teaspoon dill weed
- 1 cup butter
- 1 cup all-purpose flour
- 2 cups milk
- 2 cups chicken broth
- 1/2 pound process cheese (Velveeta)
- 1/2 teaspoon dried thyme

Pepper to taste
Additional milk, optional

1. In a Dutch oven or soup kettle, bring water and bouillon to a boil. Add potatoes, onion, rutabaga and carrots. Reduce heat; cover and simmer for 5 minutes. Add cabbage, celery and green pepper; simmer, uncovered, for 5 minutes or until vegetables are crisp-tender. Add garlic, salt and dill.

2. In a saucepan, melt butter. Stir in flour; cook and stir over medium heat until golden brown. Gradually add milk and broth, stirring until smooth. Add cheese, thyme and pepper; cook on low until cheese is melted. Stir into vegetable mixture; simmer for 5 minutes. Thin with milk if needed. **Yield:** 12-14 servings (about 3-1/2 quarts).

★ ★ ★
Barley Chicken Chili

(Also pictured on page 50)
Prep/Total Time: 25 min.

Kayleen Grew, Essexville, Michigan

After making a few changes to the original recipe, I had this zesty chili simmering on the stovetop. It was great!

- 1 cup chopped onion
- 1/2 cup chopped green pepper
- 1 teaspoon olive oil
- 2-1/4 cups water
- 1 can (15 ounces) tomato sauce
- 1 can (14-1/2 ounces) chicken broth
- 1 can (10 ounces) diced tomatoes and green chilies, undrained
- 1 cup quick-cooking barley
- 1 tablespoon chili powder
- 1/2 teaspoon ground cumin
- 1/4 teaspoon garlic powder
- 3 cups cubed cooked chicken

In a large saucepan, saute onion and green pepper in oil until tender. Add the water, tomato sauce, broth, tomatoes, barley, chili powder, cumin and garlic powder; bring to a boil. Reduce heat; cover and simmer for 10 minutes. Add chicken. Cover and simmer 5 minutes longer or until barley is tender. **Yield:** 9 servings (about 2 quarts).

★ ★ ★
Butternut Bisque

Prep: 20 min. Cook: 45 min.

Marion Tipton, Phoenix, Arizona

A delicious dinner is even more memorable when I start with this creamy soup, which has a bit of zip and super squash flavor. Serve it as a first course for a holiday feast...or as a main dish with your favorite fresh-baked bread.

- 2 medium carrots, sliced
- 2 celery ribs with leaves, chopped
- 2 medium leeks (white portion only), sliced
- 1 jalapeno pepper, seeded and minced
- 1/4 cup butter
- 2 pounds butternut squash, peeled, seeded and cubed (about 6 cups)
- 2 cans (14-1/2 ounces *each*) chicken broth
- 1/2 teaspoon ground ginger
- 1/2 cup half-and-half cream
- 1/2 teaspoon salt
- 1/4 teaspoon white pepper
- 1/2 cup chopped pecans, toasted

1. In a large saucepan, saute carrots, celery, leeks and jalapeno in butter for 10 minutes. Add the squash, broth and ginger; bring to a boil. Reduce heat; cover and simmer until squash is tender, about 25 minutes.

2. Cool until lukewarm. In a blender or food processor, puree squash mixture in small batches until smooth; return to pan. Add cream, salt and pepper;

mix well. Heat through but do not boil. Garnish with pecans. **Yield:** 8 servings (2 quarts).

Editor's Note: When cutting or seeding hot peppers, use rubber or plastic gloves to protect your hands. Avoid touching your face.

Neighborhood Bean Soup

Prep: 30 min. + standing
Cook: 3 hours

Cheryl Trowbridge, Windsor, Ontario

I like to make big batches of everything, and that tendency has helped me get to know my neighbors. The local ladies always volunteer to try out my new recipes.

- 2 cups dried great northern beans
- 5 cups chicken broth
- 3 cups water
- 1 meaty ham bone *or* 2 smoked ham hocks
- 2 to 3 tablespoons chicken bouillon granules
- 1 teaspoon dried thyme
- 1/2 teaspoon dried marjoram
- 1/2 teaspoon pepper
- 1/4 teaspoon rubbed sage
- 1/4 teaspoon dried savory
- 2 medium onions, chopped
- 3 medium carrots, chopped
- 3 celery ribs, chopped
- 1 tablespoon vegetable oil

1. Place beans in a Dutch oven or soup kettle; add water to cover by 2 in. Bring to a boil; boil for 2 minutes. Remove from the heat; cover and let stand for 1 hour. Drain.

2. Add broth, water, ham bone, bouillon and seasonings; bring to a boil. Reduce heat; cover and simmer for 2 hours. Meanwhile, saute the onions, carrots and celery in oil; add to the soup. Cover and simmer 1 hour longer.

3. Debone ham and cut into chunks; return to soup. Skim fat. **Yield:** 10 servings (2-3/4 quarts).

Zucchini Garden Chowder

Prep/Total Time: 30 min.

Nanette Jordan, Canton, Michigan

When my husband and I put in our first garden, we planted zucchini. I used it in this cheesy chowder, and it was a hit!

- 2 medium zucchini, chopped
- 1 medium onion, chopped
- 2 tablespoons minced fresh parsley
- 1 teaspoon dried basil
- 1/3 cup butter
- 1/3 cup all-purpose flour
- 1 teaspoon salt
- 1/4 teaspoon pepper
- 3 cups water
- 3 chicken bouillon cubes
- 1 teaspoon lemon juice
- 1 can (14-1/2 ounces) diced tomatoes, undrained
- 1 can (12 ounces) evaporated milk
- 1 package (10 ounces) frozen corn
- 1/4 cup grated Parmesan cheese
- 2 cups (8 ounces) shredded cheddar cheese
- Pinch sugar, optional
- Additional chopped parsley, optional

1. In a Dutch oven or soup kettle, saute the zucchini, onion, parsley and basil in butter until vegetables are tender. Stir in flour, salt and pepper. Gradually stir in water. Add the chicken bouillon and lemon juice; mix well. Bring to a boil; cook and stir for 2 minutes or until thickened.

2. Add tomatoes, milk and corn; bring to a boil. Reduce heat; cover and simmer for 5 minutes or until corn is tender. Just before serving, add cheeses; stir until melted. Add sugar and garnish with parsley if desired. **Yield:** 8-10 servings (about 2-1/2 quarts).

Chicken Tortilla Chowder

Prep/Total Time: 20 min.

Jennifer Gouge, Lubbock, Texas

Years ago, when I was a student attending college full-time, my time in the kitchen was limited. This recipe helped me have a hot meal on the table when my husband got home. He's a real meat-and-potatoes man, but he absolutely loves this thick, creamy chowder full of flour tortilla strips.

- 1 can (14-1/2 ounces) chicken broth
- 1 can (10-3/4 ounces) condensed cream of chicken soup, undiluted
- 1 can (10-3/4 ounces) condensed cream of potato soup, undiluted
- 1-1/2 cups milk
- 2 cups cubed cooked chicken
- 1 can (11 ounces) Mexicorn
- 1 jar (4-1/2 ounces) sliced mushrooms, drained
- 1 can (4 ounces) chopped green chilies
- 1/4 cup thinly sliced green onions
- 4 flour tortillas (6 to 7 inches), cut into 1/2-inch strips
- 1-1/2 cups (6 ounces) shredded cheddar cheese

In a Dutch oven or soup kettle, combine the broth, soups and milk. Add the chicken, corn, mushrooms, chilies and onions; mix well. Bring to a boil. Add the tortilla strips. Reduce heat; simmer, uncovered, for 8-10 minutes or until heated through. Add cheese; stir just until melted. Serve immediately. **Yield:** 8-10 servings (2-1/2 quarts).

Three-Bean Soup

(Also pictured on page 51)

Prep/Total Time: 30 min.

Joni Voit, Champlin, Minnesota

This chili-like soup is delicious and very low in fat. Salsa, cumin and chili powder spice it up nicely.

✓ Uses less fat, sugar or salt. Includes Nutrition Facts and Diabetic Exchanges.

 1 large onion, chopped
 1 medium green pepper, chopped
 4 garlic cloves, minced
 2 teaspoons olive oil
 1 can (16 ounces) kidney beans, rinsed and drained
 1 can (16 ounces) fat-free refried beans
 1 can (15 ounces) black beans, rinsed and drained
 1 can (14-1/2 ounces) reduced-sodium chicken broth
 1 can (14-1/2 ounces) stewed tomatoes, cut up
 3/4 cup salsa
 2 teaspoons chili powder
 1/2 teaspoon pepper
 1/4 teaspoon ground cumin

In a large saucepan, saute the onion, green pepper and garlic in oil until tender. Add the remaining ingredients; mix well. Bring to a boil. Reduce heat; cover and simmer for 10 minutes. **Yield:** 8 servings.

Nutrition Facts: 1 cup equals 201 calories, 1 g fat (trace saturated fat), 0 cholesterol, 755 mg sodium, 36 g carbohydrate, 10 g fiber, 12 g protein. **Diabetic Exchanges:** 2 starch, 1 lean meat.

Green Chili Pork Stew

Prep: 25 min. Cook: 65 min.

Carrie Burton, Sierra Vista, Arizona

Anyone living in or visiting the Southwest knows green chilies are a staple. They're put to terrific use in this zesty stew. Cumin, garlic and fresh cilantro also provide fantastic flavor, and plenty of pork means no one leaves the table hungry.

 2-1/2 to 3 pounds boneless pork shoulder *or* butt, trimmed
 1 tablespoon vegetable oil
 1 cup chopped onion
 3 garlic cloves, minced
 2 cups water
 1 can (28 ounces) stewed tomatoes
 1 to 2 cans (4 ounces *each*) chopped green chilies
 2 cups cubed peeled potatoes
 1 tablespoon chopped fresh cilantro
 2 teaspoons ground cumin
 2 teaspoons dried oregano
 2 teaspoons fennel seed
 1 teaspoon salt
 1/4 teaspoon pepper
 1 can (15 ounces) pinto beans, rinsed and drained

Cut pork into 1-in. cubes; brown in oil in a soup kettle or Dutch oven over medium heat. Add onion and garlic; saute for 3-5 minutes. Drain. Add water, tomatoes, chilies, potatoes and seasonings; bring to a boil. Reduce heat; cover and simmer for 45 minutes. Add beans; cover and simmer for 20-30 minutes or until the meat and vegetables are tender. **Yield:** 8-10 servings.

❧❧❧ Marvelous Mushroom Soup

Prep/Total Time: 30 min.

Beverly Rafferty, Winston, Oregon

Soup is tops on the list of things I love to cook. I've used this one as a first course and as a Sunday supper with rolls.

1/2 **pound fresh mushrooms, sliced**
1 **large onion, finely chopped**
1 **garlic clove, minced**
1/2 **teaspoon dried tarragon**
1/4 **teaspoon ground nutmeg**
3 **tablespoons butter**
1/4 **cup all-purpose flour**
2 **cans (14-1/2 ounces *each*) beef *or* vegetable broth**
1 **cup (8 ounces) sour cream**
1/2 **cup half-and-half cream**
1/2 **cup evaporated milk**
1 **teaspoon lemon juice**
Dash hot pepper sauce
Salt and pepper to taste

1. In a Dutch oven or soup kettle, saute the mushrooms, onion, garlic, tarragon and nutmeg in butter until the vegetables are tender. Stir in the flour until smooth. Gradually add the broth; bring to a boil, stirring constantly.

2. Reduce heat to low; slowly add sour cream. Cook and stir until smooth. Stir in cream and milk. Add lemon juice, hot pepper sauce, salt and pepper. Heat through but do not boil. **Yield:** 6 servings.

❧❧❧ Turkey Meatball Soup

Prep: 25 min. Cook: 30 min.

Carol Losier, Baldwinsville, New York

You don't need to cook the homemade meatballs or boil the egg noodles separately, so this soup comes together in no time. I usually double the recipe, and the big batch never lasts long.

2 **cans (14-1/2 ounces *each*) chicken broth**
1 **celery rib with leaves, thinly sliced**
1 **medium carrot, thinly sliced**
1/4 **cup chopped onion**
1 **tablespoon butter**
1 **egg, beaten**
1/2 **cup dry bread crumbs**
2 **tablespoons dried parsley flakes**
1 **tablespoon Worcestershire sauce**
1/4 **teaspoon pepper**
1/2 **pound lean ground turkey**
1 **cup uncooked egg noodles**

1. In a large saucepan, bring the chicken broth, celery and carrot to a boil. Reduce heat; cover and simmer for 10 minutes.

2. Meanwhile, in a small skillet, saute onion in butter until tender. Transfer to a large bowl. Add the beaten egg, bread crumbs, parsley, Worcestershire sauce and pepper. Crumble turkey over mixture and mix

well. Shape into 1-in. balls.

3. Add meatballs to the simmering broth. Bring to a boil. Reduce heat; cover and simmer for 15 minutes. Add noodles. Cover and simmer for 5 minutes or until noodles are tender. **Yield:** 5 servings.

2 cans (10-3/4 ounces *each*) condensed cream of mushroom soup, undiluted
1 can (10-3/4 ounces) condensed cream of celery soup, undiluted
2-2/3 cups milk
4 green onions, chopped
1/2 cup finely chopped celery
1 garlic clove, minced
1 teaspoon Worcestershire sauce
1/4 teaspoon hot pepper sauce
1-1/2 pounds uncooked medium shrimp, peeled and deveined
1 can (6 ounces) crabmeat, drained, flaked and cartilage removed
1 jar (4-1/2 ounces) whole mushrooms, drained
3 tablespoons Madeira wine *or* chicken broth
1/2 teaspoon salt
1/2 teaspoon pepper
Minced fresh parsley

🎖🎖🎖
Seafood Bisque

Prep/Total Time: 30 min.

Pat Edwards, Dauphin Island, Alabama

We live on the Gulf Coast, where fresh seafood is plentiful. I adapted several recipes to come up with this rich bisque.

In a Dutch oven or soup kettle, combine the first eight ingredients; mix well. Bring to a boil. Reduce heat; add the shrimp, crab and mushrooms. Simmer, uncovered, for 10 minutes. Stir in the wine or broth, salt and pepper; cook 2-3 minutes longer. Garnish with parsley. **Yield:** 10 servings (2-1/2 quarts).

🎖🎖🎖
Spicy Split Pea Soup

Prep: 10 min. **Cook:** 2-1/2 hours

Cathy Dobbins, Rio Rancho, New Mexico

After moving to New Mexico years ago, I discovered folks here put peppers or chilies in almost everything. So I decided to add some to this zippy pea soup recipe.

1 package (16 ounces) dried green split peas
6 cups water
1 meaty ham bone *or* 2 smoked ham hocks *or* shanks
4 chicken bouillon cubes
3 to 5 medium Anaheim peppers, roasted, peeled, seeded and chopped *or* 2 to 3 cans (4 ounces *each*) chopped green chilies
2 medium carrots, sliced
2 celery ribs, sliced
1 medium onion, chopped
1 garlic clove, minced
1-1/2 teaspoons dried oregano
1/4 teaspoon pepper
1/8 teaspoon ground cumin

In a Dutch oven or soup kettle, combine the peas, water, ham bone and bouillon; bring to a boil. Reduce heat; cover and simmer for 1-1/2 hours. Add the remaining ingredients; bring to a boil. Reduce heat; cover and simmer 1 hour longer. Remove ham bone and cut meat from bone. Return to the soup and heat through. **Yield:** 8-10 servings (about 2-1/2 quarts).

🎀 🎀 🎀
Hearty Chili Mac
(Also pictured on page 50)

Prep: 20 min. **Cook:** 1 hour 15 min.

Fannie Wehmas, Saxon, Wisconsin

Everyone at the dinner table asks for another bowl of this chunky, beefy soup packed with macaroni. Luckily, the recipe makes a lot, so no one is disappointed!

- 2 pounds ground beef
- 1 medium onion, chopped
- 1 can (46 ounces) tomato juice
- 1 can (28 ounces) diced tomatoes, undrained
- 2 celery ribs without leaves, chopped
- 3 tablespoons brown sugar
- 2 tablespoons chili powder
- 1 teaspoon salt
- 1 teaspoon prepared mustard
- 1/4 teaspoon pepper
- 2 cans (16 ounces *each*) kidney beans, rinsed and drained
- 1/2 cup uncooked elbow macaroni

In a Dutch oven or large kettle, cook beef and onion over medium heat until meat is no longer pink; drain. Stir in tomato juice, tomatoes, celery, sugar, chili powder, salt, mustard and pepper. Bring to a boil. Reduce heat; simmer, uncovered, for 1 hour, stirring occasionally. Add beans and pasta; simmer 15-20 minutes longer or until pasta is tender. **Yield:** 10-12 servings.

🎀 🎀 🎀
Cheeseburger Chowder
Prep/Total Time: 25 min.

Lori Risdal, Sioux City, Iowa

After tasting a wonderful chowder at a restaurant, I dressed up a can of cheese soup to see if I could capture the same flavors. Then I took things a step further by adding chilies and Southwestern spices.

- 1/2 pound ground beef
- 1 can (10-3/4 ounces) condensed cheddar cheese soup, undiluted
- 1-3/4 cups milk
- 1 cup frozen shredded hash brown potatoes
- 1 can (4 ounces) chopped green chilies
- 1 tablespoon taco seasoning
- 1 tablespoon dried minced onion
- 1/2 teaspoon chili powder
- Coarsely crushed corn chips, shredded Monterey Jack cheese and chopped green onions, optional

In a large saucepan, cook beef over medium heat until no longer pink; drain. Stir in the soup, milk, potatoes, chilies, taco seasoning, onion and chili powder until blended. Bring to a boil. Reduce heat; simmer, uncovered, for 5 minutes or until heated through. Garnish with corn chips, cheese and green onions if desired. **Yield:** 4 servings.

Taco Twist Soup

Prep/Total Time: 20 min.

Colleen Zertler, Menomonie, Wisconsin

I changed the original recipe for this soup by substituting beans for the beef and by using reduced-fat garnishes.

- 1 medium onion, chopped
- 2 garlic cloves, minced
- 2 teaspoons olive oil
- 3 cups vegetable broth *or* reduced-sodium beef broth
- 1 can (15 ounces) black beans, rinsed and drained
- 1 can (14-1/2 ounces) diced tomatoes
- 1-1/2 cups picante sauce
- 1 cup uncooked spiral pasta
- 1 small green pepper, chopped
- 2 teaspoons chili powder
- 1 teaspoon ground cumin
- 1/2 cup shredded reduced-fat cheddar cheese
- 3 tablespoons reduced-fat sour cream

1. In a large saucepan, saute the onion and garlic in oil until tender. Add the vegetable broth, black beans, tomatoes, picante sauce, spiral pasta, green pepper, chili powder and cumin. Bring soup to a boil, stirring frequently.

2. Reduce heat; cover and simmer for 10-12 minutes or until pasta is tender, stirring occasionally. Serve with cheese and sour cream. **Yield:** 6 servings.

5 cups chicken broth
2-1/4 cups sliced fresh mushrooms
1/2 cup chopped celery
1/2 cup sliced carrots
1/2 cup chopped onion
1/4 teaspoon pepper

NOODLES:
2-1/2 cups all-purpose flour, *divided*
1 teaspoon salt
2 eggs
1 can (5 ounces) evaporated milk
1 tablespoon olive oil

1. Combine the first four ingredients; rub over chickens. Place in an ungreased 13-in. x 9-in. x 2-in. baking pan. Cover and bake at 350° for 1-1/4 hours or until tender. Drain and reserve drippings. Skim fat. Cool chicken; debone and cut into chunks. Cover and refrigerate chicken.

2. In a Dutch oven or soup kettle, bring chicken broth and reserved drippings to a boil. Add mushrooms, celery, carrots, onion and pepper; simmer for 30 minutes.

3. Meanwhile, for noodles, set aside 1/3 cup of flour. Combine salt and remaining flour in a bowl. Beat eggs, milk and oil; stir into dry ingredients. Sprinkle kneading surface with reserved flour; knead dough until smooth. Divide into thirds. Roll out each portion to 1/8-in. thickness; cut to desired width.

4. Freeze two portions to use at another time. Bring soup to a boil. Add one portion of noodles; cook for 7-9 minutes or until almost tender. Add chicken; heat through. **Yield:** 10 servings (2-3/4 quarts).

Best Chicken Noodle Soup

Prep: 2 hours Cook: 30 min.

Cheryl Rogers, Ames, Iowa

I experimented to come up with my own recipe for chicken noodle soup. People really like the vegetables and rosemary.

1 tablespoon dried rosemary, crushed
2 teaspoons garlic powder
2 teaspoons pepper
2 teaspoons seasoned salt
2 broiler/fryer chickens (3 to 3-1/2 pounds *each*)

Onion Cream Soup

Prep/Total Time: 30 min.

Janice Hemond, Lincoln, Rhode Island

My whole family loves this hearty soup, especially on cold winter evenings. It has a mild onion-cheese flavor.

2 cups thinly sliced sweet onions
6 tablespoons butter, *divided*
1 can (14-1/2 ounces) chicken broth
2 teaspoons chicken bouillon granules
1/4 teaspoon pepper
3 tablespoons all-purpose flour
1-1/2 cups milk
1/4 cup diced process cheese (Velveeta)
Shredded cheddar cheese and minced fresh parsley

1. In a large skillet, cook onions in 3 tablespoons butter over medium-low heat until tender. Add the broth, bouillon and pepper; bring to a boil. Remove from the heat.

2. In a large saucepan, melt the remaining butter. Stir in flour until smooth; gradually add milk. Bring to a boil; cook and stir for 1-2 minutes or until thickened. Reduce heat; add process cheese and onion mixture. Cook and stir until heated through and cheese is melted. Sprinkle with cheddar cheese and parsley. **Yield:** 4 servings.

This soup is perfect for a group after an autumn outing. The combination of squash, applesauce and spices is terrific.

✓ Uses less fat, sugar or salt. Includes Nutrition Facts and Diabetic Exchanges.

1-1/2 **cups chopped onions**
 1 **tablespoon vegetable oil**
 4 **cups mashed cooked butternut squash**
 3 **cups reduced-sodium chicken broth**
 2 **cups unsweetened applesauce**
1-1/2 **cups fat-free milk**
 1 **bay leaf**
 1 **tablespoon sugar**
 1 **tablespoon lime juice**
 1 **teaspoon curry powder**
 1/2 **teaspoon salt, optional**
 1/2 **teaspoon ground cinnamon**
 1/4 **teaspoon ground nutmeg**
 1/4 **teaspoon pepper**

In a Dutch oven, saute onions in oil until tender. Add the remaining ingredients. Bring to a boil. Reduce heat; simmer, uncovered, for 30 minutes. Discard bay leaf before serving. **Yield:** 10 servings (2-1/2 quarts).

Nutrition Facts: 1 cup (prepared without salt) equals 113 calories, 2 g fat (0 saturated fat), 1 mg cholesterol, 60 mg sodium, 22 g carbohydrate, 0 fiber, 4 g protein.
Diabetic Exchanges: 1 starch, 1 vegetable.

🎀 🎀 🎀
Harvest Squash Soup
Prep: 15 min. **Cook:** 30 min.
Mrs. H.L. Sosnowski, Grand Island, New York

🎀 🎀 🎀
Southwestern Bean Soup
Prep/Total Time: 25 min.

Jackie Hacker, Seville, Ohio

When a friend needs a night off from cooking, I deliver this one-pot meal with tortilla chips, shredded cheese and sour cream for garnish. The amount of pepper sauce can be adjusted, and the broth can be omitted for a thicker batch.

 1 **large onion, chopped**
 1 **teaspoon vegetable oil**
 2 **cans (15 ounces *each*) black beans, rinsed and drained**
 2 **cans (14-1/2 ounces *each*) diced tomatoes with garlic and onion**
 2 **cans (14-1/2 ounces *each*) chicken *or* vegetable broth**
 1 **can (16 ounces) kidney beans, rinsed and drained**
 1 **can (15 ounces) cannellini *or* white kidney beans, rinsed and drained**
1-1/2 **cups fresh *or* frozen corn**
 4 **garlic cloves, minced**
1-1/2 **teaspoons ground cumin**
1-1/2 **teaspoons chili powder**
 1/8 to 1/4 **teaspoon hot pepper sauce**

In a Dutch oven or soup kettle, saute the onion in oil until tender. Stir in the remaining ingredients; bring to a boil. Reduce the heat; simmer, uncovered, for 5 minutes or until soup is heated through. **Yield:** 12 servings (3 quarts).

Blueberry Almond Coffee Cake, p. 88

Italian Sausage Strata, p. 81

Apple Nut Hotcakes, p. 84

Breakfast & Brunch

What could be better than starting off the day with contest-winning breakfast dishes? This sunny chapter gives you dozens of morning recipes that are so good, you'll want to make them for lunch and dinner, too!

Vegetable Oven Pancake, p. 72

🎀🎀🎀
Asparagus Bacon Quiche

Prep: 20 min. **Bake:** 35 min.

Suzanne McKinley, Lyons, Georgia

Lovely asparagus peeks out from every slice of this hearty quiche, which is delicious and a little different. I like to make it for holidays and other special occasions.

1 unbaked pastry shell (9 inches)
1 pound fresh asparagus, trimmed and cut into
    1-inch pieces
6 bacon strips, cooked and crumbled
3 eggs
1-1/2 cups half-and-half cream
1 cup grated Parmesan cheese, *divided*
1 tablespoon sliced green onions
1 teaspoon sugar
1/2 teaspoon salt
1/4 teaspoon pepper
Pinch ground nutmeg

1. Line the unpricked pastry shell with a double thickness of heavy-duty foil. Bake at 450° for 5 minutes; remove foil. Bake 5 minutes longer; remove from the oven and set aside.

2. Cook asparagus in a small amount of water until crisp-tender, about 3-4 minutes; drain well. Arrange the bacon and asparagus in the crust.

3. In a bowl, beat eggs; add cream, 1/2 cup cheese, onions, sugar, salt, pepper and nutmeg. Pour over asparagus. Sprinkle with remaining cheese. Bake at 400° for 10 minutes. Reduce heat to 350°; bake 23-25 minutes longer or until a knife inserted near the center comes out clean. **Yield:** 6-8 servings.

🎀🎀🎀
Vegetable Oven Pancake

(Also pictured on page 71)

Prep: 15 min. **Bake:** 20 min.

Mirien Church, Aurora, Colorado

I clipped this recipe when I was first married, but my husband was actually first to prepare it. The puffy pancake looks beautiful and tastes even better.

1 teaspoon butter
1/2 cup all-purpose flour
2 eggs, beaten
1/2 cup milk
1/2 teaspoon salt, *divided*
2 cups fresh broccoli florets
1 cup chopped green pepper
1 cup chopped tomato
1/2 cup chopped red onion
2 tablespoons water
1/8 teaspoon pepper
1-1/2 cups (6 ounces) shredded cheddar cheese

1. Place butter in a 9-in. pie plate; heat in a 450° oven until melted. Carefully tilt pan to coat bottom and sides. In a bowl, beat the flour, eggs, milk and 1/4 teaspoon salt until smooth. Pour into pie plate. Bake for 14-16 minutes or until puffed around the edges and golden brown.

2. Meanwhile, in a skillet, cook the broccoli, green pepper, tomato and onion in water for 8-10 minutes or until crisp-tender; drain well. Add pepper and remaining salt.

3. Sprinkle 1/2 cup cheese over pancake; top with vegetables and remaining cheese. Bake 3-4 minutes longer or until cheese is melted. Cut into four wedges; serve immediately. **Yield:** 4 servings.

Raspberry Streusel Coffee Cake

Prep: 25 min. + cooling
Bake: 40 min.

Amy Mitchell, Sabetha, Kansas

One of my mother's friends used to bring this over at Christmastime, and the pretty treat never lasted long. With a tangy raspberry filling, tender cake and crunchy topping, it has become a favorite at our house.

3-1/2 cups unsweetened raspberries
   1 cup water
   2 tablespoons lemon juice
1-1/4 cups sugar
   1/3 cup cornstarch
BATTER:
   3 cups all-purpose flour
   1 cup sugar
   1 teaspoon baking powder
   1 teaspoon baking soda
   1 cup cold butter
   2 eggs, lightly beaten
   1 cup (8 ounces) sour cream
   1 teaspoon vanilla extract

TOPPING:
   1/2 cup all-purpose flour
   1/2 cup sugar
   1/4 cup butter, softened
   1/2 cup chopped pecans
GLAZE:
   1/2 cup confectioners' sugar
   2 teaspoons milk
   1/2 teaspoon vanilla extract

1. In a large saucepan, cook raspberries and water over medium heat for 5 minutes. Add lemon juice. Combine sugar and cornstarch; stir into fruit mixture. Bring to a boil; cook and stir for 2 minutes or until thickened. Cool.

2. In a large bowl, combine the flour, sugar, baking powder and baking soda. Cut in the butter until the mixture resembles coarse crumbs. Stir in the eggs, sour cream and vanilla (the batter will be stiff).

3. Spread half into a greased 13-in. x 9-in. x 2-in. baking dish. Spread raspberry filling over batter; spoon remaining batter over filling. Combine topping ingredients; sprinkle over top. Bake at 350° for 40-45 minutes or until golden brown. Combine the glaze ingredients; drizzle over warm cake. **Yield:** 12-16 servings.

Grand Prize Winner

🎀🎀🎀
Creamy Cranberry Coffee Cake

Prep: 15 min. **Bake:** 70 min. + cooling

Nancy Roper, Etobicoke, Ontario

Chopped cranberries and orange peel give this coffee cake bursts of tart flavor, but a cream cheese layer sweetens it nicely.

  2 cups all-purpose flour
  1 cup sugar
  1-1/2 teaspoons baking powder
  1/2 teaspoon baking soda
  1 egg
  3/4 cup orange juice
  1/4 cup butter, melted
  1 teaspoon vanilla extract
  2 cups coarsely chopped fresh *or* frozen cranberries
  1 tablespoon grated orange peel
CREAM CHEESE LAYER:
  1 package (8 ounces) cream cheese, softened
  1/3 cup sugar
  1 egg
  1 teaspoon vanilla extract
TOPPING:
  3/4 cup all-purpose flour
  1/2 cup sugar, cubed
  1/2 cup cold butter

1. In a large bowl, combine the first four ingredients. Combine egg, orange juice, butter and vanilla; stir into dry ingredients until well combined. Fold in berries and peel. Pour into a greased 9-in. springform pan.

2. In a small mixing bowl, beat cream cheese and sugar until smooth. Beat in egg and vanilla. Spread over batter. Combine flour and sugar; cut in butter until the mixture resembles coarse crumbs. Sprinkle over top.

3. Place pan on a baking sheet. Bake at 350° for 70-75 minutes or until golden brown. Cool on a wire rack for 15 minutes before removing the sides of pan. **Yield:** 12 servings.

🎀🎀🎀
Sausage Garden Quiche

Prep: 20 min. **Bake:** 30 min.

Janet Jackson, Bakers Mills, New York

This hearty quiche is my all-time favorite! Sometimes I omit the sausage links and add to the garden-fresh ingredients.

Pastry for single-crust pie (9 inches)
  5 eggs
  3/4 cup milk
  1/2 cup chopped fresh spinach *or* Swiss chard
  1/3 cup shredded cheddar cheese
  1 tablespoon dried minced onion
  1 tablespoon minced chives
  1/8 teaspoon salt
  1/8 teaspoon garlic powder
Dash pepper
  6 brown-and-serve sausage links
  3 slices fresh tomato, halved

1. Line a 9-in. pie plate with pastry. Trim pastry to 1/2 in. beyond edge of pie plate; flute edges. Line un-pricked pastry shell with a double thickness of heavy-duty foil. Bake at 450° for 8 minutes. Remove the foil; bake 5 minutes longer. Cool on a wire rack.

2. In a large bowl, whisk eggs and milk. Stir in spinach, cheese, onion, chives, salt, garlic powder and pepper. Carefully pour into crust.

3. Cook sausage according to package directions. Arrange sausage in a spoke pattern in egg mixture; place tomato slices between links. Bake, uncovered, at 350° for 30-35 minutes or until a knife inserted near the center comes out clean. Let stand for 10 minutes before cutting. **Yield:** 6 servings.

🎀🎀🎀
Blueberry Brunch Bake

Prep: 15 min. + chilling **Bake:** 50 min.

Carol Forcum, Marion, Illinois

Especially nice for overnight guests, this recipe is simple to make the day before and then pop in the oven in the morning.

> 1 loaf (1 pound) day-old French bread, cut into 1/2-inch cubes
> 1-1/2 cups fresh *or* frozen unsweetened blueberries
> 12 ounces cream cheese, softened

> 8 eggs
> 1/2 cup plain yogurt
> 1/3 cup sour cream
> 1 teaspoon vanilla extract
> 1/2 teaspoon ground cinnamon
> 1/2 cup milk
> 1/3 cup maple syrup
> Additional blueberries, optional
> Additional maple syrup

1. Place half of the bread cubes in a greased shallow 3-qt. baking dish. Sprinkle with blueberries.

2. In a large mixing bowl, beat cream cheese until smooth. Beat in the eggs, yogurt, sour cream, vanilla and cinnamon. Gradually add milk and 1/3 cup maple syrup until blended. Pour half over the bread. Top with the remaining bread and cream cheese mixture. Cover and refrigerate overnight.

3. Remove from the refrigerator 30 minutes before baking. Cover and bake at 350° for 30 minutes. Uncover; bake 20-25 minutes longer or until a knife inserted near the center comes out clean. Sprinkle with additional blueberries if desired. Let stand for 5 minutes. Serve with maple syrup. **Yield:** 6-8 servings.

Editor's Note: If using frozen blueberries, do not thaw before adding to batter.

🎀🎀🎀
Cinnamon-Swirl Coffee Ring

Prep: 10 min. **Bake:** 55 min. + cooling

Stell Pierce, Franklin, Virginia

I first sampled this irresistible coffee cake at an inn that serves a marvelous breakfast for its guests. The ring has a pretty cinnamon swirl and a hint of cardamom flavor.

> 3 cups all-purpose flour
> 2 cups sugar
> 1 teaspoon baking powder
> 1 teaspoon baking soda
> 1/2 teaspoon salt
> 1/2 teaspoon ground cardamom
> 1 package (8 ounces) cream cheese, softened
> 3 eggs
> 1 cup milk
> 1/2 cup butter, melted
> 1 teaspoon vanilla extract
> **FILLING:**
> 1/2 cup 4% cottage cheese
> 2/3 cup sugar
> 2 teaspoons ground cinnamon
> Confectioners' sugar

1. In a large mixing bowl, combine the first six ingredients. In another mixing bowl, beat cream cheese until smooth. Beat in the eggs, milk, butter and vanilla.

Gradually add to dry ingredients, beating until combined. For filling, combine cottage cheese, sugar and cinnamon in a small mixing bowl. Beat on medium speed for 2 minutes.

2. Spoon half of the batter into a greased 10-in. fluted tube pan; top with filling and remaining batter. Bake at 350° for 55-65 minutes or until a toothpick inserted near the center comes out clean. Cool for 10 minutes before removing from pan to a wire rack. Dust with confectioners' sugar if desired. **Yield:** 12-14 servings.

🏵 🏵 🏵
Cherry Cheese Blintzes

Prep: 30 min. + chilling   **Bake:** 10 min.

Jessica Vantrease, Anderson, Alaska

A ruby-red cherry sauce gives these elegant blintzes delightful flavor and eye-catching color. I sometimes replace the sweet cherries with raspberries, blueberries or peaches. No matter which fruit I choose, this recipe is special enough for holidays yet easy enough for lazy weekend mornings.

- 2/3 cup all-purpose flour
- 1/2 teaspoon salt
- 1-1/2 cups milk
- 3 eggs
- 2 tablespoons butter, melted

FILLING:
- 1 cup (8 ounces) 4% cottage cheese
- 1 package (3 ounces) cream cheese, softened
- 1/4 cup sugar
- 1/2 teaspoon vanilla extract

CHERRY SAUCE:
- 1 pound fresh *or* frozen pitted sweet cherries
- 2/3 cup plus 1 tablespoon water, *divided*
- 1/4 cup sugar
- 1 tablespoon cornstarch

1. In a small mixing bowl, combine flour, salt, milk, eggs and butter. Cover and refrigerate for 2 hours.

2. Heat a lightly greased 8-in. nonstick skillet; pour 2 tablespoons batter into the center of skillet. Lift and tilt pan to evenly coat bottom. Cook until top appears dry; turn and cook 15-20 seconds longer. Remove to a wire rack. Repeat with remaining batter. When cool, stack crepes with waxed paper or paper towels in between. Wrap in foil; refrigerate.

3. In a blender, process cottage cheese until smooth. Transfer to a small mixing bowl; add cream cheese and beat until smooth. Add sugar and vanilla; mix well. Spread about 1 rounded tablespoonful onto each crepe. Fold opposite sides of crepe over filling, forming a little bundle.

4. Place seam side down in a greased 15-in. x 10-in. x 1-in. baking pan. Bake, uncovered, at 350° for 10 minutes or until heated through.

5. Meanwhile, in a large saucepan, bring cherries, 2/3 cup water and sugar to a boil over medium heat. Reduce heat; cover and simmer for 5 minutes or until heated through. Combine cornstarch and remaining water until smooth; stir into cherry mixture. Bring to a boil; cook and stir for 2 minutes or until thickened. Serve over crepes. **Yield:** 9 servings.

🎗🎗🎗
Apricot Coconut Coffee Cake

Prep: 15 min. **Bake:** 35 min. + cooling

Rita Hatfield, Cisco, Illinois

One of the senior members of our church brought this to a Saturday morning wedding shower, and the fruity breakfast cake was a big hit. I've prepared it several times since then and often get requests for the recipe.

- 1 package (8 ounces) cream cheese, softened
- 1/2 cup butter, softened
- 1-1/4 cups sugar
- 2 eggs
- 1/4 cup milk
- 1 teaspoon vanilla extract
- 2 cups all-purpose flour
- 1 teaspoon baking powder
- 1/2 teaspoon baking soda
- 1/4 teaspoon salt
- 1 can (12 ounces) apricot filling

TOPPING:
- 1/3 cup butter, softened
- 2/3 cup packed brown sugar
- 1 teaspoon ground cinnamon
- 2 cups flaked coconut

1. In a large mixing bowl, beat the cream cheese, butter and sugar until fluffy. Add eggs, one at a time, beating well after each addition. Add milk and vanilla; mix well. Combine the flour, baking powder, baking soda and salt; add to creamed mixture. Beat just until moistened.

2. Spread half of the batter into a greased 13-in. x 9-in. x 2-in. baking dish. Carefully spread apricot filling over batter; spread remaining batter over the top. Bake at 350° for 35-40 minutes or until golden brown.

3. In a mixing bowl, cream butter, brown sugar and cinnamon. Stir in coconut. Spoon over the cake. Broil 4 in. from the heat for 1-2 minutes or until golden brown. Cool on a wire rack. **Yield:** 12-15 servings.

🎗🎗🎗
Onion Tart

Prep: 20 min. **Bake:** 45 min.

Christine Andreas, Huntingdon, Pennsylvania

Onion lovers are sure to be asking for second helpings of this appetizing tart—it uses two kinds of onions!

- 1 unbaked pastry shell (9 inches)
- 2 medium sweet onions, thinly sliced
- 2 tablespoons olive oil
- 3 eggs
- 1/2 cup crumbled feta cheese
- 1/2 teaspoon salt
- 1/4 teaspoon coarsely ground pepper
- 1/8 teaspoon ground nutmeg
- 1/8 teaspoon hot pepper sauce
- 3/4 cup half-and-half cream
- 1/2 cup milk
- 1 tablespoon Dijon mustard
- 6 green onions, thinly sliced
- 2 tablespoons minced chives
- 1/3 cup grated Parmesan cheese

1. Line unpricked pastry shell with a double thickness of heavy-duty foil. Bake at 450° for 8 minutes. Remove foil; bake 5 minutes longer. Cool on a wire rack.

2. In a small skillet, saute onions in oil until tender; cool. In a food processor, combine the eggs, feta cheese, salt, pepper, nutmeg and hot pepper sauce; cover and process until smooth. Gradually add cream and milk; process until blended.

3. Brush the inside of crust with mustard. Sprinkle the green onions, chives and sauteed onions over crust. Carefully pour egg mixture over onions. Top with Parmesan cheese. Bake at 375° for 30-40 minutes or until a knife inserted near the center comes out clean. **Yield:** 6 servings.

🎀 🎀 🎀
Cherry Cheese Loaves

Prep: 1-1/2 hours + chilling **Bake:** 20 min.

Carolyn Gregory, Hendersonville, Tennessee

This has become my "trademark." Cuts in the dough give this coffee cake a pretty look without the extra work of braiding it.

- **2 packages (1/4 ounce *each*) active dry yeast**
- **1/2 cup warm water (110° to 115°)**
- **1 cup (8 ounces) sour cream**
- **1/2 cup butter, cubed**
- **1/2 cup sugar**
- **2 eggs**
- **4 cups all-purpose flour**

FILLING:
- **2 packages (one 8 ounces, one 3 ounces) cream cheese, softened**
- **1/2 cup sugar**
- **1 egg**
- **1 teaspoon almond extract**
- **1 can (21 ounces) cherry pie filling**

GLAZE:
- **2 cups confectioners' sugar**
- **1/4 cup milk**
- **1 teaspoon almond extract**

1. In a large mixing bowl, dissolve yeast in warm water. In a saucepan, heat sour cream and butter to 110°-115°. Add to yeast mixture. Add sugar and eggs; mix well. Gradually add flour; mix well. Do not knead.

Cover and refrigerate overnight.

2. In a small mixing bowl, beat cream cheese, sugar, egg and extract until smooth; set aside. Turn dough onto a lightly floured surface; divide into four portions. Roll each into a 12-in. x 8-in. rectangle. Spread a fourth of cream cheese down center of each. Spoon a fourth of pie filling over cream cheese. Fold lengthwise into thirds; pinch side seam and ends to seal. Place seam side down on greased baking sheets.

3. With a sharp scissors, make several 1-in. diagonal cuts near the center of loaves. Cover and let rise in a warm place until doubled, about 1 hour.

4. Bake at 375° for 20-25 minutes or until lightly browned. Combine glaze ingredients; drizzle over warm loaves. Cool on wire racks. Refrigerate leftovers. **Yield:** 4 loaves (10 slices each).

🎀 🎀 🎀
Ham 'n' Corn Fritters

Prep: 20 min. + standing **Cook:** 15 min.

Nelda Cronbaugh, Belle Plaine, Iowa

These tasty golden fritters are a perfect addition to a down-home breakfast or brunch in place of typical pancakes.

- **2 eggs**
- **1/3 cup milk**
- **1-1/4 cups all-purpose flour**
- **1 tablespoon sugar**
- **2 teaspoons baking powder**
- **1/2 teaspoon salt**

Dash pepper
- **1 cup fresh *or* frozen corn, cooked and drained**
- **1 cup chopped fully cooked ham**

Oil for deep-fat frying

1. Separate eggs; let stand at room temperature for 30 minutes. In a mixing bowl, beat egg yolks until slightly thickened. Beat in milk. Combine the flour, sugar, baking powder, salt and pepper; add to yolk mixture and mix well. Stir in the corn and ham. In a small mixing bowl, beat egg whites on high speed until stiff peaks form. Fold into the corn mixture.

2. In an electric skillet or deep-fat fryer, heat oil to 375°. Drop batter by heaping tablespoonfuls, a few at a time, into hot oil. Fry until golden brown, about 1 minute on each side, turning with a slotted spoon. Drain on paper towels. **Yield:** 2 dozen.

🎀🎀🎀 Breakfast Pizza

Prep: 20 min. **Bake:** 25 min.

Jean Beggs, Mears, Michigan

Pizza is ideal for breakfast or brunch when it's made like this. Sometimes I put together the recipe the night before, refrigerate it and bake it in the morning.

- 2 tubes (12 ounces *each*) refrigerated buttermilk biscuits, separated into 20 biscuits
- 1 pound bulk pork sausage
- 2 cans (4 ounces *each*) mushroom stems and pieces, drained
- 1 large onion, diced
- 4-1/2 teaspoons butter
- 12 eggs
- 3 cups (12 ounces) shredded part-skim mozzarella cheese

1. Cover the bottom of a greased 13-in. x 9-in. x 2-in. baking pan with biscuits; set aside. Crumble sausage into a large skillet; cook over medium heat until no longer pink. Drain; place sausage in a bowl and set aside. In the same skillet, saute mushrooms and onion in butter for 3-5 minutes or until tender; add to the sausage.

2. In a bowl, whisk the eggs. Coat skillet with cooking spray. Add eggs; cook and stir over medium heat until nearly set. Add sausage and vegetable mixture; cook and stir until completely set.

3. Spread egg mixture over biscuits. Sprinkle with cheese. Cover and bake at 400° for 12 minutes. Uncover; bake 10-13 minutes longer or until cheese is melted and biscuits are golden brown. **Yield:** 6-8 servings.

🎀🎀🎀 Walnut Orange Coffee Cake

Prep: 25 min. **Bake:** 25 min.

Janice Satanek, Hermitage, Pennsylvania

My sister gave me this recipe about 40 years ago, and I still make it often. Everyone loves the delightful orange flavor.

- 1 cup quick-cooking oats
- 1-1/2 cups orange juice
- 1/2 cup butter, softened
- 1-1/2 cups sugar
- 1/2 cup packed brown sugar
- 2 eggs
- 1 teaspoon vanilla extract
- 1-3/4 cups all-purpose flour
- 1 teaspoon baking powder
- 1 teaspoon baking soda
- 1/2 teaspoon salt
- 1/4 teaspoon ground cinnamon
- 1/2 cup chopped walnuts
- 1 tablespoon grated orange peel

TOPPING:
- 1-1/2 cups packed brown sugar
- 3/4 cup butter, cubed
- 3 tablespoons grated orange peel
- 3 tablespoons orange juice
- 3 cups flaked coconut
- 1-1/2 cups chopped walnuts

1. In a small bowl, stir oats and orange juice until softened; set aside. In a mixing bowl, cream butter and sugars; beat in eggs and vanilla until well combined. Combine the flour, baking powder, baking soda, salt and cinnamon; add to the creamed mixture alternately with oat mixture. Stir in walnuts and orange peel. Pour into a greased 13-in. x 9-in. x 2-in. baking dish. Bake at 350° for 25-30 minutes or until a toothpick inserted near the center comes out clean.

2. In a small saucepan, combine brown sugar, butter, orange peel and juice. Bring to a boil; reduce heat. Cook for 1 minute. Remove from the heat; stir in coconut and walnuts. Gently spread over warm cake. Broil 4 in. from the heat for 2 minutes or until the topping is bubbly. **Yield:** 12-15 servings.

1/2 teaspoon baking soda
3/4 cup cold butter
2/3 cup vanilla yogurt
1 tablespoon lemon juice
2 teaspoons grated lemon peel
1 egg
1 egg yolk
1/2 cup lemon curd
GLAZE:
1/2 cup confectioners' sugar
1 teaspoon water
1 teaspoon lemon juice

1. In a small bowl, combine the flour and sugar. Cut in butter until mixture resembles coarse crumbs. Stir in coconut; set aside.

2. For batter, in a large bowl, combine the flour, salt, baking powder and baking soda. Cut in butter until mixture resembles coarse crumbs. Combine the yogurt, lemon juice, peel, egg and egg yolk; stir into crumb mixture just until moistened (batter will be stiff).

3. Spread 2 cups batter in a greased 9-in. springform pan; sprinkle with 3/4 cup of coconut mixture. Drop 1/2 teaspoonfuls of lemon curd over the top to within 1/2 in. of edge. Carefully spoon remaining batter over lemon curd; sprinkle with remaining coconut mixture.

4. Place pan on a baking sheet. Bake at 350° for 55-60 minutes or until a toothpick inserted near the center comes out clean. Cool for 10 minutes. Carefully run a knife around the edge of pan to loosen; remove sides of pan. Combine the glaze ingredients; drizzle over warm cake. **Yield:** 12 servings.

🎀🎀🎀 Lemon Curd Coffee Cake

Prep: 20 min. **Bake:** 55 min. + cooling

Anne Wickman, Endicott, New York

I tried this recipe for my son's birthday years ago and fell in love with the tart lemon filling. The powdered sugar glaze and coconut in the topping make a pretty presentation.

1/2 cup all-purpose flour
1/3 cup sugar
3 tablespoons cold butter
1/2 cup flaked coconut
BATTER:
2-1/4 cups all-purpose flour
1/2 teaspoon salt
1/2 teaspoon baking powder

🎀🎀🎀 Artichoke Cheese Oven Omelet

Prep: 10 min. **Bake:** 25 min. + standing

Bonnie Hawkins, Elkhorn, Wisconsin

My husband and his friends take turns cooking for their group in their homes. The guys love my husband's cheesy omelet.

3/4 cup salsa
1 can (14 ounces) water-packed artichoke hearts, rinsed, drained and chopped
1 cup (4 ounces) shredded Monterey Jack cheese
1 cup (4 ounces) shredded cheddar cheese
1/4 cup grated Parmesan cheese
6 eggs, beaten
1 cup (8 ounces) sour cream
Chopped fresh tomatoes, sliced ripe olives and minced chives, optional

1. Spread salsa in a greased 9-in. deep-dish pie plate. Top with the artichoke hearts and cheese. In a bowl, whisk the eggs and sour cream. Pour over the cheeses.

2. Bake, uncovered, at 350° for 25-30 minutes or until a knife inserted near the center comes out clean. Let stand for 5 minutes before cutting. Garnish with tomatoes, olives and chives if desired. **Yield:** 6-8 servings.

Italian Sausage Strata

(Also pictured on page 70)

Prep: 20 min. + chilling

Bake: 1 hour

Amanda Reid, Oakville, Iowa

When our family sits down for breakfast on days when this make-ahead dish is on the menu, I can relax and join them. I like to serve the strata with fresh fruit and homemade rolls for a satisfying meal.

   1/2 **cup butter, softened,** *divided*
   12 **to 16 slices day-old bread, crusts removed**
   1/2 **pound fresh mushrooms, sliced**
   2 **cups sliced onions**
Salt and pepper to taste
   1 **pound bulk Italian sausage, cooked and drained**
   3 **cups (12 ounces) shredded cheddar cheese**
   5 **eggs**
2-1/2 **cups milk**
   1 **tablespoon Dijon mustard**
   1 **teaspoon ground nutmeg**
   1 **teaspoon ground mustard**
   2 **tablespoons minced fresh parsley**

1. Using 1/4 cup butter, spread one side of each bread slice with butter. Place half of the bread, butter side down, in a greased 13-in. x 9-in. x 2-in. baking dish.

2. In a large skillet, saute the mushrooms and onions in remaining butter. Sprinkle with salt and pepper. Spoon half of the mushroom mixture over bread in prepared pan. Top with half of the sausage and cheese. Layer with the remaining bread, mushroom mixture, sausage and cheese.

3. In a bowl, combine the eggs, milk, Dijon mustard, nutmeg and ground mustard. Pour over cheese. Cover and refrigerate overnight.

4. Remove from the refrigerator 30 minutes before baking. Bake, covered, at 350° for 50 minutes. Uncover; bake 10-15 minutes longer or until a knife inserted near the center comes out clean. Sprinkle with parsley. **Yield:** 12 servings.

🎗🎗🎗
Sunny Asparagus Tart

Prep: 30 min. **Bake:** 55 min. + standing

Susan Kuklinski, Delafield, Wisconsin

With an appearance that'll remind you of the rays of the sun, this eye-catching tart looks as good as it tastes. The distinctive caraway crust and rich, custard-like filling dotted with tender slices of asparagus make it a dish you'll be proud to serve time after time. Try it for your next Easter or spring brunch.

1-1/2 cups all-purpose flour
  1/2 teaspoon caraway seeds
  1/8 teaspoon salt
    5 tablespoons cold butter
    2 tablespoons cold shortening
    3 to 5 tablespoons ice water
FILLING:
1-1/2 pounds fresh asparagus
    1 package (3 ounces) cream cheese, softened
    1 egg yolk
    1 cup heavy whipping cream
    3 eggs
  3/4 teaspoon salt
  1/4 teaspoon white pepper
  1/4 pound thinly sliced fully cooked ham, julienned
  1/3 cup grated Parmesan cheese

1. In a bowl, combine flour, caraway and salt; cut in butter and shortening until mixture resembles coarse crumbs. Sprinkle with water, 1 tablespoon at a time; stir with a fork until dough forms a ball. On a floured surface, roll dough to fit a 10-in. tart pan. Place dough in pan. Freeze for 10 minutes.

2. Cut the asparagus into 2-1/2-in. pieces. Set tips aside; cut remaining pieces in half. Cook all of the asparagus in a small amount of water until crisp-tender, about 3-4 minutes; drain.

3. In a mixing bowl, combine the cream cheese and egg yolk; gradually add cream (mixture will be slightly lumpy). Beat in eggs, one at a time. Add salt and pepper. Place ham and asparagus pieces (not tips) over crust; pour half of the cream cheese mixture over the top. Bake at 425° for 15 minutes.

4. Pour remaining cream cheese mixture over top. Arrange asparagus tips over tart; sprinkle with cheese. Bake at 375° for 40 minutes or until a knife inserted near the center comes out clean. Let stand for 15 minutes before cutting. **Yield:** 6-8 servings.

Creamy Banana Crepes

Prep: 10 min. + chilling **Cook:** 10 min.

Parrish Smith, Lincoln, Nebraska

My husband and I enjoy taking turns fixing weekend breakfasts. These sweet-and-sour crepes are often on our menus.

3/4 cup water
3/4 cup milk
2 eggs
2 tablespoons butter, melted
1/2 teaspoon vanilla extract
1 cup all-purpose flour
1 tablespoon sugar
1/2 teaspoon salt
BANANA FILLING:
3 tablespoons butter
3 tablespoons brown sugar
3 medium firm bananas, cut into 1/4-inch slices
SOUR CREAM FILLING:
1 cup (8 ounces) sour cream
2 tablespoons confectioners' sugar
1/2 cup slivered almonds, toasted
Additional confectioners' sugar and toasted almonds

1. In a small mixing bowl, combine the water, milk, eggs, butter and vanilla. Combine the flour, sugar and salt; add to milk mixture and mix well. Cover and refrigerate for 1 hour.

2. Heat a lightly greased 8-in. nonstick skillet; pour 3 tablespoons batter into the center of skillet. Lift and tilt pan to evenly coat bottom. Cook for 1-2 minutes or until top appears dry; turn and cook 15-20 seconds longer. Remove to a wire rack. Repeat with remaining batter. When cool, stack crepes with waxed paper or paper towels in between.

3. In a small skillet, heat butter and brown sugar over medium heat until sugar is dissolved. Add bananas; toss to coat. Remove from the heat; keep warm.

4. In a small bowl, combine sour cream and confectioners' sugar. Spread over each crepe. Spoon banana filling over sour cream filling; sprinkle with almonds. Roll up crepes; sprinkle with additional confectioners' sugar and toasted almonds. **Yield:** 1 dozen.

Creamed Ham in Toast Cups

Prep/Total Time: 30 min.

Catherine Crandall, Amity, Oregon

My grandmother taught me many of her recipes in show-and-cook sessions. Usually, we had this dish for breakfast on Mondays, following a Sunday lunch of ham, peas and corn.

8 slices bread
1/2 cup butter, softened, *divided*
1/4 cup all-purpose flour
1/8 teaspoon white pepper
1 cup milk
1 cup heavy whipping cream
2 cups chopped fully cooked ham
1 cup frozen green peas, thawed
1 cup whole kernel corn
Paprika

1. Remove and discard the crusts from the bread slices; using a rolling pin, flatten to 1/8-in. thickness. Butter both sides of each bread slice, using 1/4 cup of butter. Press the slices into eight greased muffin cups or 6-oz. custard cups. Bake at 350° for 15-18 minutes or until golden brown.

2. Meanwhile, in a saucepan, melt the remaining butter. Stir in the flour and white pepper. Gradually stir in the milk and heavy whipping cream. Bring to a boil; cook and stir for 2 minutes or until thickened. Reduce the heat. Stir in the ham, peas and corn. Cook and stir for 5 minutes or until heated through. Pour into the warm toast cups; sprinkle with the paprika. **Yield:** 4 servings.

1 cup all-purpose flour
2 tablespoons sugar
2 teaspoons baking powder
1/2 teaspoon salt
1/2 teaspoon ground cinnamon
3/4 cup milk
3 tablespoons butter, melted
2 teaspoons vanilla extract
2 egg whites
1/2 cup shredded peeled apple
1/2 cup chopped walnuts

APPLE SYRUP:
1/4 cup sugar
4 teaspoons cornstarch
1/4 teaspoon ground allspice
1-1/2 cups apple juice

1. In a large bowl, combine flour, sugar, baking powder, salt and cinnamon. In another bowl, combine milk, butter and vanilla; mix well. Stir into dry ingredients just until combined. Beat egg whites until stiff peaks form; fold into batter with apple and nuts.

Pour batter by 1/4 cupfuls onto a lightly greased hot griddle; turn when bubbles form on top. Cook until second side is golden brown.

2. For syrup, combine sugar, cornstarch and allspice in a medium saucepan; stir in apple juice. Cook and stir over medium heat until thickened, about 6-8 minutes. Serve over hotcakes. **Yield:** 10-12 hotcakes.

🎖 🎖 🎖
Apple Nut Hotcakes

(Also pictured on page 70)
Prep/Total Time: 30 min.

Barbara Nowakowski, North Tonawanda, New York

Not only are these a family favorite, they're a favorite in the neighborhood as well. Apple syrup is the perfect complement.

🎖 🎖 🎖
Coconut Chip Coffee Cake

Prep: 15 min. Bake: 45 min. + cooling

Char Frickle, St. Charles, Illinois

Plenty of coconut, chocolate chips and chopped walnuts go into the filling of this yummy breakfast treat.

1/2 cup butter, softened
1 cup sugar
2 eggs
1 teaspoon vanilla extract
2 cups all-purpose flour
1 teaspoon baking powder
1 teaspoon baking soda
1/4 teaspoon salt
1 cup (8 ounces) sour cream

FILLING/TOPPING:
1/2 cup sugar
1/2 cup flaked coconut
1/2 cup semisweet chocolate chips
1/2 cup chopped walnuts

1. In a large mixing bowl, cream butter and sugar until light and fluffy. Add the eggs, one at a time, beating well after each addition. Beat in vanilla. Com-

bine the flour, baking powder, baking soda and salt; gradually add to the creamed mixture alternately with sour cream.

2. Spoon half of the batter into a greased 10-in. tube pan. Combine the filling ingredients; sprinkle half over the batter. Repeat layers. Bake at 350° for 45-50 minutes or until a toothpick inserted near the center comes out clean. Cool for 10 minutes before removing from pan to a wire rack. **Yield:** 12-16 servings.

Eggs Florentine

Prep/Total Time: 30 min.

Bobbi Trautman, Burns, Oregon

I wanted to serve impressive yet healthy fare for brunch, so I lightened up the hollandaise sauce a bit in this classic recipe.

- 2 tablespoons reduced-fat stick margarine
- 1 tablespoon all-purpose flour
- 1/2 teaspoon salt, *divided*
- 1-1/4 cups fat-free milk
- 1 egg yolk
- 2 teaspoons lemon juice
- 1/2 teaspoon grated lemon peel
- 1/2 pound fresh spinach
- 1/8 teaspoon pepper
- 4 eggs
- 2 English muffins, split and toasted

Dash paprika

1. In a saucepan, melt margarine. Stir in flour and 1/4 teaspoon salt until smooth. Gradually add milk. Bring to a boil; cook and stir for 1-2 minutes or until thickened. Remove from the heat.

2. Stir a small amount of sauce into egg yolk; return all to the pan, stirring constantly. Bring to a gentle boil; cook and stir for 2 minutes. Remove from the heat; stir in lemon juice and peel. Set aside and keep warm.

3. Place spinach in a steamer basket. Sprinkle with pepper and remaining salt. Place in a saucepan over 1 in. of water. Bring to a boil; cover and steam for 3-4 minutes or until wilted and tender.

4. Meanwhile, in a skillet or omelet pan with high sides, bring 2 to 3 in. water to a boil. Reduce heat; simmer gently. Break cold eggs, one at a time, into a custard cup or saucer. Holding the dish close to the surface of the simmering water, slip the eggs, one at a time, into the water. Cook, uncovered, for 3-5 minutes or until whites are completely set and yolks begin to thicken. Lift out of the water with a slotted spoon.

5. Place spinach on each muffin half; top with an egg. Spoon 3 tablespoons sauce over each egg. Sprinkle with paprika. Serve immediately. **Yield:** 4 servings.

Editor's Note: This recipe was tested with Parkay Light stick margarine.

Egg and Broccoli Casserole

Prep: 10 min. **Cook:** 3-1/2 hours

Janet Sliter, Kennewick, Washington

I rely on my slow cooker for this filling casserole. It's an unusual recipe for that appliance but is welcomed wherever I serve it.

- 3 cups (24 ounces) 4% cottage cheese
- 3 cups frozen chopped broccoli, thawed and drained
- 2 cups (8 ounces) shredded cheddar cheese
- 6 eggs, beaten
- 1/3 cup all-purpose flour
- 1/4 cup butter, melted
- 3 tablespoons finely chopped onion
- 1/2 teaspoon salt

Additional shredded cheddar cheese, optional

1. In a large bowl, combine the first eight ingredients. Pour into a greased 3-qt. slow cooker. Cover and cook on high for 1 hour. Stir.

2. Reduce heat to low; cover and cook 2-1/2 to 3 hours longer or until a thermometer placed in the center reads 160° and the eggs are set. Sprinkle with cheese if desired. **Yield:** 6 servings.

🎀🎀🎀
Maple Butter Twists

Prep: 35 min. + rising **Bake:** 25 min. + cooling

June Gilliland, Hope, Indiana

My stepmother passed on the recipe for this scrumptious yeast coffee cake that's shaped into impressive rings.

3-1/4 to 3-1/2 cups all-purpose flour
    3 tablespoons sugar
1-1/2 teaspoons salt
    1 package (1/4 ounce) active dry yeast
    3/4 cup milk
    1/4 cup butter
    2 eggs
FILLING:
    1/3 cup packed brown sugar
    1/4 cup sugar
    3 tablespoons butter, softened
    3 tablespoons maple syrup
4-1/2 teaspoons all-purpose flour
    3/4 teaspoon ground cinnamon
    3/4 teaspoon maple flavoring
    1/3 cup chopped walnuts
GLAZE:
    1/2 cup confectioners' sugar
    1/4 teaspoon maple flavoring
    2 to 3 teaspoons milk

1. In a mixing bowl, combine 1-1/2 cups flour, sugar, salt and yeast. In a saucepan, heat milk and butter to 120°-130°. Add to dry ingredients; beat just until moistened. Add eggs; beat on medium for 2 minutes. Stir in enough remaining flour to form a firm dough.

2. Turn onto a floured surface; knead until smooth and elastic, about 5-7 minutes. Place in a greased bowl, turning once to grease top. Cover and let rise in a warm place until doubled, about 70 minutes.

3. In a small mixing bowl, combine the first seven filling ingredients; beat for 2 minutes. Punch the dough down; turn onto a lightly floured surface. Divide in half; roll each into a 16-in. x 8-in. rectangle. Spread the filling to within 1/2 in. of the edges of rectangles. Sprinkle with walnuts. Roll up jelly-roll style, starting with a long side.

4. With a sharp knife, cut each roll in half lengthwise. Open halves so cut side is up; gently twist ropes together. Transfer to two greased 9-in. round baking pans. Coil into a circle. Tuck ends under; pinch to seal. Cover and let rise in a warm place until doubled, about 70 minutes.

5. Bake at 350° for 25-30 minutes or until golden brown. Cool for 10 minutes; remove from pans to wire racks. Combine glaze ingredients; drizzle over warm cakes. **Yield:** 2 coffee cakes.

🎀🎀🎀
Garden Frittata

Prep: 25 min. Bake: 45 min. + standing

Catherine Michel, St. Peters, Missouri

I created this baked dish one day to use up some fresh yellow squash, zucchini and tomato. The frittata is so easy to make because you don't have to fuss with a crust.

✓ Uses less fat, sugar or salt. Includes Nutrition Facts and Diabetic Exchanges.

- **1 small yellow summer squash, thinly sliced**
- **1 small zucchini, thinly sliced**
- **1 small onion, chopped**
- **1 cup (4 ounces) shredded part-skim mozzarella cheese**
- **1 medium tomato, sliced**
- **1/4 cup crumbled feta cheese**
- **4 eggs**
- **1 cup fat-free milk**
- **2 tablespoons minced fresh basil**
- **1 garlic clove, minced**
- **1/2 teaspoon salt**
- **1/4 teaspoon pepper**
- **1/4 cup shredded Parmesan cheese**

1. In a microwave-safe bowl, combine the squash, zucchini and onion. Cover and microwave on high for 7-9 minutes or until the vegetables are tender; drain well. Transfer to a 9-in. pie plate coated with cooking spray. Top with the mozzarella, tomato and feta cheese.

2. In a large bowl, whisk the eggs, milk, basil, garlic, salt and pepper; pour over the cheese and tomato layer. Sprinkle with Parmesan cheese.

3. Bake, uncovered, at 375° for 45-50 minutes or until a knife inserted near the center comes out clean. Let stand for 10 minutes before serving. **Yield:** 8 servings.

Nutrition Facts: 1 piece equals 126 calories, 7 g fat (4 g saturated fat), 121 mg cholesterol, 316 mg sodium, 6 g carbohydrate, 1 g fiber, 11 g protein. **Diabetic Exchanges:** 1 lean meat, 1 vegetable, 1 fat.

🎀🎀🎀
Apple Pear Coffee Cake

Prep: 15 min. Bake: 35 min.

Joanne Hoschette, Paxton, Massachusetts

A friend gave me this recipe to make for a breakfast I was hosting. The pan was empty before the party was over! The recipe is one of my most-requested, probably because it's a bit different.

- **1/2 cup butter, softened**
- **1 cup sugar**
- **2 eggs**
- **1 teaspoon vanilla extract**
- **2 cups all-purpose flour**
- **3 teaspoons baking powder**
- **1 teaspoon baking soda**
- **1/2 teaspoon salt**
- **1 cup (8 ounces) sour cream**
- **1-1/4 cups chopped peeled apples**
- **1/2 cup chopped peeled pear**
- **TOPPING:**
- **1 cup packed brown sugar**
- **1 teaspoon ground cinnamon**
- **2 tablespoons cold butter**
- **1/2 cup chopped pecans**

1. In a large mixing bowl, cream butter and sugar. Add eggs and vanilla; beat well. Combine the flour, baking powder, baking soda and salt; add to creamed mixture alternately with sour cream. Fold in apples and pear. Pour into a greased 13-in. x 9-in. x 2-in. baking dish.

2. In a small bowl, combine brown sugar and cinnamon. Cut in butter until the mixture resembles coarse crumbs. Stir in pecans. Sprinkle over batter. Bake at 350° for 35-40 minutes or until a toothpick inserted near the center comes out clean. Cool on a wire rack. **Yield:** 12-15 servings.

🎀🎀🎀

Blueberry Almond
Coffee Cake

(Also pictured on page 70)

Prep: 15 min. **Bake:** 35 min. + cooling

Brenda Carr, Houston, Texas

I've received rave reviews for this tender, not-too-sweet coffee cake. It's chock-full of blueberries and sliced almonds.

   1 **cup all-purpose flour**
1/2 **cup sugar**
3/4 **teaspoon baking powder**
1/2 **teaspoon salt**
1/4 **teaspoon baking soda**
   1 **egg**
2/3 **cup buttermilk**
   2 **tablespoons butter, melted**

   1 **teaspoon vanilla extract**
1/4 **teaspoon almond extract**
   1 **cup fresh *or* frozen blueberries, *divided***
1/2 **cup sliced almonds**
   1 **tablespoon brown sugar**
1/4 **teaspoon ground cinnamon**

1. In a large bowl, combine the flour, sugar, baking powder, salt and baking soda. In another bowl, whisk the egg, buttermilk, butter and extracts until blended. Stir into dry ingredients just until moistened. Stir in 2/3 cup blueberries.

2. Pour into a greased 8-in. square baking dish. Top with the remaining blueberries. Combine the almonds, brown sugar and cinnamon; sprinkle over top. Bake at 350° for 25-30 minutes or until a toothpick inserted near the center comes out clean. Cool on a wire rack. **Yield:** 9 servings.

Editor's Note: If using frozen blueberries, do not thaw before adding to batter.

🎖🎖🎖
Apple Oven Pancake

Prep: 25 min. **Bake:** 15 min.

Carol Gillespie, Chambersburg, Pennsylvania

Here's a puffed, golden-brown pancake that always gets compliments. It looks so pretty dusted with confectioners' sugar.

3 large Granny Smith *or* other tart apples, peeled and sliced

1 cup raisins
1/4 cup packed brown sugar
1 tablespoon honey
1/2 teaspoon ground cinnamon
1/4 teaspoon ground nutmeg
2 tablespoons butter
4 eggs
1 cup milk
1 cup all-purpose flour
1 tablespoon sugar
1/4 teaspoon salt
2 teaspoons lemon juice
3 tablespoons confectioners' sugar, optional

1. In a large bowl, combine the apples, raisins, brown sugar, honey, cinnamon and nutmeg. Melt butter in a 12-in. ovenproof skillet. Add apple mixture to skillet; saute for 15 minutes or until tender.

2. In a blender, combine the eggs, milk, flour, sugar and salt; cover and process for 10 seconds or until smooth. Pour over apple mixture; gently lift apple mixture, letting egg mixture flow underneath.

3. Bake, uncovered, at 425° for 15-20 minutes or until pancake is puffy and golden brown. Sprinkle with lemon juice and confectioners' sugar if desired. Cut into wedges. Serve warm. **Yield:** 6 servings.

🎖🎖🎖
Pumpkin Cheese Coffee Cake

Prep: 15 min. **Bake:** 35 min.

Carlene Jessop, Hildale, Utah

This is one of my favorite recipes, especially in autumn. The yummy coffee cake is much easier to make than a traditional pumpkin roll...and is always a crowd-pleaser.

2 cups sugar
2 eggs
1-1/4 cups canned pumpkin
1/4 cup vegetable oil
1/2 teaspoon vanilla extract
2-1/4 cups all-purpose flour
2 teaspoons ground cinnamon
1 teaspoon baking soda
1/2 teaspoon salt
FILLING:
1 package (8 ounces) cream cheese, softened
1 egg
1 tablespoon sugar
TOPPING:
3/4 cup flaked coconut
1/2 cup chopped pecans
1/4 cup packed brown sugar
1/4 teaspoon ground cinnamon

1. In a large mixing bowl, beat sugar, eggs, pumpkin, oil and vanilla. Combine the flour, cinnamon, baking soda and salt; add to egg mixture and mix well. Pour into a greased 13-in. x 9-in. x 2-in. baking dish.

2. In a small mixing bowl, beat cream cheese, egg and sugar until smooth. Drop tablespoonfuls over batter; cut through batter with a knife to swirl. Combine topping ingredients; sprinkle over top. Bake at 350° for 35-40 minutes or until a toothpick inserted near the center comes out clean. Cool on a wire rack. **Yield:** 12-15 servings.

Main Dishes

Whether you're looking for a family-pleasing casserole or an impressive holiday entree, you're sure to find a delicious choice in this extra-big chapter!

Roasted Garlic Pork Supper, p. 94

Caesar Chicken Wraps, p. 106

Parmesan Chicken, p. 109

Southwestern Catfish, p. 111

I make pork chops often, so I like to experiment with different ways of preparing them. I dreamed up this recipe using ingredients that I had on hand. The cherry-orange sauce makes the chops special enough for guests.

🎖🎖🎖
Sweet Cherry Pork Chops
Prep: 20 min. **Cook:** 15 min.

Shannon Mink, Columbus, Ohio

- 4 boneless pork chops (1 inch thick and 4 ounces *each*)
- 1 tablespoon vegetable oil
- 1 cup orange juice
- 3/4 cup pitted sweet cherries, halved
- 2 green onions, sliced
- 1/4 cup cherry preserves
- 4 teaspoons cornstarch
- 3 tablespoons cold water

Hot cooked rice

1. In a large skillet, brown pork chops in oil on both sides; drain. Add the orange juice, cherries and onions to skillet; bring to a boil. Reduce heat; simmer, uncovered, for 15 minutes or until a meat thermometer reads 160°, turning the chops twice.

2. Remove the chops and keep warm. Stir the cherry preserves into the pan juices. In a bowl, combine the cornstarch and cold water until smooth; stir into the pan juices. Bring to a boil; cook and stir for 1-2 minutes or until thickened. Serve over the pork and rice. **Yield:** 4 servings.

🎖🎖🎖
Reunion Steak Sandwiches
Prep: 20 min. **Grill:** 20 min.

Jan Clark, Ridgewood, New Jersey

Every year, my grandma hosts a family reunion where these flank steak subs steal the show. They're topped with a special sauce that requires only three ingredients. For a quick dinner, serve them with coleslaw and macaroni salad from the deli.

- 1 beef flank steak (1-1/2 pounds)
- 1/4 teaspoon salt
- 1/4 teaspoon pepper
- 2 tablespoons butter, softened
- 6 sesame submarine sandwich buns, split
- 2 medium tomatoes, thinly sliced
- 1 medium onion, thinly sliced
- 6 slices process American cheese

MUSTARD SAUCE:
- 1/2 cup mayonnaise
- 2 tablespoons Dijon mustard
- 4-1/2 teaspoons Worcestershire sauce

1. Sprinkle steak with salt and pepper. Grill, covered, over medium-hot heat for 6-10 minutes on each side or until meat reaches desired doneness (for medium-rare, a meat thermometer should read 145°; medium, 160°; well-done, 170°). Let stand for 5 minutes before thinly slicing.

2. Spread butter over inside of buns. Place the tomatoes, onion, sliced steak and cheese on bun bottoms. Broil 5-6 in. from the heat for 2-3 minutes or until cheese is melted.

3. In a small bowl, whisk the mayonnaise, mustard and Worcestershire sauce until blended; spoon over cheese. Replace bun tops. **Yield:** 6 servings.

Taco Lasagna

Prep: 20 min.
Bake: 25 min.

Terri Keenan, Tuscaloosa, Alabama

If you like foods with Southwestern flair, this just might become a new favorite. Loaded with cheese, meat and beans, the layered casserole comes together in a snap.

1 pound ground beef
1/2 cup chopped green pepper
1/2 cup chopped onion
2/3 cup water
1 envelope taco seasoning
1 can (15 ounces) black beans, rinsed and drained
1 can (14-1/2 ounces) Mexican diced tomatoes, undrained
6 flour tortillas (8 inches)
1 can (16 ounces) refried beans
3 cups (12 ounces) shredded Mexican cheese blend

1. In a large skillet, cook the beef, green pepper and onion over medium heat until meat is no longer pink; drain. Add water and taco seasoning; bring to a boil. Reduce heat; simmer, uncovered, for 2 minutes. Stir in the black beans and tomatoes. Simmer, uncovered, for 10 minutes.

2. Place two tortillas in a greased 13-in. x 9-in. x 2-in. baking dish. Spread with half of the refried beans and beef mixture; sprinkle with 1 cup cheese. Repeat layers. Top with remaining tortillas and cheese. Cover and bake at 350° for 25-30 minutes or until heated through and cheese is melted. **Yield:** 9 servings.

Grand Prize Winner

🎀🎀🎀

Roasted Garlic Pork Supper

(Also pictured on page 90)
Prep: 15 min. Bake: 3-1/2 hours + standing
Joseph Obbie, Webster, New York

I grow sweet onions and garlic, so they're always on hand when I want to make this mouth-watering roast. I first fixed the recipe for a church retreat, and it was a big hit.

 2 whole garlic bulbs
 2 teaspoons olive oil
 1/2 teaspoon dried basil
 1/2 teaspoon dried oregano
 2 tablespoons lemon juice
 1 boneless pork loin roast (4 to 5 pounds)
 6 medium red potatoes, quartered
 3 cups baby carrots
 1 large sweet onion, thinly sliced
1-1/2 cups water
 1 teaspoon salt
 1/2 teaspoon pepper

1. Remove papery outer skin from garlic (do not peel or separate cloves). Cut top off garlic heads, leaving root end intact. Brush with oil; sprinkle with basil and oregano. Wrap each bulb in heavy-duty foil. Bake at 425° for 30-35 minutes or until softened. Cool for 10-15 minutes. Squeeze softened garlic into a small bowl. Add lemon juice; mix well. Rub over the roast.

2. Place roast in a shallow roasting pan. Arrange potatoes, carrots and onion around roast. Pour water into the pan. Sprinkle meat and vegetables with salt and pepper. Cover and bake at 350° for 1-1/2 hours. Uncover; bake 1-1/2 hours longer or until a meat thermometer reads 160°, basting often. Cover and let stand for 10 minutes before slicing. **Yield:** 10-12 servings.

🎀🎀🎀

Southwestern Spaghetti

Prep: 15 min. Bake: 25 min.

Rose Turner Minnick, Christiansburg, Virginia

A close friend of mine made this Mexican-Italian bake for me almost 20 years ago, and I've prepared it regularly ever since. The south-of-the-border spaghetti comes together in a snap because it relies largely on convenience items.

 12 ounces uncooked spaghetti
1-1/2 pounds ground beef
 1 small onion, chopped
 1 envelope taco seasoning
 1 jar (26 ounces) spaghetti sauce
 1 jar (4-1/2 ounces) sliced mushrooms, drained
 1 can (2-1/4 ounces) sliced ripe olives, drained
 2 cups (8 ounces) shredded cheddar cheese
Shredded lettuce, diced tomatoes, sour cream and
 salsa *or* picante sauce

1. Cook spaghetti according to package directions. Meanwhile, in a large skillet, cook beef and onion over medium heat until meat is no longer pink; drain. Stir in the taco seasoning, spaghetti sauce, mushrooms and olives. Drain spaghetti; stir into the beef mixture.

2. Transfer to a greased shallow 3-qt. baking dish; sprinkle with cheese. Bake, uncovered, at 350° for 25-30 minutes or until heated through. Serve with lettuce, tomatoes, sour cream and salsa. **Yield:** 8 servings.

I am retired and always looking for fast-to-fix foods to serve when my children or grandchildren stop by. Leftover chicken, ham and a wild rice mix make this comforting casserole easy to assemble. If you have extra turkey, feel free to use it instead of the chicken.

> 1 package (6 ounces) long grain and wild rice mix
> 2 cups cubed cooked chicken
> 1 cup cubed fully cooked ham
> 1 can (10-3/4 ounces) condensed cream of chicken soup, undiluted
> 1 can (12 ounces) evaporated milk
> 1 cup (4 ounces) shredded Colby cheese
> 1/8 teaspoon pepper
> 1/4 cup grated Parmesan cheese

🎖🎖🎖
Chicken Ham Casserole

Prep: 15 min. **Bake:** 25 min.

Lovetta Breshears, Nixa, Missouri

Cook rice mix according to package directions. Transfer to a greased 2-qt. baking dish. Top with chicken and ham. In a bowl, combine the soup, milk, Colby cheese and pepper; pour over chicken mixture. Sprinkle with the Parmesan. Bake, uncovered, at 350° for 25-30 minutes or until bubbly. **Yield:** 6 servings.

🎖🎖🎖
Swordfish with Sauteed Vegetables

Prep: 20 min. + marinating **Grill:** 10 min.

Susie Thompson, Dexter, Oregon

My husband always says, "Wow!" whenever I prepare swordfish this way. The zucchini, yellow squash, red potatoes and cherry tomatoes complement the fish so well.

> 1/2 cup olive oil
> 2 green onions, sliced
> 2 tablespoons minced fresh rosemary or
>   2 teaspoons dried rosemary, crushed
> 2 tablespoons lime juice
> 2 tablespoons Dijon mustard
> 6 swordfish or halibut steaks (6 ounces each)
> **VEGETABLES:**
> 2 small zucchini
> 2 small yellow summer squash
> 1/4 cup sliced green onions
> 1 to 2 tablespoons minced fresh rosemary or
>   2 teaspoons dried rosemary, crushed
> 3 tablespoons olive oil
> 1 pound small red potatoes, cooked and cut into 1/2-inch slices
> 2 cups halved cherry tomatoes
> 1/2 to 3/4 teaspoon salt
> 1/4 teaspoon pepper

1. In a large resealable plastic bag, combine the first five ingredients; add swordfish. Seal bag and turn to coat; refrigerate for 30-45 minutes.

2. Drain and discard marinade. If grilling the fish, coat grill rack with cooking spray before starting the grill. Grill swordfish, uncovered, over medium-hot heat or broil 4-6 in. from the heat for 5-7 minutes on each side or until fish flakes easily with a fork.

3. Cut zucchini and yellow squash lengthwise into 1/4-in. slices, then widthwise into 3-in. pieces. In a large skillet, saute the onions and rosemary in oil for 1-2 minutes or until onions are tender. Add squash; saute for 5-6 minutes or until crisp-tender. Add potatoes and tomatoes; cook just until heated through. Sprinkle with salt and pepper; toss to coat. Serve with the swordfish. **Yield:** 4 servings.

Barbecue Lasagna

Prep: 35 min. **Bake:** 50 min. + standing

Hazel Selle, Hartford, Wisconsin

This beefy dish is a nice change of pace from more traditional lasagna. The barbecue flavor is fantastic!

- 1-1/2 pounds ground beef
- 1 cup ketchup
- 1 medium green pepper, chopped
- 1 medium onion, chopped
- 1/2 cup packed brown sugar
- 1/4 cup lemon juice
- 2 tablespoons cider vinegar
- 2 tablespoons Worcestershire sauce
- 1 tablespoon prepared mustard
- 1 garlic clove, minced
- 1 teaspoon salt
- 1/2 teaspoon pepper
- 1/8 teaspoon chili powder
- 1/8 teaspoon lemon-pepper seasoning
- 6 lasagna noodles, cooked and drained
- 2 cups (8 ounces) shredded part-skim mozzarella cheese
- 1 cup (4 ounces) shredded sharp cheddar cheese
- 1 cup (4 ounces) shredded Colby cheese
- 1 cup (8 ounces) 4% cottage cheese
- 1 egg

1. In a large skillet, cook beef over medium heat until no longer pink; drain. For barbecue sauce, in a large saucepan, combine the next 13 ingredients. Bring to a boil. Reduce heat; simmer, uncovered, for 10 minutes.

2. Spread about 1/4 cup barbecue sauce in a greased 13-in. x 9-in. x 2-in. baking dish. Layer with three noodles and half of the beef. Spread with half of the remaining barbecue sauce; sprinkle with half of the mozzarella, cheddar and Colby cheeses. Repeat layers.

3. Combine cottage cheese and egg; spoon evenly over the top. Bake, uncovered, at 350° for 50-60 minutes or until lightly browned. Let stand for about 10 minutes before cutting. **Yield:** 8 servings.

Grilled Salmon Steaks

Prep/Total Time: 25 min.

Robert Bishop, Lexington, Kentucky

Seasoned with herbs and lemon juice, these steaks are excellent. Sprinkle the hot coals with rosemary for additional flavor…or prepare the entree indoors using your broiler.

- 3 tablespoons dried rosemary, crushed, *divided*
- 1 tablespoon rubbed sage
- 1/4 teaspoon white pepper
- 1 tablespoon lemon juice
- 1 tablespoon olive oil
- 6 salmon steaks (6 ounces *each*)

1. In a bowl, combine 4-1/2 teaspoons rosemary, sage, pepper, lemon juice and oil. Brush over both sides of salmon steaks. Coat grill rack with cooking spray before starting the grill. Sprinkle the remaining rosemary over hot coals for added flavor.

2. Place the salmon steaks on grill rack. Grill, covered, over medium heat for 5 minutes. Turn steaks; grill 7-9 minutes longer or until the fish flakes easily with a fork. **Yield:** 6 servings.

🎗🎗🎗
Chicken with Cherry Sauce

Prep: 15 min. **Bake:** 45 min.

Linda Grubb, Poland, Indiana

This tender, moist chicken bakes in a savory sauce that combines cherries with soy sauce, orange juice and ginger. It's sure to be a big hit at your house.

> 1 **pound fresh *or* frozen pitted sweet cherries**
> 1/2 **cup orange juice**
> 1/2 **cup soy sauce**
> 1/4 **cup packed brown sugar**
> 1/4 **cup honey**
> 2 **tablespoons lemon juice**
> 1 **garlic clove, minced**
> 2 **teaspoons minced fresh gingerroot**
> 1 **broiler/fryer chicken (3 to 4 pounds), cut up**
> 3 **tablespoons butter**

1. Set aside 3/4 cup cherries. In a blender, combine orange juice and remaining cherries; cover and process until smooth. Add the soy sauce, brown sugar, honey, lemon juice, garlic and ginger; set aside.

2. In a large skillet over medium heat, brown chicken on all sides in butter. Place chicken skin side down in an ungreased 13-in. x 9-in. x 2-in. baking dish. Top with cherry sauce.

3. Bake, uncovered, at 350° for 20 minutes; turn chicken. Top with reserved cherries. Bake, uncovered, 25-30 minutes longer or until chicken juices run clear. **Yield:** 4-6 servings.

🎗🎗🎗
Dressed-Up Bacon Burgers

Prep: 10 min. **Grill:** 30 min.

Carol Mizell, Ruston, Louisiana

The tangy sauce that tops these mouth-watering burgers helps them stand out from the rest. Because the bacon cooks on the grill alongside the burgers, cleanup is a breeze, too.

> 3/4 **cup mayonnaise**
> 3 **tablespoons sweet pickle relish**
> 3 **tablespoons ketchup**

> 1 **tablespoon sugar**
> 1 **tablespoon dried minced onion**
> 1 **tablespoon Worcestershire sauce**
> 1/2 **teaspoon salt**
> 1/4 **teaspoon garlic powder**
> 1/4 **teaspoon pepper**
> 2 **pounds ground beef**
> 8 **bacon strips**
> 8 **slices cheddar cheese**
> 8 **hamburger buns, split and toasted**
> **Lettuce leaves**

1. In a small bowl, whisk the mayonnaise, pickle relish, ketchup, sugar and onion until well blended. Cover and refrigerate. In a large bowl, combine the Worcestershire sauce, salt, garlic powder and pepper. Crumble the beef over the mixture; mix well. Shape into eight patties.

2. Place bacon on a piece of heavy-duty foil on one side of the grill. Place the patties on the other side of the grill. Grill, covered, over medium-hot heat for 20 minutes or until bacon is crisp and meat patties are no longer pink, turning once.

3. Drain the bacon on paper towels. Place a cheddar cheese slice on each patty; cover and grill until cheese is melted. Layer bottom half of each bun with lettuce, patty, bacon and mayonnaise mixture. Add bun tops. **Yield:** 8 servings.

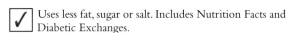

🎗️🎗️🎗️
Pepperoni Ziti Casserole
Prep: 20 min. Bake: 30 min.

Andrea Abrahamsen, Brentwood, California

I took a traditional family recipe and put my own nutritious spin on it to create this casserole. The spinach and turkey pepperoni add color and flair, pleasing both the eyes and the palate. Your gang will never guess they're eating light!

✓ Uses less fat, sugar or salt. Includes Nutrition Facts and Diabetic Exchanges.

- **1 package (1 pound) uncooked ziti *or* small tube pasta**
- **1/2 pound lean ground turkey**
- **2 cans (one 29 ounces, one 8 ounces) tomato sauce, *divided***
- **1-1/2 cups (6 ounces) shredded part-skim mozzarella cheese, *divided***
- **1 can (8 ounces) mushroom stems and pieces, drained**
- **5 ounces frozen chopped spinach, thawed and squeezed dry**
- **1/2 cup reduced-fat ricotta cheese**
- **4 teaspoons Italian seasoning**
- **2 garlic cloves, minced**
- **1/2 teaspoon garlic powder**
- **1/2 teaspoon crushed red pepper flakes**
- **1/4 teaspoon pepper**
- **1/2 cup water**
- **1 tablespoon grated Parmesan cheese**
- **1-1/2 ounces sliced turkey pepperoni**

1. Cook pasta according to package directions. Meanwhile, in a large nonstick skillet, cook turkey over medium heat until no longer pink; drain. Transfer to a large bowl. Add the 29-oz. can tomato sauce, 1 cup mozzarella cheese, mushrooms, spinach, ricotta cheese, Italian seasoning, garlic, garlic powder, pepper flakes and pepper. Drain pasta; fold into turkey mixture.

2. Transfer to a 13-in. x 9-in. x 2-in. baking dish coated with cooking spray. Combine the water and remaining tomato sauce; pour over pasta mixture. Sprinkle with Parmesan cheese and remaining mozzarella cheese. Top with pepperoni.

3. Cover and bake at 350° for 24-30 minutes or until bubbly. Uncover; bake 5 minutes longer or until cheese is melted. **Yield:** 10 servings.

Nutrition Facts: 1 cup equals 306 calories, 7 g fat (3 g saturated fat), 37 mg cholesterol, 795 mg sodium, 42 g carbohydrate, 4 g fiber, 20 g protein. **Diabetic Exchanges:** 2-1/2 starch, 2 lean meat, 1 vegetable.

1/2 cup all-purpose flour
1-1/2 teaspoons salt, *divided*
6 boneless pork loin chops (5 ounces *each*)
3 cups day-old cubed bread, toasted
1-1/2 cups chopped peeled tart apples
1/2 cup chopped celery
1/2 cup chopped onion
1 teaspoon poultry seasoning
1/4 teaspoon pepper
1/3 cup boiling water
1 teaspoon butter, melted

1. In a large resealable plastic bag, combine flour and 1/2 teaspoon salt. Add pork chops; toss to coat. In a nonstick skillet coated with cooking spray, brown chops for about 3 minutes on each side. Transfer to a shallow 2-1/2-qt. baking dish.

2. In a large bowl, combine the bread cubes, apples, celery, onion, poultry seasoning, pepper and remaining salt; toss to coat. Add water and butter; toss to coat.

3. Place 1/2 cup of stuffing on each pork chop. Cover and bake at 350° for 30 minutes. Uncover; bake 5-10 minutes longer or until a meat thermometer reads 160°. **Yield:** 6 servings.

Nutrition Facts: 1 pork chop with stuffing equals 345 calories, 11 g fat (4 g saturated fat), 88 mg cholesterol, 787 mg sodium, 25 g carbohydrate, 2 g fiber, 35 g protein. **Diabetic Exchanges:** 4 lean meat, 1 starch, 1/2 fruit.

Pork Chops with Apple Stuffing

Prep: 20 min. **Bake:** 30 min.

Alta Looney, Howard, Ohio

Here's an easy way to dress up plain pork chops—just top them with a moist apple stuffing. Apples and pork always go together so well, and this makes a wonderful fall meal.

Boston Subs

Prep/Total Time: 20 min.

Sue Erdos, Meriden, Connecticut

My mother has been making these fantastic sandwiches since she left her hometown of Boston many years ago.

1/2 cup mayonnaise
12 submarine sandwich buns, split
1/2 cup Italian salad dressing, *divided*
1/4 pound *each* thinly sliced bologna, deli ham, hard salami, pepperoni and olive loaf
1/4 pound thinly sliced provolone cheese
1 medium onion, diced
1 medium tomato, diced
1/2 cup diced dill pickles
1 cup shredded lettuce
1 teaspoon dried oregano

Spread mayonnaise on inside of buns. Brush with half of the salad dressing. Layer deli meats and cheese on bun bottoms. Top with onion, tomato, pickles and lettuce. Sprinkle with oregano and drizzle with remaining dressing. Replace bun tops. **Yield:** 12 servings.

1/4 teaspoon salt
2 cups frozen pearl onions, thawed
1-1/2 cups baby carrots, halved
1 medium parsnip, peeled, halved lengthwise
and sliced
2 tablespoons butter
3 garlic cloves, minced
1/4 cup all-purpose flour
1-1/3 cups beef broth
4-1/2 teaspoons red wine vinegar
4-1/2 teaspoons Dijon mustard
3 teaspoons minced fresh rosemary, *divided*
1 sheet frozen puff pastry, thawed
1 egg, lightly beaten

1. In a large skillet, cook beef over medium heat until no longer pink; drain. Stir in pepper and salt; remove and set aside. In the same skillet, saute the onions, carrots and parsnip in butter for 7 minutes. Add garlic; cook 2 minutes longer or until vegetables are crisp-tender. Stir in flour.

2. Combine the broth, vinegar and mustard; gradually stir into vegetable mixture. Bring to a boil; cook and stir for 2-3 minutes or until thickened. Stir in beef mixture and 2 teaspoons rosemary; heat through. Transfer to a greased 8-in. square baking dish.

3. On a lightly floured surface, roll the pastry into a 10-in. square. Sprinkle with the remaining rosemary; press into the pastry. Place over the filling; flute the edges and cut slits in the top. Brush with egg. Bake, uncovered, at 400° for 25-30 minutes or until crust is golden brown. **Yield:** 6 servings.

Vegetable Beef Potpie

Prep: 40 min. **Bake:** 25 min.

Trudy Williams, Shannonville, Ontario

This old-fashioned main dish is tried-and-true comfort food. The golden crust and savory filling make such a pretty presentation…and the taste doesn't disappoint.

1 pound ground beef
1/2 teaspoon pepper

Broccoli Turkey Supreme

Prep: 15 min. **Bake:** 1-1/4 hours

Marcene Christopherson, Miller, South Dakota

I do a lot of catering, and this easy rice casserole always gets rave reviews from my clients as well as my friends and family. The creamy main dish is loaded with chunks of turkey, broccoli and crunchy water chestnuts.

4 cups cubed cooked turkey breast
1 can (10-3/4 ounces) condensed cream of
chicken soup, undiluted
1 package (10 ounces) frozen broccoli florets,
thawed and drained
1 package (6.9 ounces) chicken-flavored rice mix
1-1/3 cups milk
1 cup chicken broth
1 cup chopped celery
1 can (8 ounces) sliced water chestnuts, drained
3/4 cup mayonnaise
1/2 cup chopped onion

In a large bowl, combine all of the ingredients. Transfer to a greased 3-qt. baking dish. Cover and bake at 325° for 1 hour. Uncover; bake 15-20 minutes longer or until rice is tender. **Yield:** 8 servings.

Chicken Pizza Packets

Prep: 15 min.
Grill: 20 min.

Amber Zurbrugg, Alliance, Ohio

Basil, garlic, pepperoni and mozzarella cheese give plenty of pizza flavor to the chicken, green pepper, zucchini and cherry tomatoes in these individual foil dinners. The grilled supper is a great way to eat your veggies.

    1   pound boneless skinless chicken breasts,
        cut into 1-inch pieces
    2   tablespoons olive oil
    1   small zucchini, thinly sliced
   16   pepperoni slices
    1   small green pepper, julienned
    1   small onion, sliced
  1/2   teaspoon dried oregano
  1/2   teaspoon dried basil
  1/4   teaspoon salt
  1/4   teaspoon garlic powder
  1/4   teaspoon pepper
    1   cup halved cherry tomatoes
  1/2   cup shredded part-skim mozzarella
        cheese
  1/2   cup shredded Parmesan cheese

1. In a large bowl, combine the first 11 ingredients. Coat four pieces of heavy-duty foil (about 12 in. square) with cooking spray. Place a quarter of the chicken mixture in the center of each piece. Fold foil around mixture and seal tightly. Grill, covered, over medium-hot heat for 15-18 minutes or until chicken juices run clear.

2. Carefully open each packet. Sprinkle with the tomatoes, mozzarella cheese and Parmesan cheese. Seal loosely; grill 2 minutes longer or until cheese is melted. **Yield:** 4 servings.

🎖🎖🎖
Southwestern Pizza

Prep: 40 min. **Bake:** 5 min.

Caroline Grooms, Dickinson, North Dakota

I dreamed up this south-of-the-border pizza for a New Year's Eve party at church. My craving for corn bread and black bean salsa was the inspiration.

1-1/4 cups all-purpose flour
3/4 cup cornmeal
1/4 cup sugar
2 teaspoons baking powder
1 teaspoon cayenne pepper
1 teaspoon chili powder
1/2 teaspoon salt
1 cup milk

1/4 cup vegetable oil
1 egg
3/4 cup shredded cheddar cheese
3/4 cup shredded Monterey Jack cheese
TOPPING:
1-1/2 pounds ground beef
2/3 cup water
2 envelopes taco seasoning, *divided*
2 cups (16 ounces) sour cream
1-3/4 cups shredded cheddar cheese
1-3/4 cups shredded Monterey Jack cheese
1 can (15-1/4 ounces) whole kernel corn, drained
1 can (15 ounces) black beans, rinsed and drained
1 cup salsa

1. In a large bowl, combine the flour, cornmeal, sugar, baking powder, cayenne, chili powder and salt. Combine the milk, oil and egg; stir into dry ingredients just until moistened. Stir in the cheeses.

2. Spread into a greased 15-in. x 10-in. x 1-in. baking pan. Bake at 400° for 10-12 minutes or until a toothpick comes out clean.

3. In a large skillet, cook beef over medium heat until no longer pink; drain. Stir in water and one envelope of taco seasoning. Bring to a boil. Reduce heat; simmer, uncovered, for 5 minutes. Set aside.

4. In a small bowl, combine the sour cream and remaining taco seasoning; mix well. Spread over crust. Sprinkle with the beef mixture and half of the cheeses. Combine the corn, beans and salsa; spoon over cheese. Sprinkle with remaining cheese. Broil 5-10 minutes or until cheese is melted. **Yield:** 12-15 servings.

🎖🎖🎖
Italian Grilled Cheese

Prep/Total Time: 15 min.

Melody Biddinger, Costa Mesa, California

Provolone cheese, tomato and basil make up the satisfying filling for these flame-broiled sandwiches. Brushed with Italian dressing, they're sure to become family favorites.

8 fresh basil leaves
8 thin tomato slices
4 slices provolone cheese
4 slices Italian bread (1/4 inch thick)
2 tablespoons prepared Italian salad dressing

Layer the basil leaves, tomato slices and provolone cheese on two slices of bread. Top with remaining bread. Brush outsides of sandwiches with salad dressing. Grill, uncovered, over medium heat for 3-4 minutes on each side. **Yield:** 2 servings.

🎖 🎖 🎖

Crispy Onion Chicken

Prep: 10 min. **Bake:** 30 min.

Charlotte Smith, McDonald, Pennsylvania

🎖 🎖 🎖

Steak and Shrimp Kabobs

Prep: 20 min. + marinating **Grill:** 15 min.

Karen Mergener, St. Croix, Minnesota

You'll make any get-together special with these attractive kabobs. Cubes of marinated steak are skewered with shrimp, mushrooms, tomatoes, peppers and onions, then grilled.

> 1 cup teriyaki sauce
> 1 can (6 ounces) pineapple juice
> 1/2 cup packed brown sugar
> 6 garlic cloves, minced
> 1/4 teaspoon Worcestershire sauce
> 1/8 teaspoon pepper
> 1 pound boneless beef sirloin steak, cut into 1-inch cubes
> 1 pound uncooked large shrimp, peeled and deveined
> 1 pound whole fresh mushrooms
> 2 large green peppers, cut into 1-inch pieces
> 2 medium onions, halved and quartered
> 1 pint cherry tomatoes
> 1-1/2 teaspoons cornstarch

1. In a large bowl, combine the first six ingredients; mix well. Pour half of the marinade into a large resealable plastic bag; add beef. Seal bag and turn to coat; refrigerate for 8 hours or overnight, turning occasionally. Cover and refrigerate remaining marinade.

2. Drain and discard marinade from beef. On metal or soaked wooden skewers, alternately thread beef, shrimp, mushrooms, green peppers, onions and toma-

My family loves chicken, and I'm always trying new ways of preparing it. This golden brown chicken has a crunchy french-fried onion coating and is great with rice, baked potatoes, macaroni salad or potato salad.

> 1/2 cup butter, melted
> 1 tablespoon Worcestershire sauce
> 1 teaspoon ground mustard
> 1/2 teaspoon garlic salt
> 1/4 teaspoon pepper
> 1 can (6 ounces) cheddar *or* original french-fried onions, crushed
> 4 boneless skinless chicken breast halves

1. In a shallow bowl, combine the butter, Worcestershire sauce, mustard, garlic salt and pepper. In another shallow bowl, place 1/2 cup french-fried onions. Dip chicken in the butter mixture, then coat with onions.

2. Place in a greased 9-in. square baking pan. Top with remaining onions; drizzle with any remaining butter mixture. Bake, uncovered, at 350° for 30-35 minutes or until chicken juices run clear. **Yield:** 4 servings.

toes; set aside. In a small saucepan, combine cornstarch and reserved marinade until smooth. Bring to a boil; cook and stir for 1-2 minutes or until sauce is thickened.

3. Grill the kabobs, covered, over indirect medium heat for 6 minutes, turning once. Baste with the sauce. Continue turning and basting for 8-10 minutes or until shrimp turn pink and beef reaches desired doneness. **Yield:** 6-8 servings.

Main Dishes **103**

1 head cabbage
1 large potato, peeled and shredded
1 large carrot, shredded
1/2 cup finely chopped celery
1/2 cup finely chopped green pepper
1/2 cup finely chopped onion
2 eggs, beaten
2 garlic cloves, minced
3/4 teaspoon salt
1/2 teaspoon pepper
1 pound lean ground beef
2 cans (8 ounces *each*) tomato sauce
1/2 teaspoon dried basil
1/2 teaspoon dried parsley flakes

1. Cook the cabbage in boiling water just until the leaves fall off the head. Cut out the thick vein from the bottom of 12 large leaves, making a V-shaped cut; set the leaves aside. (Refrigerate the remaining cabbage for another use.)

2. In a large bowl, combine the potato, carrot, celery, green pepper, onion, eggs, garlic, salt and pepper. Crumble beef over mixture; mix well. Shape into 12 logs. Place one log on each cabbage leaf; overlap cut ends of leaf. Fold in sides, beginning from the cut end. Roll up completely to enclose filling. Secure with a toothpick.

3. Place in a greased 13-in. x 9-in. x 2-in. baking dish. Pour tomato sauce over roll-ups. Sprinkle with basil and parsley. Cover and bake at 350° for 30-35 minutes or until a meat thermometer reads 160° and cabbage is tender. **Yield:** 6 servings.

Beef Cabbage Roll-Ups

Prep: 30 min. **Bake:** 30 min.

Irma Finely, Lockwood, Missouri

Cooking up original recipes is a hobby of mine. My version of classic cabbage rolls is delicious served with rice or noodles.

Italian Bow Tie Bake

Prep/Total Time: 35 min.

Lisa Blackwell, Henderson, North Carolina

Alongside a green salad and garlic bread, this cheesy casserole always pleases my family. They love the four-ingredient main dish and think I worked on it for hours.

8 ounces uncooked bow tie pasta
1 jar (16 ounces) garlic and onion spaghetti sauce
1 envelope Italian salad dressing mix
2 cups (8 ounces) shredded part-skim mozzarella cheese

1. Cook pasta according to package directions; drain. In a large bowl, combine the spaghetti sauce and salad dressing mix. Add pasta; toss to coat.

2. Transfer to a greased shallow 2-qt. baking dish. Sprinkle with cheese. Bake, uncovered, at 400° for 15-20 minutes or until heated through. **Yield:** 4 servings.

Pork with Pineapple Salsa

Prep: 10 min. **Bake:** 30 min.

Nicole Pickett, Oro Valley, Arizona

Not only does this easy entree taste terrific, but it's on the lighter side, too. A little brown sugar, ground ginger and Dijon mustard help give the moist pork tenderloin its incredible flavor, and the tangy pineapple salsa can be made in no time.

✓ Uses less fat, sugar or salt. Includes Nutrition Facts and Diabetic Exchanges.

- **1 can (20 ounces) unsweetened pineapple tidbits**
- **1 pork tenderloin (1-1/4 pounds)**
- **3 tablespoons brown sugar, *divided***
- **2 tablespoons Dijon mustard**
- **1 teaspoon paprika**
- **1/2 teaspoon ground ginger**
- **1/3 cup finely chopped sweet red or green pepper**
- **1/4 cup chopped green onions**
- **1/8 teaspoon crushed red pepper flakes, optional**

1. Drain pineapple, reserving 1/4 cup juice. Set aside 1 cup of pineapple (save remaining pineapple for another use). Place the pork on a rack in a shallow roasting pan. Combine 2 tablespoons brown sugar, mustard, paprika and ginger. Spread half over the pork.

2. Bake, uncovered, at 450° for 15 minutes. Spread with remaining brown sugar mixture. Bake 15-20 minutes longer or until a meat thermometer reads 160°.

3. Meanwhile, for salsa, in a small bowl, combine the red pepper, onions, pepper flakes if desired, remaining brown sugar, reserved pineapple and juice. Let pork stand for 5 minutes before slicing. Serve with salsa. **Yield:** 4 servings.

Nutrition Facts: 4 ounces cooked pork with 1/4 cup salsa equals 259 calories, 6 g fat (2 g saturated fat), 84 mg cholesterol, 255 mg sodium, 19 g carbohydrate, 1 g fiber, 31 g protein. **Diabetic Exchanges:** 4 lean meat, 1 fruit.

1 teaspoon garlic powder
3/4 teaspoon salt, *divided*
1/2 teaspoon ground cumin
1/2 teaspoon dried oregano
1/4 teaspoon crushed red pepper flakes
4 boneless beef sirloin steaks (about 8 ounces each and 1 inch thick)
2 large sweet onions, cut into 1/2-inch slices and separated into rings
1/4 cup olive oil
1/4 teaspoon pepper
1 medium lime, cut into quarters

1. In a bowl, combine the garlic powder, 1/2 teaspoon salt, cumin, oregano and pepper flakes. Rub over the steaks; set aside.

2. Place onions in a disposable foil pan; add oil and toss to coat. Grill, covered, over medium heat for 30-40 minutes or until golden brown, stirring occasionally. Season onions with pepper, remaining salt and a squeeze of lime.

3. Grill steaks, uncovered, over medium heat for 7-10 minutes on each side or until meat reaches desired doneness (for medium-rare, a meat thermometer should read 145°; medium, 160°; well-done, 170°). Squeeze remaining lime over the steaks; top with onions. **Yield:** 4 servings.

🎗🎗🎗 Onion-Smothered Sirloins

Prep: 10 min. **Grill:** 45 min.

Tina Michalicka, Hudson, Florida

Everyone loves these steaks and sweet onions. I usually serve them with corn and potatoes cooked on the grill as well. For spicier steaks, increase the pepper flakes and cumin.

🎗🎗🎗 Caesar Chicken Wraps

(Also pictured on page 90)
Prep/Total Time: 30 min.

Christi Martin, Elko, Nevada

When we have chicken for dinner, I cook extra for these tasty roll-ups. They're great alongside corn or a green vegetable.

1/2 cup Caesar salad dressing
1/2 cup grated Parmesan cheese, *divided*
1 teaspoon lemon juice
1 garlic clove, minced
1/4 teaspoon pepper
1 package (8 ounces) cream cheese, softened
3 cups shredded romaine
1/2 cup diced sweet red pepper
1 can (2-1/4 ounces) sliced ripe olives, drained
5 flour tortillas (10 inches)
1-3/4 cups cubed cooked chicken

1. In a small bowl, combine the salad dressing, 1/4 cup Parmesan cheese, lemon juice, garlic and pepper. In a small mixing bowl, beat cream cheese until smooth. Add half of the salad dressing mixture and mix well; set aside.

2. In a large bowl, combine the romaine, red pepper and olives. Add the remaining salad dressing mixture; toss to coat. Spread about 1/4 cup cream cheese mixture on each tortilla. Top with the romaine mixture and chicken; sprinkle with remaining Parmesan cheese. Roll up; cut in half. **Yield:** 5 servings.

❦ ❦ ❦
Creole Flounder with Seafood Sauce

Prep: 25 min. **Broil:** 10 min.

Melinda Sue Daenen, Pineville, Louisiana

This is one of my family's best-loved Creole dishes. The recipe can be prepared with flounder or sole fillets, but I sometimes use locally caught kingfish bass.

1 cup diced onion
1 cup chopped green pepper
2 garlic cloves, minced
1/2 cup minced fresh parsley
1/2 cup butter, cubed
1/4 cup all-purpose flour
2 cups half-and-half cream
8 ounces Mexican process cheese (Velveeta),
cubed
2 tablespoons lemon *or* lime juice
2 cans (6 ounces *each*) crabmeat, drained,
flaked and cartilage removed
1/4 cup Creole mustard *or* other spicy mustard
2 pounds flounder fillets
1-1/2 teaspoons Creole seasoning
2 pounds cooked shrimp, peeled and deveined

1. In a large skillet, saute the onion, green pepper, garlic and parsley in butter until tender. Stir in the flour until blended. Gradually add the cream. Bring to a boil; cook and stir for 2 minutes or until thickened. Reduce the heat; stir in the cheese and lemon juice; cook and stir until the cheese is melted. Add the crab. Cover and keep warm.

2. Spread mustard on both sides of fillets. Sprinkle with Creole seasoning. Place on a greased broiler pan. Broil 4-6 in. from the heat for 3-5 minutes on each side or until fish flakes easily with a fork. Top each fillet with four to five shrimp; serve over crab sauce. **Yield:** 4-5 servings.

Editor's Note: The following spices may be substituted for 1 teaspoon Creole seasoning: 1/4 teaspoon each salt, garlic powder and paprika; and a pinch each of dried thyme, ground cumin and cayenne pepper.

❦ ❦ ❦
Raspberry Grilled Cheese

Prep/Total Time: 15 min.

Jane Beers, Siloam Springs, Arkansas

My favorite appetizer is a raspberry-glazed cheese ball, so I used similar ingredients to dress up a plain grilled cheese sandwich. The quick combination was different but delicious, and it's become a popular request in my house.

2 tablespoons seedless red raspberry preserves
4 slices sourdough bread
2 tablespoons chopped pecans
1 to 2 tablespoons sliced green onion
4 slices Muenster *or* baby Swiss cheese
3 tablespoons butter, softened

Spread raspberry preserves on two slices of bread; top with the pecans, green onion and cheese. Top with remaining bread; butter outsides of bread. Toast on a hot griddle for 3-4 minutes on each side or until golden brown. **Yield:** 2 servings.

1 turkey (about 12 pounds)
1/2 cup butter, melted
2 tablespoons Worcestershire sauce
2 tablespoons steak sauce
1 tablespoon garlic powder
1 tablespoon onion powder
1 tablespoon lemon-pepper seasoning
1 tablespoon pepper
2 to 3 teaspoons cayenne pepper
1/4 teaspoon salt
1 cup chicken broth
12 sandwich rolls, split
Lettuce leaves and tomato slices, optional

1. Place turkey breast side up on a rack in a roasting pan. Combine the butter, Worcestershire sauce, steak sauce and seasonings; rub 3 tablespoons over turkey. Cover and refrigerate remaining butter mixture. Bake turkey, uncovered, at 325° for 3 to 3-1/2 hours or until a meat thermometer read 180°, basting occasionally with pan drippings.

2. Remove turkey; pour drippings into a saucepan. When turkey is cool enough to handle, remove meat from the bones. Shred turkey and return to the roasting pan. Add broth and remaining butter mixture to the drippings; bring to a rolling boil. Pour over shredded turkey.

3. Cover and bake at 325° for 25-30 minutes or until heated through. Serve on rolls with lettuce and tomato if desired. **Yield:** 12 servings.

Turkey Barbecue

Prep: 25 min. **Bake:** 3 hours 25 min.

Tammy Schill, Omaha, Nebraska

Cayenne and lemon-pepper add extra zip to this tantalizing shredded turkey. It'll have guests lining up for seconds.

Mushroom Crab Melts

Prep/Total Time: 30 min.

Jean Bevilacqua, Rohdodendron, Oregon

I received this recipe from my grandmother. The rich open-faced rounds are great with a green salad, but I've also cut them into quarters to serve as hors d'oeuvres.

3 bacon strips, diced
1 cup sliced fresh mushrooms
1/4 cup chopped onion
1 can (6 ounces) crabmeat, drained, flaked and cartilage removed *or* 1 cup chopped imitation crabmeat
1 cup (4 ounces) shredded Swiss cheese
1/2 cup mayonnaise
1/3 cup grated Parmesan cheese
2 tablespoons butter, softened
6 English muffins, split
Dash *each* cayenne pepper and paprika

1. In a skillet, cook bacon over medium heat until crisp; remove to paper towels. Drain, reserving 2 table-

spoons drippings. Saute mushrooms and onion in drippings until tender. In a large bowl, combine the crab, Swiss cheese, mayonnaise, mushroom mixture, Parmesan cheese and bacon.

2. Spread butter over muffin halves. Top with crab mixture; sprinkle with cayenne and paprika. Place on an ungreased baking sheet. Bake at 400° for 10-15 minutes or until lightly browned. **Yield:** 6 servings.

Parmesan Chicken

(Also pictured on page 91)

Prep: 15 min. **Bake:** 50 min.

Sharon Crider, St. Robert, Missouri

Here's the perfect main course to prepare in advance and take on a picnic. The oven-fried chicken tastes just as good cold as it does warm.

- 1 cup all-purpose flour
- 2 teaspoons salt
- 2 teaspoons paprika
- 1/4 teaspoon pepper
- 2 eggs
- 3 tablespoons milk
- 2/3 cup grated Parmesan cheese
- 1/3 cup dry bread crumbs
- 1 broiler/fryer chicken (3 to 4 pounds), cut up

1. In a shallow bowl, combine the flour, salt, paprika and pepper. In another shallow bowl, beat the eggs and milk. In a third bowl, combine the Parmesan cheese and bread crumbs. Coat chicken pieces with flour mixture, dip in egg mixture, then roll in crumb mixture.

2. Place in a well-greased 15-in. x 10-in. x 1-in. baking pan. Bake at 400° for 50-55 minutes or until chicken juices run clear. **Yield:** 4 servings.

Determining Doneness

To test for doneness when baking Parmesan Chicken, pierce the chicken pieces with a fork in several places. If the juices run clear, the chicken is thoroughly cooked.

🎖🎖🎖
Crawfish-Stuffed Pork Tenderloins

Prep: 35 min. Bake: 65 min.

Kim Bunting, Colfax, Louisiana

This is a great main dish for company. With a flavorful stuffing, the meat is so moist and bakes to a nice golden brown.

6 green onions, chopped
3/4 cup chopped green pepper
1/4 cup butter
1/2 teaspoon chicken bouillon granules
1/2 cup boiling water
2 cups seasoned stuffing croutons
1 pound cooked crawfish tails *or* cooked medium shrimp, peeled and deveined
4 pork tenderloins (1 pound *each*)
1/2 teaspoon salt
1/4 teaspoon pepper
1/4 cup molasses
GRAVY:
5 teaspoons cornstarch
2 teaspoons beef bouillon granules
1 cup plus 2 tablespoons cold water
1 can (4 ounces) mushroom stems and pieces, undrained
1/4 teaspoon browning sauce, optional

1. In a skillet, saute onions and green pepper in butter until tender. Dissolve bouillon in boiling water. Place the croutons in a large bowl; add onion mixture and bouillon mixture. Stir in crawfish tails; set aside.

2. Cut a lengthwise slit down the center of each tenderloin to within 1/2 in. of bottom. Open tenderloins so they lie flat; cover with plastic wrap. Flatten to 3/4-in. thickness. Remove plastic; sprinkle with salt and pepper. Spoon stuffing over two tenderloins. Top with remaining tenderloins; tie with kitchen string.

3. Place on a rack in a shallow roasting pan. Cover and bake at 350° for 20 minutes. Brush with half of the molasses. Bake, uncovered, 45-50 minutes longer or until a meat thermometer inserted into meat reads 160°, brushing once with remaining molasses. Let stand for 5 minutes.

4. Meanwhile, in a small saucepan, combine cornstarch, bouillon and water until smooth. Bring to a boil; cook and stir for 2 minutes or until thickened. Add mushrooms and browning sauce if desired. Slice pork; serve with gravy. **Yield:** 8-10 servings.

3 medium tomatoes, chopped
1/4 cup chopped onion
2 jalapeno peppers, seeded and finely chopped
2 tablespoons white wine vinegar
3 teaspoons salt, *divided*
3 teaspoons paprika
3 teaspoons chili powder
1 to 1-1/2 teaspoons ground cumin
1 to 1-1/2 teaspoons ground coriander
3/4 to 1 teaspoon cayenne pepper
1/2 teaspoon garlic powder
4 catfish fillets (6 ounces *each*)

1. For salsa, in a bowl, combine the tomatoes, onion, jalapenos, vinegar and 1 teaspoon salt. Cover and refrigerate for at least 30 minutes.

2. Combine the paprika, chili powder, cumin, coriander, cayenne, garlic powder and remaining salt; rub over catfish. Coat grill rack with cooking spray before starting the grill. Grill fillets, uncovered, over medium heat for 5 minutes on each side or until fish flakes easily with a fork. Serve with salsa. **Yield:** 4 servings.

Editor's Note: When cutting or seeding hot peppers, use rubber or plastic gloves to protect your hands. Avoid touching your face.

🎗 🎗 🎗
Southwestern Catfish
(Also pictured on page 91)
Prep: 15 min. + chilling **Bake:** 10 min.

Bruce Crittenden, Clinton, Mississippi

These catfish fillets are rubbed with a blend of chili powder, cumin, cayenne and more, then topped with salsa.

🎗 🎗 🎗
Grilled Roast Beef Sandwiches
Prep/Total Time: 30 min.

Jolie Goddard, Elko, Nevada

When we're short on time, I turn to this fast favorite. Deli roast beef, cheese, onion, green pepper and fresh mushrooms are sandwiched between slices of sourdough bread, then toasted on a griddle to buttery perfection.

1 medium onion, sliced
1 medium green pepper, sliced
1/2 pound fresh mushrooms, sliced
2 to 3 garlic cloves, minced
2 tablespoons vegetable oil
1/4 teaspoon salt
1/8 teaspoon pepper
8 slices sourdough bread
16 slices Colby-Monterey Jack *or* Swiss cheese, *divided*
8 slices deli roast beef
1/2 cup butter, softened
Garlic salt, optional

1. In a large skillet, saute the onion, green pepper, mushrooms and garlic in oil until tender; sprinkle with salt and pepper. On four slices of bread, layer two slices of cheese, two slices of beef and a fourth of the veg-

etable mixture. Top with the remaining cheese and bread slices.

2. Butter outside of bread; sprinkle with garlic salt if desired. On a hot griddle or large skillet, toast sandwiches for 3-4 minutes on each side or until golden brown. **Yield:** 4 servings.

🏅🏅🏅
Fruited Pork Chops

Prep: 10 min. Cook: 3 hours 10 min.

Cindy Ragan, North Huntingdon, Pennsylvania

Here's one of my favorite slow cooker recipes. I like to prepare these chops with pineapple sauce and serve them with rice.

✓ Uses less fat, sugar or salt. Includes Nutrition Facts and Diabetic Exchanges.

> **3 tablespoons all-purpose flour**
> **1-1/2 teaspoons dried oregano**
> **3/4 teaspoon salt**
> **1/4 teaspoon garlic powder**
> **1/4 teaspoon pepper**
> **6 lean boneless pork loin chops (5 ounces *each*)**
> **1 tablespoon olive oil**
> **1 can (20 ounces) unsweetened pineapple chunks**
> **3/4 cup unsweetened pineapple juice**
> **1/4 cup water**
> **2 tablespoons brown sugar**
> **2 tablespoons dried minced onion**
> **2 tablespoons tomato paste**
> **1/4 cup raisins**

1. In a large resealable plastic bag, combine the flour, oregano, salt, garlic powder and pepper; add the pork chops, one at a time, and shake to coat. In a nonstick skillet, brown chops on both sides in oil. Transfer to a 5-qt. slow cooker.

2. Drain pineapple, reserving juice; set pineapple aside. In a bowl, combine the 3/4 cup pineapple juice with reserved pineapple juice. Stir in the water, brown sugar, onion and tomato paste; pour over chops. Sprinkle with raisins. Cover and cook on high for 3 to 3-1/2 hours or until meat is tender and a meat thermometer reads 160°. Stir in reserved pineapple. Cover and cook 10 minutes longer or until heated through. **Yield:** 6 servings.

Nutrition Facts: 1 pork chop with 2/3 cup fruit equals 366 calories, 12 g fat (4 g saturated fat), 79 mg cholesterol, 353 mg sodium, 31 g carbohydrate, 2 g fiber, 32 g protein. **Diabetic Exchanges:** 4 lean meat, 2 fruit.

🏅🏅🏅
Turkey Salad on Wheat

Prep/Total Time: 15 min.

Merrijane Rice, Bountiful, Utah

Inspired by the turkey salad at a local deli, I developed this version. Serve it on croissants for an elegant luncheon.

✓ Uses less fat, sugar or salt. Includes Nutrition Facts and Diabetic Exchanges.

> **2 cups chopped romaine**
> **1-1/4 cups diced cooked turkey**
> **1/2 cup shredded Swiss cheese**
> **2 green onions, thinly sliced**
> **6 bacon strips, cooked and crumbled**
> **1/3 cup frozen peas, thawed**
> **1/2 cup mayonnaise**
> **1/4 teaspoon pepper**
> **12 slices whole wheat bread**

In a large bowl, combine the first six ingredients. Add mayonnaise and pepper; toss to coat. Spread on six slices of bread; top with remaining bread. Serve immediately. **Yield:** 6 servings.

Nutrition Facts: 1 sandwich equals 268 calories, 8 g fat (2 g saturated fat), 36 mg cholesterol, 618 mg sodium, 31 g carbohydrate, 5 g fiber, 20 g protein. **Diabetic Exchanges:** 2 starch, 2 lean meat.

1 boneless beef sirloin tip roast (about 3
   pounds), cut into large chunks
3 celery ribs, chopped
1 large onion, chopped
1 medium green pepper, chopped
1 cup ketchup
1 can (6 ounces) tomato paste
1/2 cup packed brown sugar
1/4 cup cider vinegar
3 tablespoons chili powder
2 tablespoons lemon juice
2 tablespoons molasses
2 teaspoons salt
2 teaspoons Worcestershire sauce
1 teaspoon ground mustard
8 to 10 sandwich rolls, split

🎗🎗🎗
Slow Cooker Barbecue Beef
Prep: 15 min. **Cook:** 8 hours

Colleen Nelson, Mandan, North Dakota

This juicy shredded beef is so popular at summer gatherings. The tender meat is slow cooked in a savory sauce that includes tomato paste, brown sugar, molasses and chili powder. It makes a big batch...enough for seconds!

1. Place beef in a 5-qt. slow cooker. Add the celery, onion and green pepper. In a bowl, combine the ketchup, tomato paste, brown sugar, vinegar, chili powder, lemon juice, molasses, salt, Worcestershire sauce and mustard. Pour over beef mixture. Cover and cook on low for 8-9 hours or until meat is tender.

2. Skim fat from cooking juices if necessary. Shred beef. Toast rolls if desired. Use a slotted spoon to serve beef on rolls. **Yield:** 8-10 servings.

🎗🎗🎗
Overnight Spinach Manicotti
Prep: 10 min. + chilling **Bake:** 40 min.

Tonya Fitzgerald, West Monroe, Louisiana

A friend gave me a delicious recipe for manicotti, and I set out to make it a little healthier. Now, whenever we have company, my husband asks me to fix this.

1 carton (15 ounces) reduced-fat ricotta cheese
1 package (10 ounces) frozen chopped spinach,
   thawed and squeezed dry
1-1/2 cups (6 ounces) shredded part-skim
   mozzarella cheese, *divided*
1/2 cup grated Parmesan cheese, *divided*
2 egg whites
2 teaspoons minced fresh parsley
1/2 teaspoon salt
1/2 teaspoon onion powder
1/2 teaspoon pepper
1/4 teaspoon garlic powder
4-1/2 cups meatless spaghetti sauce
3/4 cup water
1 package (8 ounces) manicotti shells

1. In a large bowl, combine the ricotta cheese, spinach, 1 cup mozzarella cheese, 1/4 cup Parmesan cheese, egg whites, parsley, salt, onion powder, pepper and garlic powder. Combine spaghetti sauce and water; spread 1 cup in an ungreased 13-in. x 9-in. x 2-in. baking dish. Stuff uncooked manicotti shells with ricotta mixture; arrange over tomato sauce. Top with remaining sauce. Cover and refrigerate overnight.

2. Remove from the refrigerator 30 minutes before baking. Sprinkle with remaining mozzarella and Parmesan cheeses. Bake, uncovered, at 350° for 40-45 minutes or until heated through. **Yield:** 7 servings.

🎖🎖🎖
Hearty Grilled Cheese

Prep/Total Time: 30 min.

Catherine Brennan, Denver, Colorado

I enjoy watching gourmet cooking shows on television. But as a mother of five, I find that those time-consuming dishes don't fit my busy schedule. After seeing a chef create a sandwich and cheese sauce on one program, I came up with this quick version. It's been a hit in my house ever since.

    12 slices dark rye bread
     6 slices American cheese
     6 slices Swiss cheese
     6 slices fully cooked ham
     6 slices fully cooked turkey
   1/4 cup butter, softened
CHEESE SAUCE:
     1 can (10-3/4 ounces) condensed cheddar
        cheese soup, undiluted
   2/3 cup water
   1/4 teaspoon Liquid Smoke, optional
   1/8 to 1/4 teaspoon onion powder
   1/8 to 1/4 teaspoon garlic powder
   1/4 teaspoon cayenne pepper, optional

1. On six slices of bread, layer one slice of American cheese, Swiss cheese, ham and turkey. Top with remaining bread; set aside.

2. In a small saucepan, combine the sauce ingredients. Cook over medium heat until heated through, stirring occasionally. Meanwhile, toast sandwiches on a hot griddle for 2-3 minutes on each side or until lightly browned. Serve with cheese sauce. **Yield:** 6 servings.

🎖🎖🎖
Bratwurst Supper

Prep: 10 min. **Grill:** 45 min.

Janice Meyer, Medford, Wisconsin

This meal-in-one grills to perfection in a heavy-duty foil bag and is ideal for camping trips. Loaded with chunks of bratwurst, red potatoes, mushrooms and carrots, it's easy to season with onion soup mix and a little soy sauce.

     3 pounds uncooked bratwurst links
     3 pounds small red potatoes, cut into wedges
     1 pound baby carrots
     1 large red onion, sliced and separated into
        rings
     2 jars (4-1/2 ounces *each*) whole mushrooms,
        drained
   1/4 cup butter, cubed
     1 envelope onion soup mix
     2 tablespoons soy sauce
   1/2 teaspoon pepper

1. Cut bratwurst links into thirds. Place the bratwurst, potatoes, carrots, onion and mushrooms in a heavy-duty foil bag (17 in. x 15 in.). Dot with butter. Sprinkle with soup mix, soy sauce and pepper. Seal tightly; turn to coat.

2. Grill, covered, over medium heat for 45-55 minutes or until vegetables are tender and sausage is no longer pink, turning once. **Yield:** 12 servings.

Onion Beef Au Jus

Prep: 20 min.
Bake: 2-1/2 hours + standing

Marilyn Brown, West Union, Iowa

These savory hot sandwiches are served with plenty of tasty, rich broth for dipping. The seasoned sliced beef makes satisfying cold sandwiches, too.

- 1 **boneless beef rump roast (4 pounds)**
- 2 **tablespoons vegetable oil**
- 2 **large sweet onions, cut into 1/4-inch slices**
- 6 **tablespoons butter, softened, *divided***
- 5 **cups water**
- 1/2 **cup soy sauce**
- 1 **envelope onion soup mix**
- 1 **garlic clove, minced**
- 1 **teaspoon browning sauce, optional**

- 1 **loaf (1 pound) French bread**
- 1 **cup (4 ounces) shredded Swiss cheese**

1. In a Dutch oven over medium-high heat, brown roast on all sides in oil; drain. In a large skillet, saute onions in 2 tablespoons of butter until tender. Add the water, soy sauce, soup mix, garlic and browning sauce if desired. Pour over roast. Cover and bake at 325° for 2-1/2 hours or until meat is tender.

2. Let stand for 10 minutes before slicing. Return meat to pan juices. Slice bread in half lengthwise; cut into 3-in. sections. Spread remaining butter over bread.

3. Place on a baking sheet. Broil 4-6 in. from the heat for 2-3 minutes or until golden brown. Top with beef and onions; sprinkle with cheese. Broil 4-6 in. from the heat for 1-2 minutes or until cheese is melted. Serve with pan juices. **Yield:** 12 servings.

1 package (8 ounces) elbow macaroni
6 tablespoons butter, *divided*
1/4 cup all-purpose flour
1/2 teaspoon salt
Dash pepper
2 cups milk
2 cups (8 ounces) shredded sharp cheddar cheese
2 cups cubed fully cooked ham
1 can (4 ounces) mushroom stems and pieces, drained
1 jar (2 ounces) diced pimientos, drained
1/2 cup crushed butter-flavored crackers (about 11 crackers)
Minced fresh parsley, optional

1. Cook the macaroni according to package directions. Meanwhile, in large saucepan, melt 4 tablespoons butter. Stir in the flour, salt and pepper until smooth; gradually whisk in milk. Bring to a boil; cook and stir for 1 minute or until thickened. Reduce heat. Add the cheese; cook and stir until melted. Stir in the ham, mushrooms and pimientos. Drain macaroni; stir into ham mixture.

2. Transfer to a greased shallow 2-1/2-qt. baking dish. Sprinkle with cracker crumbs; dot with remaining butter. Bake, uncovered, at 350° for 25-30 minutes or until heated through and bubbly. Sprinkle with parsley if desired. **Yield:** 8 servings.

🎗 🎗 🎗
Cheesy Ham Macaroni

Prep: 25 min. **Bake:** 25 min.

Molly Seidel, Edgewood, New Mexico

I'm often asked to bring this comforting casserole to potluck dinners, and it's a favorite of my family's, too. The rich, creamy dish is a great way to use up leftover baked ham.

🎗 🎗 🎗
Chicken Italian

Prep: 15 min. **Bake:** 2 hours

Ann Walsh, Maple Park, Illinois

This hearty chicken dish is sure to please. A friend gave me the recipe, and I've since added a few ingredients of my own.

1 can (28 ounces) crushed tomatoes
1 can (18 ounces) Italian diced tomatoes
1 cup chicken broth
1/4 cup red wine vinegar
1 can (8 ounces) tomato sauce
1 medium green pepper, julienned
1 medium sweet red pepper, julienned
1 medium onion, chopped
6 garlic cloves, minced
1 tablespoon brown sugar
1 teaspoon dried oregano
1 teaspoon salt
1 teaspoon pepper
2 broiler/fryer chickens (3 to 4 pounds *each*), cut up and skin removed
1 pound Italian sausage links, sliced
Hot cooked spaghetti

In a large roasting pan, combine the first 13 ingredients. Place the chicken and sausage over the tomato mixture. Bake, uncovered, at 350° for 2 hours or until the chicken is tender and the juices run clear, basting occasionally with the sauce. Serve over spaghetti. **Yield:** 10 servings.

Jamaican Pork Tenderloin

Prep: 10 min. + marinating **Grill:** 20 min.

Rosetta Hockett, Colorado Springs, Colorado

Here's an ideal recipe for barbecues and parties. A spicy marinade adds plenty of flavor to the tenderloin overnight. Then you can grill the meat in just minutes the next day.

✓ Uses less fat, sugar or salt. Includes Nutrition Facts and Diabetic Exchange.

1/3 **cup orange juice**
1/3 **cup reduced-sodium soy sauce**
3 **tablespoons lemon juice**
2 **tablespoons olive oil**
1 **large onion, chopped**
1 **cup chopped green onions**
1 **jalapeno pepper**
3 **tablespoons minced fresh thyme** *or* 2
teaspoons dried thyme
3/4 **teaspoon salt**
3/4 **teaspoon** *each* **ground allspice, cinnamon**
and nutmeg
1/4 **teaspoon ground ginger**
1/4 **teaspoon pepper**
2 **pork tenderloins (1 pound** *each*)

1. In a food processor, combine the orange juice, soy sauce, lemon juice, oil, onion, green onions, jalapeno, thyme, salt, allspice, cinnamon, nutmeg, ginger and pepper. Cover and process until smooth. Pour into a large resealable plastic bag; add the pork. Seal bag and turn to coat; refrigerate overnight.

2. Drain and discard marinade. Coat grill rack with cooking spray before starting the grill. Prepare the grill for indirect heat. Grill, covered, over indirect medium-hot heat for 20-25 minutes or until a meat thermometer reads 160°. Let stand for 5 minutes before slicing. **Yield:** 6 servings.

Nutrition Facts: 4 ounces cooked pork equals 225 calories, 8 g fat (2 g saturated fat), 90 mg cholesterol, 481 mg sodium, 4 g carbohydrate, 1 g fiber, 33 g protein. **Diabetic Exchange:** 4 lean meat.

Editor's Note: When cutting or seeding hot peppers, use rubber or plastic gloves to protect your hands. Avoid touching your face.

Zesty Onion Burgers

Prep/Total Time: 30 min.

Mary Welle, Lake Elmo, Minnesota

My mother found this simple recipe on a soup can over 40 years ago. The oniony sandwiches starred in many of our Sunday suppers. I carry on the tradition today, making the burgers for my husband and our two grown sons.

1 **pound ground beef**
1 **cup chopped celery**
1 **can (10-1/2 ounces) condensed onion soup,**
undiluted
1/2 **cup water**
1/4 **cup ketchup**
1 **teaspoon Worcestershire sauce**
1 **teaspoon prepared mustard**
Dash pepper
6 **hamburger buns, split**
3 **tablespoons butter, softened**

In a large skillet, cook beef and celery over medium heat until meat is no longer pink; drain. Add the soup, water, ketchup, Worcestershire sauce, mustard and pepper. Bring to a boil. Reduce heat; simmer, uncovered, for 20-25 minutes or until thickened, stirring occasionally. Spread cut sides of buns with butter; toast the buns. Top with beef mixture. **Yield:** 4 servings.

Catfish Po'boys

Prep/Total Time: 30 min.

Mildred Sherrer, Fort Worth, Texas

When my neighbor prepared these big, full-flavored sandwiches, I had to have the recipe. Strips of catfish are treated to a zesty Cajun cornmeal breading, then served on a bun with packaged broccoli coleslaw mix dressed in a homemade sauce.

- 2 tablespoons fat-free mayonnaise
- 1 tablespoon fat-free sour cream
- 1 tablespoon white wine vinegar
- 1 teaspoon sugar
- 2 cups broccoli coleslaw mix
- 1/4 cup cornmeal
- 2 teaspoons Cajun seasoning
- 1/2 teaspoon salt
- 1/8 teaspoon cayenne pepper
- 2 tablespoons fat-free milk
- 1 pound catfish fillets, cut into 2-1/2-inch strips
- 2 teaspoons olive oil
- 4 kaiser rolls, split

1. In a small bowl, whisk the mayonnaise, sour cream, vinegar and sugar until smooth. Add coleslaw mix; toss to coat. Set aside.

2. In a large resealable plastic bag, combine the cornmeal, Cajun seasoning, salt and cayenne. Place the milk in a shallow bowl. Dip a few pieces of fish at a time in milk mixture, then place in bag; seal and shake to coat.

3. In a large nonstick skillet, cook the catfish over medium heat in oil for 4-5 minutes on each side or until the fish flakes easily with a fork and the coating is golden brown. Spoon the coleslaw onto rolls; top with the catfish. **Yield:** 4 servings.

Apple-Smothered Pork Chops

Prep: 20 min. **Bake:** 1 hour

Bonnie Riffle, New Lexington, Ohio

With a touch of sweetness from molasses and raisins, this dinner always brings lots of compliments and recipe requests.

- 6 bone-in pork loin chops (3/4 inch thick)
- 3/4 teaspoon salt
- 1/4 teaspoon rubbed sage
- 1 tablespoon vegetable oil
- 3 medium tart apples, peeled and sliced
- 3 tablespoons molasses
- 3 tablespoons all-purpose flour
- 2 cups water
- 1 tablespoon white vinegar
- 1/3 cup golden raisins

1. Sprinkle pork chops with salt and sage. In a large skillet, brown chops on both sides in oil. Transfer to a greased shallow 3-qt. baking dish. Layer apples over the meat; drizzle with molasses.

2. Add flour to pan drippings in skillet; stir until blended. Gradually stir in water. Bring to a boil; cook and stir for 2 minutes or until thickened. Remove from the heat; stir in the vinegar and raisins. Pour over apples

and chops. Bake, uncovered, at 350° for 1 hour or until a meat thermometer reads 160°. **Yield:** 6 servings.

Picante Cranberry Meatballs

Prep: 20 min. **Bake:** 30 min.

Marge Wyse, Winfield, British Columbia

These zippy, ground beef meatballs are my favorites. The cranberry, chili and picante sauces sound like an unusual combination, but the flavors blend deliciously.

2 eggs, lightly beaten
1/3 cup ketchup
1/3 cup minced fresh parsley
2 tablespoons soy sauce
2 tablespoons dried minced onion
1/2 teaspoon garlic powder
1/4 teaspoon pepper
1 cup crushed saltines (about 30 crackers)
2 pounds lean ground beef

SAUCE:

1 can (16 ounces) jellied cranberry sauce
1 cup chili sauce
1/4 cup picante sauce
2 tablespoons brown sugar
1 tablespoon lemon juice

1. In a bowl, combine the eggs, ketchup, parsley, soy sauce, onion, garlic powder and pepper. Add cracker crumbs. Crumble beef over mixture; mix well. Shape into 1-1/2-in. balls. In a skillet, brown meatballs over medium heat. Transfer to a greased 13-in. x 9-in. x 2-in. baking dish.

2. In a saucepan, combine the cranberry sauce, chili sauce, picante sauce, brown sugar and lemon juice. Cook and stir until cranberry sauce is melted and mixture is heated through. Pour over meatballs. Cover and bake at 350° for 30-35 minutes or until meat is no longer pink. **Yield:** 8 servings.

8 ounces uncooked elbow macaroni
3 eggs
1 cup (4 ounces) shredded cheddar cheese
1 pound ground beef
3/4 cup chopped onion
1 can (15 ounces) pizza sauce
1 can (4 ounces) mushroom stems and pieces, drained
28 pepperoni slices
1 cup (4 ounces) shredded Mexican cheese blend

1. Cook macaroni according to package directions; drain. Meanwhile, in a large bowl, beat the eggs; stir in cheddar cheese and macaroni.

2. Spread onto a greased 14-in. pizza pan. Bake at 375° for 15 minutes. Meanwhile, in a large skillet, cook beef and onion over medium heat until meat is no longer pink; drain. Stir in pizza sauce.

3. Spread over macaroni crust. Sprinkle with mushrooms, pepperoni and Mexican cheese. Bake for 15-20 minutes or until the cheese is melted. Let stand for 5-10 minutes before slicing. **Yield:** 6-8 servings.

🎗🎗🎗
Macaroni 'n' Cheese Pizza

Prep: 35 min. **Bake:** 15 min. + standing

Edna Havens, Bartlesville, Oklahoma

Here's a fun dish for anyone who likes pizza as well as macaroni and cheese. Feel free to try other pizza toppings.

🎗🎗🎗
Pork Soft-Shell Tacos

Prep/Total Time: 20 min.

Margaret Steele, North Vancouver, British Columbia

It's hard to find recipes that have enough flavor to satisfy my husband without overwhelming our kids. This Southwestern take on pork tenderloin earned a thumbs-up from them all!

 Uses less fat, sugar or salt. Includes Nutrition Facts and Diabetic Exchanges.

1 pork tenderloin (1 pound), cut into 1-inch strips
1 small onion, chopped
1 teaspoon canola oil
MOLE SAUCE:
2/3 cup enchilada sauce
1 tablespoon dry roasted peanuts
1 tablespoon semisweet chocolate chips
1 tablespoon raisins
1 garlic clove, minced
1 teaspoon ground cumin
1/4 teaspoon crushed red pepper flakes
1/2 cup frozen corn, thawed
8 corn tortillas (6 inches), warmed
1 cup shredded lettuce
1/4 cup reduced-fat sour cream
1/4 cup sliced green onions

1. In a large nonstick skillet or wok, stir-fry pork and onion in oil for 3-4 minutes or until pork is no longer pink; drain and keep warm.

2. In the same skillet, combine the enchilada sauce, peanuts, chocolate chips, raisins, garlic, cumin and red pepper flakes. Cook and stir over medium heat for 2-3 minutes or until chocolate is melted. Pour into a blender; cover and process until smooth. Return to skillet. Stir in corn and pork mixture; cook until heated through.

3. Spoon pork mixture down one half of each tortilla; fold remaining side over filling. Serve with lettuce, sour cream and green onions **Yield:** 4 servings.

Nutrition Facts: 2 tacos equals 370 calories, 10 g fat (3 g saturated fat), 67 mg cholesterol, 263 mg sodium, 41 g carbohydrate, 5 g fiber, 30 g protein. **Diabetic Exchanges:** 3 lean meat, 2-1/2 starch.

🎗️ 🎗️ 🎗️
Barbecued Country Ribs

Prep: 5 min. **Bake:** 2 hours

Barbara Gerriets, Topeka, Kansas

I created this sauce more than 45 years ago when I adapted a recipe I saw in a magazine. I usually triple the sauce and keep some in my freezer to use on chicken, beef or pork.

2-1/2 pounds boneless country-style pork ribs
   2 teaspoons Liquid Smoke, *optional*
1/2 teaspoon salt
   1 cup water
BARBECUE SAUCE:
 2/3 cup chopped onion
   1 tablespoon canola oil
3/4 cup *each* water and ketchup
1/3 cup lemon juice
   3 tablespoons sugar
   3 tablespoons Worcestershire sauce
   2 tablespoons prepared mustard
1/2 teaspoon salt
1/2 teaspoon pepper
1/4 teaspoon Liquid Smoke, *optional*

1. Place ribs in an 11-in. x 7-in. x 2-in. baking dish coated with cooking spray. Sprinkle with Liquid Smoke if desired and salt. Pour water over ribs. Cover and bake at 350° for 1 hour. Meanwhile, in a saucepan, saute onion in oil until tender. Add the remaining sauce ingredients; bring to a boil. Reduce heat; simmer, uncovered, for 15 minutes or until slightly thickened.

2. Drain ribs; top with half of the barbecue sauce. Cover and bake 1 hour longer or until meat is tender, basting every 20 minutes. Serve with remaining sauce. **Yield:** 8 servings.

🎗️ 🎗️ 🎗️
Corn Bread Taco Bake

Prep: 20 min. **Bake:** 25 min.

Vicki Good, Oscoda, Michigan

The corn bread and beef bake together in the same dish, making this casserole convenient. It's packed with seasonings, and the french-fried onions make a tempting topping.

1-1/2 pounds ground beef
   1 can (15-1/4 ounces) whole kernel corn, drained
   1 can (8 ounces) tomato sauce
1/2 cup water
1/2 cup chopped green pepper
   1 envelope taco seasoning
   1 package (8-1/2 ounces) corn bread/muffin mix
   1 can (2.8 ounces) french-fried onions, *divided*
1/3 cup shredded cheddar cheese

1. In a large skillet, cook beef over medium heat until no longer pink; drain. Stir in the corn, tomato sauce, water, green pepper and taco seasoning. Spoon into a greased 2-qt. baking dish.

2. Prepare corn bread mix according to package directions for corn bread. Stir in half of the onions. Spread over the beef mixture. Bake, uncovered, at 400° for 20 minutes.

3. Sprinkle with cheese and remaining onions. Bake 3-5 minutes longer or until cheese is melted and a toothpick inserted into corn bread layer comes out clean. **Yield:** 6 servings.

🎀🎀🎀
Chili Flank Steak

Prep: 10 min. + marinating **Grill:** 15 min.

Karma Henry, Glasgow, Kentucky

I started making this recipe when we moved from Idaho to Kentucky. It gets so hot here that we use our outdoor grill as often as possible to keep the kitchen cool. My husband loves this juicy steak and its flavorful sauce.

- 2/3 cup packed brown sugar
- 2/3 cup V8 juice
- 2/3 cup soy sauce
- 1/2 cup olive oil
- 4 garlic cloves, chopped
- 2 tablespoons chili powder
- 1/4 teaspoon ground cumin
- 1 beef flank steak (about 1-1/2 pounds)

1. In a large bowl, combine the first seven ingredients; mix well. Pour half of the marinade into a large resealable plastic bag; add the steak. Seal bag and turn to coat; refrigerate for 8 hours or overnight, turning occasionally. Cover and refrigerate remaining marinade.

2. Drain and discard marinade from steak. Grill steak, covered, over medium-hot heat for 6-10 minutes on each side or until meat reaches desired doneness (for medium-rare, a meat thermometer should read 145°; medium, 160°; well-done, 170°). Serve with reserved marinade. **Yield:** 4-6 servings.

🎀🎀🎀
Meatball Sandwich Slices

Prep: 15 min. **Bake:** 20 min.

Heidi Coomer, Fort Smith, Arkansas

These sandwiches are ideal for everything from rushed family dinners to movie nights with friends. Three types of cheese give each slice a savory lasagna flavor, while frozen meatballs and jarred spaghetti sauce keep preparation simple.

- 2-1/2 cups shredded part-skim mozzarella cheese, divided
- 1 cup ricotta cheese
- 3 tablespoons grated Parmesan cheese
- 1 tablespoon Italian seasoning
- 1/2 teaspoon garlic powder

Salt and pepper to taste
- 1 unsliced loaf (1 pound) Italian bread
- 12 frozen cooked Italian meatballs (1/2 ounce each), thawed
- 1 jar (14 ounces) meatless spaghetti sauce

Pickled pepper rings, optional

1. In a bowl, combine 1/4 cup mozzarella cheese, ricotta, Parmesan, Italian seasoning, garlic powder, salt and pepper; set aside. Cut loaf of bread in half lengthwise. Cut a 2-in.-wide strip down the center of each half to within an inch of the bottom of the bread. Remove cut portion and save for another use. If desired, toast bread under the broiler until lightly browned.

2. Spread the cut side of bread with cheese mixture. Place six meatballs in each half; top with spaghetti sauce. Place on a baking sheet. Bake at 400° for 20-25 minutes or until heated through. Sprinkle with remaining mozzarella cheese. Cut into slices; top with pepper rings if desired. **Yield:** 6-8 servings.

🎖🎖🎖 Honey Lemon Chicken

Prep: 10 min. + marinating **Grill:** 15 min.

Tamara McFarlin, Mondovi, Wisconsin

When I told our daughter that we were grilling chicken, she asked to make a marinade. Now we use her blend of honey, lemon, garlic and seasonings every time we grill chicken.

- 1/2 cup lemon juice
- 1/3 cup honey
- 1/4 cup soy sauce
- 2 tablespoons finely chopped onion
- 4 garlic cloves, minced
- 2 teaspoons dried parsley flakes
- 2 teaspoons dried basil
- 1 teaspoon salt-free seasoning blend
- 1 teaspoon white pepper
- 1 teaspoon lime juice
- 6 boneless skinless chicken breast halves

1. In a bowl, combine the first 10 ingredients; mix well. Pour 2/3 cup marinade into a large resealable plastic bag; add the chicken. Seal bag and turn to coat; refrigerate for at least 4 hours or overnight. Cover and refrigerate the remaining marinade.

2. Drain and discard the marinade from the chicken. Coat the grill rack with cooking spray before starting the grill. Grill the chicken, uncovered, over medium heat for 12-15 minutes or until the juices run clear, turning once and basting occasionally with the reserved marinade. **Yield:** 6 servings.

🎖🎖🎖 Savory Pork Roast

Prep: 5 min. **Bake:** 1-3/4 hours

Edith Fisher, Leyden, Massachusetts

Seasoned with a rub of sage, oregano, thyme and nutmeg, this mouth-watering roast is perfect for special occasions.

☑️ Uses less fat, sugar or salt. Includes Nutrition Facts and Diabetic Exchanges.

- 2 teaspoons dried rosemary, crushed
- 2 teaspoons salt
- 1-1/2 teaspoons dried oregano
- 1-1/2 teaspoons dried thyme
- 1-1/2 teaspoons rubbed sage
- 1/4 teaspoon ground nutmeg
- 1/4 teaspoon pepper
- 1 bone-in pork loin roast (5 pounds)
- 1 cup sliced onion
- 1 cup sliced carrots

1. In a small bowl, combine the first seven ingredients. With a sharp knife, cut 1/2-in.-deep slits in fat side of roast. Rub spice mixture into slits and over roast. Place roast fat side up in a shallow roasting pan. Place onion and carrots around roast.

2. Bake, uncovered, at 350° for 1-3/4 to 2-1/4 hours or until a meat thermometer reads 160°. Let stand for 10 minutes before carving. **Yield:** 12 servings.

Nutrition Facts: 4 ounces cooked pork equals 219 calories, 10 g fat (4 g saturated fat), 83 mg cholesterol, 459 mg sodium, 1 g carbohydrate, 1 g fiber, 29 g protein. **Diabetic Exchange:** 4 lean meat.

Pork Pointers

Avoid overcooking lean, fresh pork—it can become dry and tough. Pork is done when it reaches 160°. At that temperature, bone-in roasts may appear slightly pink near the bone.

🎀🎀🎀
Cheesy Sausage Penne
Prep: 25 min. **Bake:** 30 min.

Dallas McCord, Reno, Nevada

This lasagna-like entree takes me back to my childhood. I got the recipe from a friend's mother, who fixed it for us when we were kids. I made a few changes to it over the years, but it's still a quick and delicious dinner.

- 1 pound bulk Italian sausage
- 1 garlic clove, minced
- 1 jar (26 ounces) spaghetti sauce
- 1 package (16 ounces) uncooked penne pasta
- 1 package (8 ounces) cream cheese, softened
- 1 cup (8 ounces) sour cream
- 4 green onions, sliced
- 2 cups (8 ounces) shredded cheddar cheese

1. In a large skillet, cook the sausage and garlic over medium heat until meat is no longer pink; drain. Stir in spaghetti sauce; bring to a boil. Reduce heat; cover and simmer for 20 minutes.

2. Cook pasta according to package directions; drain. Meanwhile, in a small mixing bowl, combine the cream cheese, sour cream and onions.

3. In a greased shallow 3-qt. baking dish, layer half of the pasta and sausage mixture. Dollop with half of the cream cheese mixture; sprinkle with half of the cheddar cheese. Repeat layers. Bake, uncovered, at 350° for 30-35 minutes or until bubbly. **Yield:** 12 servings.

🎀🎀🎀
Colorful Chicken and Rice
Prep: 20 min. **Bake:** 25 min.

Dana Wise, Quinter, Kansas

Topped with crushed corn chips, shredded lettuce and chopped tomatoes, this marvelous casserole is as attractive as it is tasty. I serve it along with fresh-baked bread and dessert for a crowd-pleasing meal every time.

- 1 can (10-3/4 ounces) condensed cream of chicken soup, undiluted
- 1 cup (8 ounces) sour cream
- 1/2 cup 4% cottage cheese
- 1 package (3 ounces) cream cheese, cubed
- 3 cups cubed cooked chicken
- 3 cups cooked rice
- 1-1/2 cups (6 ounces) shredded Monterey Jack cheese
- 1 can (4 ounces) chopped green chilies
- 1 can (2-1/4 ounces) sliced ripe olives, drained
- 1/8 teaspoon garlic salt
- 1-1/2 cups crushed corn chips
- 2 cups shredded lettuce
- 2 medium tomatoes, chopped

1. In a blender, combine the soup, sour cream, cottage cheese and cream cheese; cover and process until smooth. Transfer to a large bowl. Stir in the chicken,

rice, Monterey Jack cheese, chilies, ripe olives and garlic salt.

2. Pour into a greased 2-qt. baking dish. Bake, uncovered, at 350° for 25-30 minutes or until heated through. Just before serving, top with corn chips, lettuce and tomatoes. **Yield:** 6-8 servings.

Pork Loin with Currant Sauce

Prep: 5 min.

Bake: 2-1/2 hours + standing

Edie Urso, Spokane, Washington

I make this roast often for my family and friends, and someone at the table always asks for the recipe. To complete the meal, I prepare stir-fried green beans and a lightened-up version of twice-baked potatoes.

✓ Uses less fat, sugar or salt. Includes Nutrition Facts and Diabetic Exchanges.

- 3/4 **cup sherry or apple juice**
- 3/4 **cup reduced-sodium soy sauce**
- 6 **garlic cloves, minced**
- 4 **teaspoons ground mustard**
- 1-1/2 **teaspoons ground ginger**
- 1-1/2 **teaspoons dried thyme**
- 1 **bone-in pork loin roast (5 pounds)**

SAUCE:
- 2/3 **cup currant jelly**
- 1 **tablespoon sherry or apple juice**
- 1-1/2 **teaspoons reduced-sodium soy sauce**

1. In a bowl, combine the first six ingredients; mix well. Pour 1-1/4 cups marinade into a 2-gal. resealable plastic bag; add the pork roast. Seal bag and turn to coat; refrigerate overnight. Cover and refrigerate remaining marinade.

2. Drain and discard marinade from roast. Place on a rack in a shallow roasting pan. Bake, uncovered, at 325° for 2-1/2 to 3 hours or until a meat thermometer reads 160°, basting every 30 minutes with reserved marinade. Let stand for 10 minutes before slicing.

3. In a small saucepan, combine sauce ingredients; bring to a boil over medium heat. Serve with the pork. **Yield:** 10 servings.

Nutrition Facts: 4 ounces cooked pork with 1 tablespoon sauce equals 298 calories, 11 g fat (4 g saturated fat), 91 mg cholesterol, 481 mg sodium, 15 g carbohydrate, trace fiber, 33 g protein. **Diabetic Exchanges:** 4 lean meat, 1 starch.

Southern Barbecue Spaghetti Sauce

Prep: 10 min. **Cook:** 4 hours

Rhonda Melanson, Sarnia, Ontario

I revamped our favorite sloppy joe recipe into this thick spaghetti sauce that simmers in the slow cooker.

✓ Uses less fat, sugar or salt. Includes Nutrition Facts.

- **1 pound lean ground turkey**
- **2 medium onions, chopped**

- **1-1/2 cups sliced fresh mushrooms**
- **1 medium green pepper, chopped**
- **2 garlic cloves, minced**
- **1 can (14-1/2 ounces) diced tomatoes, undrained**
- **1 can (12 ounces) tomato paste**
- **1 can (8 ounces) tomato sauce**
- **1 cup ketchup**
- **1/2 cup beef broth**
- **2 tablespoons Worcestershire sauce**
- **2 tablespoons brown sugar**
- **1 tablespoon ground cumin**
- **2 teaspoons chili powder**
- **12 cups hot cooked spaghetti**

In a large nonstick skillet, cook turkey, onions, mushrooms, pepper and garlic over medium heat until meat is no longer pink; drain. Transfer to a slow cooker. Stir in tomatoes, tomato paste, tomato sauce, ketchup, broth, Worcestershire sauce, brown sugar, cumin and chili powder; mix well. Cover and cook on low for 4-5 hours. Serve over spaghetti. **Yield:** 12 servings.

Nutrition Facts: 2/3 cup sauce with 1 cup spaghetti equals 342 calories, 4 g fat (1 g saturated fat), 30 mg cholesterol, 491 mg sodium, 60 g carbohydrate, 5 g fiber, 17 g protein.

Cajun Stir-Fry

Prep/Total Time: 20 min.

Sharon Clemens, Groveland, Illinois

Cubes of chicken and chunks of smoked turkey kielbasa, plus plenty of herbs and veggies, make this a hearty stir-fry.

✓ Uses less fat, sugar or salt. Includes Nutrition Facts and Diabetic Exchanges.

- **3/4 pound boneless skinless chicken breasts, cut into 1-inch cubes**
- **1/2 pound reduced-fat smoked turkey kielbasa, cut into 1/2-inch slices**
- **1 medium onion, chopped**
- **3 garlic cloves, minced**
- **1 tablespoon olive oil**
- **1 *each* medium green, sweet red and yellow pepper, coarsely chopped**
- **1 pound fresh mushrooms, sliced**
- **2 medium tomatoes, diced**
- **1/4 cup *each* minced fresh basil, oregano and parsley *or* 4 teaspoons *each* dried basil, oregano and parsley flakes**
- **1-1/2 teaspoons Cajun seasoning**
- **1/2 teaspoon salt**
- **1/4 teaspoon pepper**
- **1 tablespoon cornstarch**

- **2 tablespoons cold water**
- **Hot cooked spaghetti**

In a large nonstick skillet, stir-fry chicken, kielbasa, onion and garlic in oil until onion is tender. Add peppers, mushrooms, tomatoes, herbs, Cajun seasoning, salt and pepper. Cook and stir until chicken juices run clear and vegetables are crisp-tender. Combine cornstarch and cold water until smooth; add to skillet. Bring to a boil; cook and stir for 2 minutes or until thickened. Serve over spaghetti. **Yield:** 8 servings.

Nutrition Facts: 1 cup stir-fry without spaghetti equals 140 calories, 4 g fat (1 g saturated fat), 40 mg cholesterol, 555 mg sodium, 11 g carbohydrate, 2 g fiber, 17 g protein. **Diabetic Exchanges:** 2 lean meat, 2 vegetable.

8 chicken drumsticks
1/4 cup butter
1/2 cup barbecue sauce
1 tube (8 ounces) refrigerated crescent rolls
1 egg, lightly beaten
2 teaspoons grated Parmesan cheese
2 teaspoons Italian seasoning
2 teaspoons sesame seeds, toasted

1. Remove and discard skin from drumsticks. In a large skillet, melt butter over medium heat; stir in the barbecue sauce. Add drumsticks. Bring to a boil. Reduce heat; cover and simmer for 30 minutes or until a meat thermometer reads 170°, turning occasionally. Remove chicken from pan; cool slightly.

2. Separate crescent dough into eight triangles; place in a lightly greased 15-in. x 10-in. x 1-in. baking pan. Brush dough with some of the beaten egg; sprinkle with Parmesan cheese and Italian seasoning. Place meaty portion of each drumstick at the tip of each triangle, with bony portion extended beyond one long side of triangle. Wrap drumstick in dough; place seam side down. Brush with remaining egg; sprinkle with sesame seeds.

3. Bake at 375° for 13-15 minutes or until golden brown and a meat thermometer reads 180°. **Yield:** 4 servings (2 drumsticks each).

🎗🎗🎗
Crescent-Wrapped Drumsticks

Prep: 50 min. **Bake:** 15 min.

Paula Plating, Colorado Springs, Colorado

Looking for a different way to do drumsticks? These are simmered in barbecue sauce, then wrapped in crescent dough that's sprinkled with Parmesan and Italian seasoning.

🎗🎗🎗
Italian Turkey Burgers

Prep/Total Time: 30 min.

Mary Tallman, Arbor Vitae, Wisconsin

Seasoned with oregano and cheese, these plump burgers are a delicious change-of-pace entree. I like to serve them on crusty Italian bread with warmed spaghetti sauce.

✓ Uses less fat, sugar or salt. Includes Nutrition Facts and Diabetic Exchanges.

1/4 cup canned crushed tomatoes
2 tablespoons grated Parmesan cheese
1/2 teaspoon garlic powder
1/2 teaspoon dried oregano
1/4 teaspoon salt
1/4 teaspoon pepper
1 pound lean ground turkey
8 slices Italian bread, toasted
1/2 cup meatless spaghetti sauce, warmed

1. In a large bowl, combine the first six ingredients. Crumble turkey over mixture and mix well. Shape into four 3/4-in.-thick oval-shaped patties.

2. Coat grill rack with cooking spray before starting the grill. Grill patties, uncovered, over medium heat for 6-8 minutes on each side or until a meat thermome-ter reads 165°. Place a patty on each of four slices of bread. Drizzle with spaghetti sauce; top with remaining bread. **Yield:** 4 servings.

Nutrition Facts: 1 burger equals 306 calories, 12 g fat (3 g saturated fat), 92 mg cholesterol, 680 mg sodium, 24 g carbohydrate, 2 g fiber, 25 g protein. **Diabetic Exchanges:** 3 lean meat, 1-1/2 starch, 1 fat.

2 cups finely chopped sweet onion
1 cup chopped fresh basil
4 garlic cloves, minced
1 tablespoon olive oil
5 cups chopped seeded tomatoes
1 can (6 ounces) tomato paste
1/2 teaspoon crushed red pepper flakes
1/2 teaspoon salt
1/4 teaspoon pepper
1 package (16 ounces) spiral pasta
3 cups cubed cooked chicken
1/2 cup shredded Parmesan cheese

1. In a large saucepan or Dutch oven, saute the onion, basil and garlic in oil until onion is tender. Stir in the tomatoes, tomato paste, red pepper flakes, salt and pepper. Bring to a boil. Reduce heat; cover and simmer for 30-45 minutes.

2. Meanwhile, cook pasta according to package directions. Add chicken to the tomato mixture; heat through. Drain pasta. Top with chicken mixture; sprinkle with Parmesan cheese. **Yield:** 8 servings.

Nutrition Facts: 1 cup chicken mixture with 1 cup pasta equals 373 calories, 6 g fat (2 g saturated fat), 44 mg cholesterol, 291 mg sodium, 53 g carbohydrate, 5 g fiber, 27 g protein. **Diabetic Exchanges:** 3 vegetable, 2-1/2 starch, 2 lean meat.

🎗🎗🎗
Tomato-Basil Chicken Spirals

Prep: 5 min. **Cook:** 35 min.

Sandra Giguere, Bremen, Maine

After tasting a wonderful pasta dish at an Italian restaurant, I experimented until I came up with this recipe.

✓ Uses less fat, sugar or salt. Includes Nutrition Facts and Diabetic Exchanges.

🎗🎗🎗
Rio Grande Pork Roast

Prep: 5 min. **Bake:** 70 min.

Konnie McKown, Ringgold, Georgia

Years ago, I used this mouth-watering recipe for promotions when I was the Nebraska Pork Industry Queen. No one guesses that the delicious roast needs only five simple ingredients.

✓ Uses less fat, sugar or salt. Includes Nutrition Facts and Diabetic Exchanges.

1 garlic clove, minced
1/2 teaspoon salt
1 teaspoon chili powder, *divided*
1 lean boneless top loin pork roast (3 pounds)
1/2 cup apple jelly
1/2 cup barbecue sauce

1. Rub garlic, salt and 1/2 teaspoon chili powder over roast. Place on a rack in a shallow roasting pan. Bake, uncovered, at 350° for 30 minutes. In a small saucepan, combine the apple jelly, barbecue sauce and remaining chili powder; bring to a boil. Reduce heat; simmer, uncovered, for 2 minutes. Pour over roast. Bake 40-50 minutes longer or until a meat thermometer reads 160°, basting occasionally. Remove roast and keep warm.

2. Stir drippings in pan to loosen browned bits; pour into a 2-cup measuring cup. Skim fat. Add enough water to measure 1-1/4 cups. Transfer to a small saucepan; bring to a boil. Remove from the heat; serve with the roast. **Yield:** 10 servings.

Nutrition Facts: 4 ounces cooked pork with 2 tablespoons pan juices equals 286 calories, 8 g fat (3 g saturated fat), 89 mg cholesterol, 346 mg sodium, 15 g carbohydrate, trace fiber, 35 g protein. **Diabetic Exchanges:** 4 lean meat, 1 fruit.

Honey Rosemary Chicken

Prep: 5 min. + marinating
Bake: 55 min.

Elsie Barton, Hoover, Alabama

A rosemary marinade sweetened with honey gives this moist chicken great taste and a pretty golden sheen.

✓ Uses less fat, sugar or salt. Includes Nutrition Facts and Diabetic Exchanges.

- 1/4 cup honey
- 1/4 cup balsamic vinegar
- 1/4 cup minced fresh rosemary
- 2 tablespoons olive oil
- 6 bone-in skinless chicken breast halves (7 ounces *each*)
- 1 teaspoon salt
- 1/4 teaspoon pepper

1. In a bowl, combine honey, vinegar, rosemary and oil; mix well. Pour half of marinade into a large resealable plastic bag; add chicken. Seal bag and turn to coat; refrigerate for 2 hours. Cover and refrigerate the remaining marinade.

2. Drain and discard marinade from chicken. Place chicken bone-side down in a 13-in. x 9-in. x 2-in. baking pan. Sprinkle with salt and pepper. Bake, uncovered, at 350° for 55-65 minutes or until juices run clear, basting occasionally with reserved marinade. **Yield:** 6 servings.

Nutrition Facts: 1 serving equals 200 calories, 6 g fat (1 g saturated fat), 79 mg cholesterol, 462 mg sodium, 7 g carbohydrate, trace fiber, 29 g protein. **Diabetic Exchanges:** 4 very lean meat, 1/2 starch, 1/2 fat.

1 tube (13.8 ounces) refrigerated pizza crust
3/4 pound boneless skinless chicken breasts, cut into strips
2 teaspoons canola oil
1/2 cup fat-free Caesar salad dressing
1/2 cup shredded Parmesan cheese, *divided*
1 teaspoon salt-free lemon-pepper seasoning
1 garlic clove, minced
1 package (8 ounces) fat-free cream cheese, cubed
4 cups thinly sliced romaine
1/2 cup diced sweet red pepper
1 can (2-1/4 ounces) sliced ripe olives, drained

1. Unroll pizza crust onto a 12-in. pizza pan coated with cooking spray; flatten dough and build up edges slightly. Prick with a fork. Bake at 400° for 11 minutes or until lightly browned. Cool on a wire rack.

2. In a nonstick skillet, cook chicken in oil over medium heat until no longer pink; cool. In a small bowl, combine the dressing, 1/4 cup Parmesan, lemon-pepper and garlic. Combine cream cheese and half of the dressing mixture until well blended.

3. Combine romaine, red pepper and olives. Add remaining dressing mixture; toss. Spread cream cheese mixture over crust. Top with romaine mixture, chicken and remaining Parmesan. **Yield:** 6 servings.

🏵 🏵 🏵

Chicken Caesar Salad Pizza

Prep/Total Time: 30 min.

Amber Zurbrugg, Alliance, Ohio

Lighten up your pizza a bit with this delectable cold version. A refrigerated crust is baked, spread with seasoned cream cheese and topped with dressed salad fixings and moist chicken.

🏵 🏵 🏵

Kung Pao Wings

Prep/Total Time: 30 min.

Kathy Evans, Lacey, Washington

Served as an entree over hot cooked rice, these delicious drummettes have plenty of personality, with sweet red pepper for color, red pepper flakes for zip and peanuts for crunch. They're quick and easy to fix, too.

8 whole chicken wings (about 1-1/2 pounds)
2 tablespoons sugar
2 teaspoons cornstarch
1/4 cup water
1/4 cup soy sauce
2 tablespoons lemon juice
1/4 teaspoon crushed red pepper flakes
1 tablespoon vegetable oil
1 small sweet red pepper, diced
1/2 cup diced onion
1 to 2 garlic cloves, minced
1/3 cup peanuts
Hot cooked rice

1. Cut chicken wings into three sections; discard wing tip section. Set the wings aside. In a small bowl, combine the sugar, cornstarch, water, soy sauce, lemon juice and pepper flakes until blended; set aside.

2. In a large skillet, cook chicken wings, uncovered, over medium-high heat for 10-15 minutes or until chicken juices run clear, turning occasionally.

3. Add the red pepper, onion and garlic; cook, uncovered, for 3-5 minutes or until vegetables are crisp-tender. Stir cornstarch mixture; gradually add to skillet. Bring to a boil; cook and stir for 2 minutes or until sauce is thickened and vegetables are tender. Sprinkle with peanuts. Serve with rice. **Yield:** 4 servings.

⚜⚜⚜
Pork Cabbage Stir-Fry

Prep/Total Time: 25 min.

Marcie Nor, Macungie, Pennsylvania

The ginger comes through nicely in this colorful stir-fry that is lower in fat and sodium than many other versions. It's great served over steamed rice or cooked noodles.

    4 teaspoons cornstarch
1-1/2 teaspoons sugar
  1/4 cup white wine *or* chicken broth
    3 tablespoons reduced-sodium soy sauce
    1 pound boneless pork loin, cut into 2-inch strips
    4 teaspoons canola oil
    1 cup thinly sliced carrots
    2 garlic cloves, minced
    1 teaspoon ground ginger
1-1/2 pounds Chinese *or* napa cabbage, thinly sliced
Hot cooked rice

In a bowl, combine the cornstarch and sugar. Stir in wine or broth and soy sauce until smooth; set aside. In a large nonstick skillet or wok, stir-fry pork in oil until lightly browned. Add carrots, garlic and ginger; stir-fry for 2 minutes. Add cabbage; stir-fry until cabbage is wilted. Stir soy sauce mixture; add to the skillet. Bring to a boil; cook and stir for 2 minutes or until thickened. Serve with rice. **Yield:** 4 servings.

Nutrition Facts: 1 cup stir-fry mixture (calculated without rice) equals 312 calories, 12 g fat (3 g saturated fat), 63 mg cholesterol, 550 mg sodium, 19 g carbohydrate, 6 g fiber, 30 g protein. **Diabetic Exchanges:** 3 lean meat, 3 vegetable, 1 fat.

⚜⚜⚜
Cranberry Turkey Burgers

Prep: 15 min. **Grill:** 20 min.

Barbara Lindauer, New Athens, Illinois

These turkey burgers are so good, you might give up traditional beef hamburgers altogether! The thick grilled patties are topped with prepared cranberry sauce and served on toasted English muffins for a tongue-tingling change of pace.

    1 small tart apple, peeled and finely chopped
    1 celery rib, chopped
    1 small onion, chopped
    1 teaspoon poultry seasoning
  3/4 teaspoon salt
  1/4 teaspoon pepper
1-1/4 pounds ground turkey
  1/2 cup mayonnaise
    6 English muffins, split and toasted
    6 lettuce leaves
    1 cup whole-berry cranberry sauce

1. In a large bowl, combine the first six ingredients. Crumble turkey over mixture and mix well. Shape into six patties.

2. Coat grill rack with cooking spray before starting the grill. Grill patties, covered, over medium heat for 10 minutes on each side or until a meat thermometer reads 165°.

3. Spread mayonnaise over the muffin halves. Place lettuce, turkey burgers and cranberry sauce on muffin bottoms; replace tops. **Yield:** 6 servings.

🎗️🎗️🎗️
Light Chicken Cordon Bleu

Prep: 20 min. **Bake:** 25 min.

Shannon Strate, Salt Lake City, Utah

I love chicken cordon bleu, but because I'm watching my cholesterol, I couldn't afford to indulge in it often. Then I found a recipe I received in my high school home economics class years ago, and I substituted some lighter ingredients.

> 8 **boneless skinless chicken breast halves (4 ounces *each*)**
> 1/2 **teaspoon pepper**
> 8 **slices (1 ounce *each*) lean deli ham**

> 1-1/2 **cups (6 ounces) shredded part-skim mozzarella cheese**
> 2/3 **cup fat-free milk**
> 1 **cup crushed cornflakes**
> 1 **teaspoon paprika**
> 1/2 **teaspoon garlic powder**
> 1/4 **teaspoon salt**
> **SAUCE:**
> 1 **can (10-3/4 ounces) reduced-fat reduced-sodium condensed cream of chicken soup, undiluted**
> 1/2 **cup fat-free sour cream**
> 1 **teaspoon lemon juice**

1. Flatten chicken to 1/4-in. thickness. Sprinkle with pepper; place a ham slice and 3 tablespoons of cheese down the center of each piece. Roll up and tuck in ends; secure with toothpicks. Pour milk into a shallow bowl. In another bowl, combine the cornflakes, paprika, garlic powder and salt. Dip chicken in milk, then roll in crumbs.

2. Place in a 13-in. x 9-in. x 2-in. baking dish coated with cooking spray. Bake, uncovered, at 350° for 25-30 minutes or until juices run clear.

3. Meanwhile, in a small saucepan, whisk the soup, sour cream and lemon juice until blended; heat through. Discard toothpicks from chicken; serve with sauce. **Yield:** 8 servings.

🎗️🎗️🎗️
Lobster Newburg

Prep/Total Time: 25 min.

Wendy Cornell, Hudson, Maine

We live in Maine, so we like to use fresh lobster in this time-honored recipe. However, it can also be made with frozen, canned or imitation lobster. No matter how you prepare it, guests will think you fussed when you treat them to these rich, individual seafood casseroles.

> 3 **cups cooked lobster meat *or* canned flaked lobster meat *or* imitation lobster chunks**
> 3 **tablespoons butter**
> 1/4 **teaspoon paprika**
> 3 **cups heavy whipping cream**
> 1/2 **teaspoon Worcestershire sauce**
> 3 **egg yolks, lightly beaten**
> 1 **tablespoon sherry, optional**
> 1/4 **teaspoon salt**
> 1/3 **cup crushed butter-flavored crackers (about 8 crackers)**

1. In a large skillet, saute the lobster in butter and paprika for 3-4 minutes; set aside. In a large saucepan, bring cream and Worcestershire sauce to a gentle

boil. Meanwhile, in a bowl, combine egg yolks, sherry if desired and salt.

2. Remove the cream from the heat; stir a small amount into the egg yolk mixture. Return all to the pan, stirring constantly. Bring to a gentle boil; cook and stir for 5-7 minutes or until slightly thickened. Stir in the lobster.

3. Divide lobster mixture between four 10-oz. baking dishes. Sprinkle with cracker crumbs. Broil 6 in. from the heat for 2-3 minutes or until golden brown. **Yield:** 4 servings.

Pizza Loaf

Prep: 20 min.
Bake: 35 min.

Jenny Brown, West Lafayette, Indiana

This savory stromboli relies on frozen bread dough, so it comes together in no time. The golden loaf is stuffed with cheese, pepperoni, mushrooms, peppers and olives.

- 1 loaf (1 pound) frozen bread dough, thawed
- 2 eggs, *separated*
- 1 tablespoon grated Parmesan cheese
- 1 tablespoon olive oil
- 1 teaspoon minced fresh parsley
- 1 teaspoon dried oregano
- 1/2 teaspoon garlic powder
- 1/4 teaspoon pepper
- 8 ounces sliced pepperoni
- 2 cups (8 ounces) shredded part-skim mozzarella cheese
- 1 can (4 ounces) mushroom stems and pieces, drained
- 1/4 to 1/2 cup pickled pepper rings
- 1 medium green pepper, diced
- 1 can (2-1/4 ounces) sliced ripe olives
- 1 can (15 ounces) pizza sauce

1. On a greased baking sheet, roll out dough into a 15-in. x 10-in. rectangle. In a small bowl, combine the egg yolks, Parmesan cheese, oil, parsley, oregano, garlic powder and pepper. Brush over the dough.

2. Sprinkle with pepperoni, mozzarella cheese, mushrooms, pepper rings, green pepper and olives. Roll up the dough jelly-roll style, starting with a long side; pinch the seam to seal and tuck the ends under.

3. Place seam side down; brush with egg whites. Do not let rise. Bake at 350° for 35-40 minutes or until golden brown. Warm the pizza sauce; serve with sliced loaf. **Yield:** 10-12 slices.

Asparagus Mornay, p. 145

Southwestern Onion Rings, p. 150

Triple-Onion Baked Potatoes, p. 140

Side Dishes & Condiments

Whatever main course you'll be serving, you're sure to find an outstanding accompaniment right here. Choose from loaded baked potatoes, crispy onion rings, tongue-tingling relish, cheesy pasta…and much more!

Jalapeno Cranberry Jelly, p. 152

🎗🎗🎗
Broccoli Brown Rice Pilaf

Prep: 5 min. **Cook:** 50 min.

Marie Condit, Brooklyn Center, Minnesota

This is one of my favorite dishes—it's terrific! Rosemary, garlic, almonds and sunflower kernels flavor the broccoli and rice. For a main course, add cooked cubed chicken.

  1 **cup uncooked brown rice**
2-1/4 **cups reduced-sodium chicken broth or vegetable broth**
  2 **tablespoons minced fresh rosemary or 2 teaspoons dried rosemary, crushed**
  2 **garlic cloves, minced**
  2 **cups chopped fresh broccoli**
1/4 **cup slivered almonds**
1/4 **cup unsalted sunflower kernels**
1/2 **teaspoon salt**
1/8 **teaspoon pepper**

1. In a large nonstick skillet coated with cooking spray, saute the rice until lightly browned. Add the broth, rosemary and garlic; bring to a boil. Reduce the heat; cover and simmer for 40 minutes or until the rice is almost tender.

2. Stir in the broccoli, almonds, sunflower kernels, salt and pepper. Cover and cook 3-5 minutes longer or until rice is tender and broccoli is crisp-tender. Fluff with a fork. **Yield:** 6 servings.

Nutrition Facts: 2/3 cup equals 202 calories, 6 g fat (1 g saturated fat), 0 cholesterol, 414 mg sodium, 31 g carbohydrate, 2 g fiber, 7 g protein. **Diabetic Exchanges:** 2 starch, 1 fat.

🎗🎗🎗
Shoepeg Corn Casserole

Prep: 15 min. **Bake:** 20 min.

Lori Talamao, Baton Rouge, Louisiana

Creamy and cheesy, this bake makes a comforting side dish. Plus, the recipe is really versatile. Not only can you double it for larger crowds, but you can also substitute reduced-fat or low-sodium ingredients if you prefer.

  2 **cans (11 ounces each) shoepeg or white corn, drained**
  1 **can (10-3/4 ounces) condensed cream of celery soup, undiluted**
  1 **cup (8 ounces) sour cream**
  1 **cup (4 ounces) shredded cheddar cheese**
1/2 **cup chopped onion**
1/2 **cup chopped celery**
1/4 **cup chopped green pepper**
3/4 **cup crushed butter-flavored crackers (about 18 crackers)**
  2 **tablespoons butter, melted**

In a large bowl, combine the first seven ingredients. Transfer to a greased 2-qt. baking dish. Sprinkle with the cracker crumbs; drizzle with butter. Bake, uncovered, at 350° for 20-25 minutes or until bubbly. **Yield:** 6 servings.

Rhubarb Corn Bread Stuffing

Prep: 20 min.
Bake: 40 min.

Kathy Petrullo, Long Island City, New York

I've been a rhubarb fan since I was a girl, so when a friend suggested this recipe, I had to try it. The distinctive stuffing is awesome alongside ham, chicken or turkey. Whenever I serve this side dish, my guests are curious about my special ingredient...and they love it!

> 5 cups chopped fresh *or* frozen rhubarb (1/2-inch pieces), thawed
> 1/2 cup sugar
> 1 medium onion, chopped
> 1/2 cup butter, *divided*

> 3 cups crushed corn bread stuffing
> 1/2 cup chopped walnuts

1. In a large bowl, toss rhubarb and sugar; set aside. In a large skillet, saute onion in 2 tablespoons butter until tender; add to rhubarb mixture. Stir in stuffing and walnuts.

2. In a small skillet, melt the remaining butter over medium heat; pour over the stuffing mixture and toss lightly. Spoon into a greased 2-qt. shallow baking dish. Bake, uncovered, at 325° for 40-45 minutes or until the stuffing is heated through and the top is lightly browned. Serve warm. **Yield:** 6-8 servings.

Editor's Note: If using frozen rhubarb, measure rhubarb while still frozen, then thaw completely. Drain in a colander, but do not press liquid out.

Grand Prize Winner

I've presented these rich, satisfying potatoes as both an appetizer and a change-of-pace side dish. I think they're perfect for a late-afternoon or evening get-together when something a little heartier is needed. Guests seem to enjoy the distinctive taste of the Monterey Jack cheese and basil.

1-1/2 pounds small red potatoes
    2 to 3 tablespoons vegetable oil
    1 cup (4 ounces) shredded Monterey Jack cheese
1/2 cup sour cream
    1 package (3 ounces) cream cheese, softened
1/3 cup minced green onions
    1 teaspoon dried basil
    1 garlic clove, minced
1/2 teaspoon salt
1/4 to 1/2 teaspoon pepper
1/2 pound sliced bacon, cooked and crumbled

1. Pierce potatoes; rub skins with oil. Place in a baking pan. Bake, uncovered, at 400° for 50 minutes or until tender. Allow to cool to the touch.

2. In a mixing bowl, combine the Monterey Jack cheese, sour cream, cream cheese, green onions, basil, garlic, salt and pepper. Cut the potatoes in half; carefully scoop out the pulp, leaving a thin shell. Add the pulp to the cheese mixture and mash; stir in the bacon. Stuff the potato shells. Broil for 7-8 minutes or until heated through. **Yield:** about 2 dozen.

🎗 🎗 🎗
Twice-Baked New Potatoes

Prep: 70 min. **Broil:** 10 min.

Susan Herbert, Aurora, Illinois

🎗 🎗 🎗
Tangy Cherry Relish

Prep: 10 min. + chilling **Cook:** 5 min. + cooling

Sue Bellamy, Roblin, Manitoba

This flavorful combination of dried cherries, onion, green pepper and carrot perks up plain chicken or turkey wonderfully. When my mother first served the relish at a holiday meal, I just had to have the recipe...and then was thrilled to discover how simple it is to fix.

    1 cup cherry preserves
    1 cup dried cherries
    2 tablespoons cider vinegar
1/2 cup chopped onion
1/4 cup chopped green pepper
1/4 cup shredded carrot
1/2 teaspoon salt
1/2 teaspoon dried basil

1. Cut cherries in preserves into small pieces; place preserves in a saucepan. Add the dried cherries and vinegar. Bring to a boil.

2. Reduce heat; simmer, uncovered, for 5 minutes. Remove from the heat; cool. Stir in the remaining ingredients. Cover and refrigerate overnight. Serve with turkey or chicken. **Yield:** 2 cups.

1 pound fresh green beans, trimmed
1-1/2 cups sliced fresh mushrooms
2 tablespoons chopped green onion
2 tablespoons butter
2 tablespoons minced fresh savory *or* 2
  teaspoons dried savory
2 tablespoons minced fresh parsley
1 tablespoon lemon juice
1 tablespoon cider vinegar
1 tablespoon vegetable oil
1 teaspoon sugar
1 teaspoon salt
1/8 teaspoon pepper
4 bacon strips, cooked and crumbled

1. Place beans in a steamer basket; place in a saucepan over 1 in. of water. Bring to a boil; cover and steam for 7-9 minutes or until crisp-tender.

2. Meanwhile, in a large skillet, saute mushrooms and onion in butter until tender. Remove from the heat; stir in the savory, parsley, lemon juice, vinegar, oil, sugar, salt and pepper. Add beans; toss to coat. Sprinkle with bacon. **Yield:** 4 servings.

🎗🎗🎗
Savory Green Beans

Prep/Total Time: 20 min.

Devon Brown, San Jose, California

When we have family get-togethers, this is the side dish I'm always asked to bring. The whole gang loves the savory beans.

🎗🎗🎗
Lemony Acorn Slices

Prep/Total Time: 30 min.

Nell Fletcher, Sedalia, Colorado

I discovered this recipe a long time ago and have used it often. With the skins on the slices, plus a lemon sauce drizzled over them, this side dish looks as good as it tastes.

2 large acorn squash (about 2-1/4 pounds
  each)
1 cup plus 2 tablespoons water, **divided**
1/2 cup sugar
2 tablespoons lemon juice
1 tablespoon butter
1/4 teaspoon salt
1/8 teaspoon pepper
Lemon wedges and fresh mint, optional

1. Cut squash in half lengthwise; remove and discard the seeds and membrane. Cut each half widthwise into 1/2-in. slices; discard ends. Place slices in a large skillet. Add 1 cup water; bring to a boil. Reduce heat; cover and simmer for 20 minutes or until tender.

2. Meanwhile, in a heavy saucepan, combine sugar and remaining water. Cook over medium heat until sugar melts and syrup is golden, stirring occasionally. Remove from the heat; carefully add the lemon juice, butter, salt and pepper. Cook and stir over low heat until butter melts. Place squash on a serving plate; top with syrup. Garnish with lemon and mint if desired. **Yield:** 6 servings.

Triple-Onion Baked Potatoes

(Also pictured on page 134)

Prep: 20 min. **Bake:** 1-1/2 hours

Char Shanahan, Schererville, Indiana

I've been making twice-baked potatoes for over 20 years. This rich version features onions, bacon, sour cream and cheese.

> **4 large baking potatoes**
> **1 pound sliced bacon, diced**
> **1/2 cup finely chopped red onion**
> **1/2 cup finely chopped yellow onion**
> **1/2 cup sour cream**
> **2 tablespoons milk**
> **1 cup diced American cheese**
> **1/2 cup shredded cheddar cheese**
> **4 green onions, finely sliced**

1. Bake potatoes at 400° for 1 hour or until tender. Meanwhile, in a large skillet, cook the bacon over medium heat until crisp; remove to paper towels. Drain, reserving 1 tablespoon drippings. In the drippings, saute red and yellow onions until tender; set aside.

2. When potatoes are cool enough to handle, cut in half lengthwise. Scoop out pulp, leaving an 1/8-in. shell. In a mixing bowl, beat the pulp, sour cream and milk until creamy. Stir in sauteed onions, American cheese and 1 cup of bacon. Spoon into potato shells.

3. Place on a baking sheet. Bake at 400° for 25 minutes. Sprinkle with cheddar cheese, green onions and remaining bacon. Bake 5-10 minutes longer or until cheese is melted. **Yield:** 8 servings.

🎀🎀🎀
Cranberry Pearl Onions

Prep/Total Time: 30 min.

Lesley Tragesser, Charleston, Missouri

This unusual combination of pearl onions, canned cranberry sauce and cranberry juice is surprisingly delicious. There's plenty of thick ruby-red sauce, and the onions have a sweet-tangy taste. They absolutely melt in your mouth!

        8 cups water
        3 packages (10 ounces *each*) fresh pearl onions
        1 tablespoon butter
        1 tablespoon vegetable oil
   1-1/2 cups cranberry juice
      1/2 teaspoon salt
        1 can (16 ounces) jellied cranberry sauce
      1/2 teaspoon lemon juice

1. In a large saucepan, bring water to a boil. Add onions; boil for 3 minutes. Drain and rinse in cold water; peel.

2. In a large skillet, cook onions in butter and oil over medium heat until lightly browned, about 5 minutes. Add cranberry juice and salt. Bring to a boil. Reduce heat to medium-low; cover and cook just until onions are tender. Add cranberry sauce and lemon juice; cook and stir until mixture is thick and syrupy. **Yield:** 6 servings.

🎀🎀🎀
Hearty Corn Pudding

Prep: 15 min. Bake: 35 min. + standing

Linda Hutmacher, Teutopolis, Illinois

Every year, we grow corn in our backyard garden, and corn is a staple around our house in summer. I keep several packages of our homegrown corn in the freezer so I can make recipes like this comforting dish anytime.

        4 eggs
      1/2 cup heavy whipping cream
        3 tablespoons sugar
        3 tablespoons cornstarch
      1/2 to 1 teaspoon vanilla extract
      1/2 teaspoon salt
      1/8 teaspoon cayenne pepper
        1 can (15-1/4 ounces) whole kernel corn, drained
        1 can (14-3/4 ounces) cream-style corn
        4 bacon strips, cooked and crumbled
        4 green onions, chopped
      1/2 cup shredded cheddar cheese
   Maple syrup, optional

1. In a large mixing bowl, beat the eggs, cream, sugar, cornstarch, vanilla, salt and cayenne until smooth. Stir in the corn, cream-style corn, bacon and onions. Pour into a greased 1-1/2-qt. baking dish. Sprinkle with cheese.

2. Bake, uncovered, at 350° for 35-40 minutes or until a knife inserted near the center comes out clean. Let stand for 5-10 minutes before serving. Serve with syrup if desired. **Yield:** 8 servings.

🏅🏅🏅 Potato Spinach Pie

Prep: 10 min. **Bake:** 45 min.

Lola Kauffmann, Goshen, Indiana

I combined two recipes to come up with this dish, which is terrific for either brunch or dinner. Reduced-fat cheese, egg whites and a shredded potato crust help lighten it up a bit.

- 3 cups coarsely shredded peeled potatoes
- 2 tablespoons olive oil, *divided*
- 1 teaspoon salt, *divided*
- 1/3 cup chopped onion
- 1 package (10 ounces) frozen chopped spinach, thawed and squeezed dry
- 1 cup (4 ounces) shredded reduced-fat Swiss cheese
- 1/2 cup fat-free evaporated milk
- 2 eggs, lightly beaten
- 2 egg whites, lightly beaten
- 1/2 to 1 teaspoon dried oregano
- 1/4 teaspoon ground nutmeg

1. In a bowl, combine the potatoes, 4 teaspoons oil and 1/2 teaspoon salt. Press onto the bottom and up the sides of a 9-in. pie plate coated with cooking spray. Bake at 425° for 20-25 minutes or until the crust is lightly browned. Cool on a wire rack. Reduce temperature to 350°.

2. In a nonstick skillet, saute onion in remaining oil until tender. In a bowl, combine the spinach, Swiss cheese, milk, eggs, egg whites, oregano, nutmeg, onion and remaining salt. Pour into crust.

3. Bake for 25-30 minutes or until top begins to brown and a knife inserted near the center comes out clean. Let stand for 10 minutes before cutting. **Yield:** 6 servings.

🏅🏅🏅 Seafood Stuffing

Prep/Total Time: 20 min.

Marcy Thrall, Haddam Neck, Connecticut

For an easy and elegant side dish, I add canned crab, canned shrimp and lemon juice to packaged stuffing mix. When I served this to my mom as part of her birthday dinner, she said it was the best stuffing she had ever tasted...and that, next time, she wanted just the stuffing for her meal!

- 1 package (6 ounces) instant chicken-flavored stuffing mix
- 1 can (6 ounces) crabmeat, drained and cartilage removed or 1 cup imitation crabmeat
- 1 can (6 ounces) small shrimp, rinsed and drained or 1 cup frozen small cooked shrimp
- 1 teaspoon lemon juice

Prepare stuffing according to the package directions. Gently stir in crab, shrimp and lemon juice. Serve immediately. **Yield:** 4-6 servings.

🎖🎖🎖
Cranberry Sweet Potato Bake
Prep/Total Time: 30 min.

Martha Nadelhoffer, Algona, Iowa

This recipe is a different but delicious way to serve sweet potatoes. It goes well with ham, turkey or chicken.

> 2 cans (15 ounces *each*) cut sweet potatoes,
>   drained
> 1 cup fresh *or* frozen cranberries
> 1/4 cup coarsely chopped pecans
> 1/2 cup orange marmalade, warmed

Place the sweet potatoes in a greased 11-in. x 7-in. x 2-in. baking dish. Sprinkle with cranberries and pecans; spoon marmalade over top. Cover and bake at 350° for 25-30 minutes or until heated through. **Yield:** 4-6 servings.

🎖🎖🎖
Christmas Pickles
Prep: 10 min. **Cook:** 25 min. + chilling

Patricia Martin, Shelbyville, Tennessee

My pickle recipe was adapted from one a dear family friend shared. These morsels are great any time of year, but the green, red and white colors of the pickles, cherries and onions make them ideal for Christmas gift giving.

> 1 gallon whole dill pickles
> 11-1/4 cups sugar
> 1 cup white vinegar
> 1 tablespoon mustard seed
> 1 tablespoon whole cloves
> 3 to 4 jalapeno peppers, chopped
> 4 to 5 garlic cloves, minced
> 5 to 6 whole cinnamon sticks
> 1 pound whole candied cherries
> 3 jars (15 ounces *each*) pearl onions, drained
> 1 teaspoon olive oil

1. Drain pickles, reserving juice; set juice aside. Cut pickles into 1/2-in. slices; set aside. In a large kettle, combine the sugar, vinegar, mustard seed, cloves, peppers, garlic, cinnamon sticks and pickle juice.

2. Cook over medium heat for 10 minutes or until sugar is dissolved, stirring occasionally. Bring to a boil. Reduce heat; simmer, uncovered, for 10 minutes. Remove from the heat; cool slightly. Discard cinnamon sticks.

3. In a large bowl, combine the candied cherries, pearl onions and pickle slices. Pour the liquid over pickle mixture. Stir in oil. Cover and refrigerate for 48 hours, stirring occasionally. Divide mixture among jars. Cover and store in the refrigerator for up to 1 month. **Yield:** 6-1/2 quarts.

Editor's Note: When cutting or seeding hot peppers, use rubber or plastic gloves to protect your hands. Avoid touching your face.

Perfect Pickles

When making Christmas Pickles, make sure to use fresh spices for maximum flavor. Spices that have been in your pantry for longer than 1 year begin to lose their strength.

The tartness of cranberry juice is a tongue-tingling contrast to the sweet brown sugar and molasses in these baked beans.

3 cups dried navy beans
5 cups cranberry juice
1/2 pound lean salt pork, diced
3/4 cup chopped onion
1/2 cup ketchup
1/4 cup molasses
5 teaspoons dark brown sugar
1-1/2 teaspoons ground mustard
1-1/2 teaspoons salt
1/8 teaspoon ground ginger

1. Place beans in a Dutch oven or soup kettle; add water to cover by 2 in. Bring to a boil; boil for 2 minutes. Remove from the heat; cover and let stand for 1-4 hours or until softened.

2. Drain beans and discard liquid. Return beans to Dutch oven. Add cranberry juice; bring to a boil. Reduce heat; cover and simmer for 1 hour or until beans are almost tender.

3. Drain, reserving the cranberry liquid. Place the beans in a 2-1/2-qt. casserole or bean pot; add the remaining ingredients and 1-1/2 cups of cranberry liquid. Cover and bake at 350° for 3 hours or until the beans are tender and of desired consistency, stirring every 30 minutes. Add the reserved cranberry liquid as needed. **Yield:** 10-12 servings.

🎀 🎀 🎀

Cranberry Baked Beans

Prep: 1 hour 10 min. + standing **Bake:** 3 hours

Wendie Osipowicz, New Britain, Connecticut

🎀 🎀 🎀

Nutty Brussels Sprouts

Prep/Total Time: 20 min.

Laura Hamrick, Buena Park, California

Even my son will eat Brussels sprouts when I make this simple but tasty side dish. The traditional English recipe was made with chestnuts, but I use chopped pecans. They give a nice, nutty crunch to a plain green vegetable.

1 pound fresh *or* frozen Brussels sprouts, thawed and halved
1/2 teaspoon salt
1/4 teaspoon pepper
3 tablespoons butter
1/4 cup chopped pecans

1. Trim Brussels sprouts and cut an x in the core of each. In a large saucepan, bring 1 in. water, salt and Brussels sprouts to a boil. Reduce heat. Cover and cook for 8-10 minutes or until crisp-tender; drain. Sprinkle with pepper.

2. Meanwhile, in a small skillet, melt butter over medium heat until golden brown. Add pecans; cook for 1-2 minutes or until lightly browned. Add Brussels sprouts; toss to coat. **Yield:** 4-6 servings.

🎀 🎀 🎀
Asparagus Mornay

(Also pictured on page 134)
Prep/Total Time: 25 min.

Linda McKee, Big Prairie, Ohio

When I was growing up on my parents' dairy farm, we always had a large asparagus patch. I still love asparagus, but my husband and children weren't eager to eat it until I found this recipe. Now everyone enjoys these savory spears.

1-1/2 pounds fresh asparagus, trimmed
    1 tablespoon butter
    1 tablespoon all-purpose flour
    1 cup half-and-half cream
  1/2 teaspoon chicken bouillon granules
  1/8 teaspoon ground nutmeg
  1/8 teaspoon salt
  1/2 cup shredded Swiss cheese
    2 tablespoons crushed butter-flavored crackers

1. In a skillet, cook asparagus in a small amount of water until crisp-tender, about 6-8 minutes; drain. Arrange spears in the bottom of a greased 1-1/2-qt. baking dish; set aside and keep warm.

2. In a small saucepan, melt butter. Stir in flour until smooth. Gradually whisk in the cream, bouillon, nutmeg and salt. Bring to a boil over medium heat; cook and stir for 2 minutes or until thickened.

3. Remove from the heat; add cheese and stir until melted. Pour over asparagus. Sprinkle with cracker crumbs. Broil 6 in. from the heat for 3-5 minutes or until lightly browned. **Yield:** 4-6 servings.

🎖 🎖 🎖
Pickled Peppers

Prep: 20 min. + chilling

Heather Prendergast, Sundre, Alberta

Always popular at potlucks, this colorful and tasty dish adds zest to the menu. I also make the peppers as a salad.

- **2 *each* medium green, sweet red and yellow peppers, cut into 1-inch pieces**
- **1 large red onion, halved and thinly sliced**
- **1 cup cider vinegar**
- **1 cup sugar**
- **1/3 cup water**
- **2 teaspoons mixed pickling spices**
- **1/2 teaspoon celery seed**

1. In a large glass bowl, combine the peppers and onion; set aside. In a saucepan, combine the cider vinegar, sugar and water. Place the pickling spices and celery seed in a double thickness of cheesecloth; bring up the corners of the cheesecloth and tie with string to form a bag. Add to the saucepan. Bring to a boil; boil for 1 minute.

2. Transfer spice bag to pepper mixture. Pour the vinegar mixture over all. Cover and refrigerate for 24 hours, stirring occasionally.

3. Discard spice bag. Peppers may be stored in the refrigerator for up to 1 month. **Yield:** 4 cups.

Acorn Squash Feta Casserole

Prep: 25 min. **Bake:** 1 hour 35 min.

Maisy Vliet, Holland, Michigan

I get loads of compliments on this unusual side-dish casserole whenever I serve it. The recipe combines squash and feta cheese with onion, garlic, peppers and sunflower kernels.

- 2 large acorn squash (about 1-1/2 pounds each)
- 1 medium onion, chopped
- 2 garlic cloves, minced
- 3 tablespoons butter
- 1/2 cup chopped green pepper
- 1/2 cup chopped sweet red pepper
- 2 eggs
- 1 cup (8 ounces) plain yogurt
- 1 cup (4 ounces) crumbled feta cheese
- 1-1/4 teaspoons salt
- 1/2 teaspoon pepper
- Dash cayenne pepper, optional
- 1/4 cup sunflower kernels

1. Cut squash in half; discard seeds. Place squash cut side down in a greased 15-in. x 10-in. x 1-in. baking pan; add 1/2 in. of hot water. Bake, uncovered, at 350° for 35-40 minutes. Drain water from pan; turn squash cut side up. Bake 10 minutes longer or until squash is tender; cool slightly. Carefully scoop out squash; place in a large bowl and mash. Set aside.

2. In a large skillet, saute onion and garlic in butter until tender. Add peppers; saute until crisp-tender. In a large bowl, whisk eggs and yogurt until blended. Stir in the squash, onion mixture, feta cheese, salt, pepper and cayenne if desired.

3. Transfer to a greased 11-in. x 7-in. x 2-in. baking dish. Sprinkle with sunflower kernels. Cover and bake at 375° for 25 minutes. Uncover; bake 25-30 minutes longer or until a knife inserted near the center comes out clean. **Yield:** 6-8 servings.

Three-Cheese Spirals

Prep: 15 min. **Bake:** 30 min.

Deb Collette, Holland, Ohio

Sour cream and three kinds of cheese create the creamy coating for this tasty twist on macaroni and cheese. It calls for only six ingredients and can be served as a side dish or entree.

- 1 package (16 ounces) spiral pasta
- 1 egg
- 1-1/2 cups (12 ounces) sour cream
- 1-1/2 cups (12 ounces) 4% cottage cheese
- 1 pound process American cheese (Velveeta), cubed
- 2 cups (8 ounces) shredded cheddar cheese

1. Cook pasta according to package directions. Meanwhile, in a blender, combine the egg, sour cream and cottage cheese; cover and process until smooth. Transfer to a large bowl; add American and cheddar cheeses. Drain pasta; stir into cheese mixture until evenly coated.

2. Transfer to a greased shallow 3-qt. baking dish. Bake, uncovered, at 350° for 15 minutes; stir. Bake 15-20 minutes longer or until bubbly and edges begin to brown. **Yield:** 8-10 servings.

1/2 cup butter, melted
1-1/4 teaspoons *each* minced fresh parsley, basil and
     chives
3/4 teaspoon salt
1/4 teaspoon pepper
  3 medium ears sweet corn, husks removed, cut
     into 2-inch pieces
  1 medium sweet red pepper, cut into 1-inch
     pieces
  1 medium sweet yellow pepper, cut into 1-inch
     pieces
  1 medium zucchini, cut into 1/4-inch slices
 10 large fresh mushrooms

In a large bowl, combine the butter, parsley, basil, chives, salt and pepper. Add the vegetables; toss to coat. Place vegetables in a disposable foil pan. Grill, covered, over medium-high heat for 5 minutes; stir. Grill 5 minutes longer or until the vegetables are tender. **Yield:** 6-8 servings.

🏅🏅🏅
Summer Vegetable Medley
Prep/Total Time: 15 min.

Maria Regakis, Somerville, Massachusetts

This swift side dish is as beautiful as it is delicious. Red and yellow peppers, zucchini, corn and mushrooms are seasoned with garden-fresh herbs. Grilled in a foil pan, it's no-fuss cooking.

Corn Clue

Remove the husks on an ear of corn by pulling them down the ear. Either use your hand to pull out the silk between the kernel rows or remove the silk using a dry vegetable brush.

🏅🏅🏅
Hearty Baked Beans
Prep: 15 min. Bake: 1 hour

Cathy Swancutt, Junction City, Oregon

Chock-full of ground beef, bacon and four varieties of beans, this saucy dish is terrific. I've had the recipe for over 10 years and make it often at home and for potlucks.

  1 pound ground beef
  2 large onions, chopped
3/4 pound sliced bacon, cooked and crumbled
  4 cans (15 ounces *each*) pork and beans
  1 bottle (18 ounces) honey barbecue sauce
  1 can (16 ounces) kidney beans, rinsed and
     drained
  1 can (15-1/4 ounces) lima beans, rinsed and
     drained
  1 can (15 ounces) black beans, rinsed and
     drained
1/2 cup packed brown sugar
  3 tablespoons cider vinegar
  1 tablespoon Liquid Smoke, optional

  1 teaspoon salt
1/2 teaspoon pepper

In a large skillet, cook the beef and onions over medium heat until meat is no longer pink; drain. Transfer to a 5-qt. Dutch oven. Stir in the remaining ingredients. Cover and bake at 350° for 1 hour or until heated through. **Yield:** 18 servings.

🎀🎀🎀 Creamy Sweet Onions

Prep: 10 min. + chilling

Ethel Lowey, Fort Frances, Ontario

Well-coated with a tangy dressing, these sweet-sour onions will really dress up a burger. Plus, they're so easy to make, you'll want to have them every time burgers are on the menu. But the onions can also be enjoyed other ways—my sister serves them as a side salad when our family gets together in summer.

  5 **large white onions, thinly sliced**
2-1/4 **cups sugar**
1-1/2 **cups cider vinegar**
1-1/2 **cups water**
  4 **teaspoons salt**
  1 **cup (8 ounces) sour cream**
  3 **tablespoons mayonnaise**
 1/4 **teaspoon celery seed**
Salt and pepper to taste

1. Place the onions in a large bowl; set aside. In a small saucepan, combine the sugar, vinegar, water and salt. Bring to a boil; pour over onions. Cover and refrigerate overnight.

2. Drain the onions, discarding the liquid. In a large bowl, combine the sour cream, mayonnaise, celery seed, salt and pepper. Add the onions; toss to coat. **Yield:** 4 cups.

🎀🎀🎀 Cheesy Squash

Prep/Total Time: 20 min.

Randy Lawrence, Clinton, Mississippi

With my busy schedule, I rely on speedy side dishes like this one. The squash retains its fresh taste and cooks to a perfect tender crispness, smothered in plenty of golden mozzarella and Parmesan cheese. This recipe is so good, you'll want to try it with other fresh vegetables, too.

 1 **small zucchini**
 1 **small yellow summer squash**
Salt and pepper to taste
 1 **cup (4 ounces) shredded part-skim**
  mozzarella cheese
 1/4 **cup grated Parmesan cheese**

1. Cut the zucchini and yellow squash into 1/4-in. slices. Place in a greased shallow 1-qt. baking dish. Sprinkle with salt and pepper. Top with mozzarella and Parmesan cheese.

2. Broil 4 in. from the heat for 7-10 minutes or until squash is crisp-tender and cheese is bubbly. Serve immediately. **Yield:** 2 servings.

🎗️🎗️🎗️
Southwestern Onion Rings

(Also pictured on page 134)

Prep: 10 min. + soaking **Cook:** 10 min.

Tamra Kriedeman, Enderlin, North Dakota

These light, crispy onion rings are sliced thin and spiced just right with garlic powder, cayenne pepper, chili powder and cumin. My family likes them best alongside grilled burgers. The rings are even good as leftovers.

        2 **large sweet onions**
2-1/2 **cups buttermilk**
        2 **eggs**
        3 **tablespoons water**
1-3/4 **cups all-purpose flour**
        2 **teaspoons salt**

2 **teaspoons chili powder**
1 to 2 **teaspoons cayenne pepper**
1 **teaspoon sugar**
1 **teaspoon garlic powder**
1 **teaspoon ground cumin**
Oil for deep-fat frying

1. Cut onions into 1/4-in. slices; separate into rings. Place in a large bowl; cover with buttermilk and soak for 30 minutes, stirring twice.

2. In a shallow bowl, beat eggs and water. In another shallow bowl, combine the flour, salt, chili powder, cayenne, sugar, garlic powder and cumin. Drain onion rings; dip in egg mixture, then roll in flour mixture.

3. In an electric skillet or deep-fat fryer, heat 1 in. of oil to 375°. Fry onion rings, a few at a time, for 1 to 1-1/2 minutes on each side or until golden brown. Drain on paper towels. **Yield:** 8 servings.

🏵 🏵 🏵
Calico Squash Casserole

Prep: 20 min. **Bake:** 30 min.

Lucille Terry, Frankfort, Kentucky

I have a thriving country garden and try a lot of recipes using my squash. It's a pleasure to present this beautiful casserole as part of a holiday menu...or any time at all.

2 cups sliced yellow summer squash (1/4 inch thick)

1 cup sliced zucchini (1/4 inch thick)
1 medium onion, chopped
1/4 cup sliced green onions
1 cup water
1 teaspoon salt, *divided*
2 cups crushed butter-flavored crackers
1/2 cup butter, melted
1 can (10-3/4 ounces) condensed cream of chicken soup, undiluted
1 can (8 ounces) sliced water chestnuts, drained
1 large carrot, shredded
1/2 cup mayonnaise
1 jar (2 ounces) diced pimientos, drained
1 teaspoon rubbed sage
1/2 teaspoon white pepper
1 cup (4 ounces) shredded sharp cheddar cheese

1. In a large saucepan, combine the first five ingredients; add 1/2 teaspoon salt. Cover and cook until squash is tender, about 6 minutes. Drain well; set aside.

2. Combine the cracker crumbs and butter; spoon half into a greased shallow 1-1/2-qt. baking dish. In a large bowl, combine the soup, water chestnuts, carrot, mayonnaise, pimientos, sage, white pepper and remaining salt; fold into the squash mixture. Spoon over the crumbs.

3. Sprinkle with cheese and the remaining crumb mixture. Bake, uncovered, at 350° for 30 minutes or until lightly browned. **Yield:** 8 servings.

🏵 🏵 🏵
Cheddar Taters

Prep: 5 min. **Bake:** 30 min.

Ruth Van Nattan, Kingston, Tennessee

Potato chips are the fun topping that's sprinkled over this irresistible Tater Tot dish. With its garlic, onion and cheese flavors, leftovers will be hard to come by!

1 can (10-3/4 ounces) condensed cream of chicken soup, undiluted
1 can (12 ounces) evaporated milk
1 cup (8 ounces) sour cream
1/2 cup butter, melted
1 teaspoon garlic powder
1 teaspoon onion powder
1 package (32 ounces) frozen Tater Tots
1-1/2 cups (6 ounces) shredded cheddar cheese
1 cup crushed potato chips

In a large bowl, combine the first six ingredients. Gently stir in the Tater Tots. Transfer to a greased 13-in. x 9-in. x 2-in. baking dish. Sprinkle with cheese and potato chips. Bake, uncovered, at 350° for 30-35 minutes or until bubbly. **Yield:** 8-10 servings.

🎀 🎀 🎀
Jalapeno Cranberry Jelly

(Also pictured on page 135)

Prep: 30 min. **Process:** 5 min. + standing

Karen Bunzow, Saginaw, Michigan

The thing that inspires most of my recipes is getting an ingredient that I don't know what to do with. When my brother gave me some jalapeno peppers, I created this jelly. Fortunately, my husband is a willing guinea pig for my experiments!

- 3 cups cranberry juice
- 1 cup chopped seeded jalapeno peppers
- 1 cup white vinegar
- 7 cups sugar
- 2 pouches (3 ounces *each*) liquid fruit pectin
- 10 drops red food coloring, optional

1. Place the cranberry juice and jalapeno peppers in a blender; cover and process until the peppers are fully chopped. Strain through a double thickness of cheesecloth. Pour the strained juice into a large kettle; add the vinegar. Stir in the sugar. Bring to a full rolling boil, stirring constantly.

2. Stir in pectin; return to a full rolling boil. Boil for 1 minute, stirring constantly. Remove from the heat; skim foam. Add food coloring if desired. Pour into hot sterilized jars, leaving 1/4-in. headspace. Adjust caps.

3. Process for 5 minutes in a boiling-water bath. Serve the jelly with cream cheese on crackers or use as a condiment with meat or poultry. **Yield:** 8 half-pints.

Editor's Note: When cutting or seeding hot peppers, use rubber or plastic gloves to protect your hands. Avoid touching your face.

🎀 🎀 🎀
Mushroom Wild Rice Bake

Prep: 15 min. + soaking **Bake:** 1 hour 25 min.

Jann Marie Foster, Minneapolis, Minnesota

Wild rice adds a wonderful flavor to this casserole, which I like to serve on special occasions throughout the year.

- 1 cup uncooked wild rice
- 2 cups boiling water
- 1 pound sliced fresh mushrooms
- 1 medium onion, chopped
- 2 tablespoons butter
- 3/4 cup uncooked long grain rice
- 1/2 cup sliced almonds
- 3 cups chicken broth
- 1-1/2 cups heavy whipping cream
- 1 teaspoon salt
- 1/8 teaspoon pepper
- 3 tablespoons grated Parmesan cheese

1. Place wild rice in a bowl and cover with boiling water; soak for 1 hour. Drain and set aside.

2. In a large skillet, saute mushrooms and onion in butter until tender. In a large bowl, combine the mushroom mixture, wild rice, long grain rice, almonds, broth, whipping cream, salt and pepper.

3. Transfer to a greased 2-1/2-qt. baking dish. Cover and bake at 350° for 75 minutes. Uncover; sprinkle with Parmesan cheese. Bake 10 minutes longer or until rice is tender. **Yield:** 8-10 servings.

🎖🎖🎖
Never-Fail Egg Noodles
Prep/Total Time: 20 min.

Kathryn Roach, Edgemont, Arkansas

Some 30 years ago, the small church I attended held a chicken and noodles supper as a fundraiser. I was put in charge of noodles for 200 people! A dear lady shared this great recipe.

> 1 **egg plus 3 egg yolks**
> 3 **tablespoons cold water**
> 1 **teaspoon salt**
> 2 **cups all-purpose flour**
> **Chopped fresh parsley, optional**

1. In a mixing bowl, beat the egg and egg yolks until light and fluffy. Add the water and salt; mix well. Stir in the flour. Turn onto a floured surface; knead until smooth. Divide into thirds. Roll out each portion to 1/8-in. thickness.

2. Cut noodles to desired width (noodles shown in the photo were cut 2 in. x 1/2 in.). Cook immediately in boiling salted water or chicken broth for 7-9 minutes or until tender. Drain; sprinkle with parsley if desired. **Yield:** about 5-1/2 cups.

🎖🎖🎖
Creamed Spinach
Prep/Total Time: 15 min.

Susan Geddie, Harker Heights, Texas

The inspiration for this creamy side dish came from a local restaurant. I lightened up the original recipe a bit by using fat-free half-and-half and cream cheese.

> 1/4 **cup diced onion**
> 1 **garlic clove, minced**
> 1 **tablespoon butter**
> 1 **tablespoon all-purpose flour**
> 1-1/4 **cups fat-free half-and-half**
> 4 **ounces fat-free cream cheese, cubed**
> 3/4 **teaspoon salt**
> 1/8 **teaspoon ground nutmeg**
> 1/8 **teaspoon pepper**
> 1 **package (16 ounces) frozen leaf spinach, thawed and squeezed dry**
> 1/4 **cup plus 1 tablespoon shredded Parmesan cheese, *divided***

1. In a large nonstick skillet, saute onion and garlic in butter until tender. Stir in flour until blended. Gradually whisk in half-and-half until blended. Bring to a boil over medium-low heat; cook and stir for 2 minutes or until slightly thickened.

2. Add the cream cheese, salt, nutmeg and pepper, stirring until cream cheese is melted. Stir in spinach and 1/4 cup Parmesan cheese; heat through. Sprinkle with remaining Parmesan cheese. Serve immediately. **Yield:** 5 servings.

Pineapple Cheese Braid, p. 167

Apricot Cranberry Bread, p. 170

Surprise Sausage Bundles, p. 161

Breads & Rolls

Treat your family and friends to the golden loaves, yummy muffins and other fresh-baked favorites in this chapter. Chances are, you'll get lots of rave reviews...and requests for more!

Cherry Chip Scones, p. 157

🎀🎀🎀
Orange-Hazelnut Spiral Rolls

Prep: 30 min. + rising **Bake:** 20 min.

Loraine Meyer, Bend, Oregon

By adapting a popular coffee cake recipe, I came up with these scrumptious rolls. I make them for family throughout the year.

 5 to 5-1/2 cups all-purpose flour, *divided*
 1 cup mashed potato flakes
1/4 cup sugar
 2 packages (1/4 ounce *each*) quick-rise yeast
 1 teaspoon salt
 2 teaspoons grated orange peel
 1 cup milk
1/2 cup butter, cubed
1/2 cup sour cream
1/4 cup water
 2 eggs
FILLING:
 1/3 cup butter, softened
  1 cup confectioners' sugar
  1 cup ground hazelnuts
GLAZE:
 1/2 cup sugar
 1/4 cup orange juice concentrate
 1/4 cup sour cream
  2 tablespoons butter

1. In a large mixing bowl, combine 4 cups flour, potato flakes, sugar, yeast, salt and orange peel. In saucepan, heat the milk, butter, sour cream and water to 120°-130°. Add to dry ingredients; beat just until moistened. Add eggs; beat until smooth. Stir in enough remaining flour to form a stiff dough.

2. Turn onto floured surface; knead until smooth and elastic, about 6-8 minutes. Place in greased bowl, turning once to grease top. Cover; let dough rest in a warm place for 20 minutes. Punch dough down. Turn onto a floured surface; roll into a 22-in. x 14-in. rectangle.

3. For filling, combine butter, confectioners' sugar and nuts. Spread lengthwise over half of the dough. Fold dough over filling, forming a 22-in. x 7-in. rectangle. Cut into 7-in. x 3/4-in. strips. Twist each strip 4 or 5 times and shape into a ring. Pinch ends together. Place on two greased 15-in. x 10-in. x 1-in. baking pans. Cover and let rise for 30 minutes or until doubled. Bake at 375° for 17-20 minutes or until golden brown. Remove to wire racks.

4. Meanwhile, in a saucepan, combine glaze ingredients over medium heat. Bring to boil; boil and stir for 3 minutes or until thickened. Remove from the heat. Drizzle over warm rolls. **Yield:** about 2 dozen.

🎀🎀🎀
Herbed Garlic Bread

Prep/Total Time: 30 min.

Wendy Smith, Hartford, Wisconsin

I've used both French and Vienna bread for this recipe. The Parmesan cheese complements the garlic nicely.

 1 unsliced loaf (1 pound) French bread
1/2 cup butter, softened
 2 tablespoons grated Parmesan cheese
 2 tablespoons minced fresh parsley
 4 garlic cloves, minced
1/2 teaspoon dried oregano
1/8 teaspoon garlic salt

Slice bread, but not all the way through, leaving slices attached at the bottom. In a small mixing bowl, cream butter. Add the Parmesan cheese, parsley, garlic, oregano and garlic salt; mix well. Spread between slices. Wrap loaf in a large piece of heavy-duty foil (about 28 in. x 18 in.). Bake at 325° for 15-20 minutes or until heated through. **Yield:** 8-10 servings.

Cherry Chip Scones

(Also pictured on page 155)

Prep: 15 min. **Bake:** 20 min.

Pamela Brooks, South Berwick, Maine

These buttery scones, dotted with plenty of dried cherries and vanilla chips, are so sweet and flaky that I even serve them for dessert...and everyone loves them.

>   3 cups all-purpose flour
> 1/2 cup sugar
> 2-1/2 teaspoons baking powder
> 1/2 teaspoon baking soda
>   6 tablespoons cold butter
>   1 cup (8 ounces) vanilla yogurt
> 1/4 cup plus 2 tablespoons milk, *divided*
> 1-1/3 cups dried cherries
> 2/3 cup vanilla or white chips

1. In a large bowl, combine the flour, sugar, baking powder and baking soda. Cut in butter until the mixture resembles coarse crumbs. Combine yogurt and 1/4 cup milk; stir into crumb mixture just until moistened. Knead in the cherries and chips.

2. On a greased baking sheet, pat the dough into a 9-in. circle. Cut into eight wedges; separate wedges. Brush with the remaining milk. Bake at 400° for 20-25 minutes or until golden brown. Serve warm. **Yield:** 8 servings.

🎗🎗🎗
Whole Wheat Honey Rolls

Prep: 25 min. + rising **Bake:** 15 min.

Linda Gunn, Reynolds, Georgia

These airy, golden-brown yeast rolls get a bit of sweetness from the creamy honey butter and the honey in the dough.

    2 packages (1/4 ounce *each*) active dry yeast
    2 cups warm buttermilk (110° to 115°)
    1/2 cup butter, melted
    1/3 cup honey
    3 cups whole wheat flour
    1 teaspoon salt
    1 teaspoon baking soda
    1-1/2 to 2-1/2 cups all-purpose flour
    Additional melted butter
    HONEY BUTTER:
    1 cup butter, softened
    1/2 cup honey

1. In a large mixing bowl, dissolve yeast in warm buttermilk. Add the butter, honey, whole wheat flour, salt and baking soda. Beat until smooth. Stir in enough all-purpose flour to form a soft dough.

2. Turn onto a floured surface; knead until smooth and elastic, about 6-8 minutes. Place in a greased bowl, turning once to grease top. Cover and let rise in a warm place until doubled, about 1 hour.

3. Punch dough down. Turn onto a lightly floured surface; divide into seven portions. Divide each portion into six pieces; shape each into a ball. Place 2 in. apart on greased baking sheets. Cover and let rise in a warm place until doubled, about 30 minutes.

4. Brush with melted butter. Bake at 400° for 12-16 minutes or until golden brown. Remove to wire racks to cool. In a small mixing bowl, beat butter and honey until smooth; serve with rolls. **Yield:** 3-1/2 dozen.

Editor's Note: Warmed buttermilk will appear curdled.

🎗🎗🎗
Maple Sticky Buns

Prep: 30 min. + rising **Bake:** 25 min.

Priscilla Rossi, East Barre, Vermont

My family has a small sugaring operation in our backyard. This recipe makes great use of the maple syrup we make.

    2 packages (1/4 ounce *each*) active dry yeast
    2 cups warm water (110° to 115°)
    1/4 cup shortening
    1/2 cup sugar
    1 egg
    2 teaspoons salt
    6 to 6-1/2 cups all-purpose flour
    6 tablespoons butter, softened
    3/4 cup packed brown sugar
    1 tablespoon ground cinnamon
    3/4 cup chopped walnuts
    1-1/2 cups maple syrup
    Additional brown sugar

1. In a mixing bowl, dissolve yeast in water. Add shortening, sugar, egg, salt and enough flour to form a soft dough. Cover and refrigerate for 24 hours.

2. Punch dough down. Turn onto a floured surface; knead until smooth and elastic, about 6-8 minutes, adding more flour if needed. Divide into thirds. Roll each portion into a 16-in. x 10-in. rectangle. On each rectangle, spread 2 tablespoons butter and sprinkle with 1/4 cup brown sugar, 1 teaspoon cinnamon and 1/4 cup walnuts.

3. Pour syrup into three greased 9-in. round baking pans. Sprinkle with brown sugar. Tightly roll up each rectangle jelly-roll style, starting with a short side. Slice each roll into 10 pieces; place over the syrup in pans. Cover and let rise until doubled, about 30 minutes. Bake at 350° for 25-30 minutes or until golden brown. Cool in pans for 5 minutes; invert onto a wire rack. **Yield:** 2-1/2 dozen.

⚜ ⚜ ⚜
Herbed Swirl Bread

Prep: 30 min. + rising **Bake:** 40 min.

Laura Dennison, Pensacola, Florida

This yeast bread is so pretty, with its swirl of herbs in every slice. Try it with soups or stews...or toasted with butter.

✓ Uses less fat, sugar or salt. Includes Nutrition Facts and Diabetic Exchange.

  3 packages (1/4 ounce *each*) active dry yeast
2-1/2 cups warm water (110° to 115°), *divided*
  1 teaspoon sugar
3-1/4 cups whole wheat flour
  1 tablespoon salt
2-3/4 to 3-1/2 cups bread flour
  6 green onions, finely chopped
  1 garlic clove, minced
  1 cup minced fresh parsley
  2 tablespoons minced fresh rosemary
  1 tablespoon *each* minced fresh basil and oregano
  1 teaspoon minced fresh thyme
1/4 teaspoon pepper
  2 tablespoons butter
  1 egg, beaten

1. In a large mixing bowl, dissolve yeast in 3/4 cup warm water. Add sugar; let stand for 5 minutes. Add the whole wheat flour, salt and remaining water; beat until smooth. Stir in enough bread flour to form a soft dough (dough will be sticky).

2. Turn onto a floured surface; knead until smooth and elastic, about 6-8 minutes. Place in a bowl coated with cooking spray; turn once to coat top. Cover and let rise in a warm place until doubled, about 1 hour. In a nonstick skillet, saute onions, garlic, herbs and pepper in butter until tender. Set aside.

3. Punch dough down and turn onto a floured surface; divide in half. Roll each piece into a 14-in. x 9-in. rectangle. Brush with some of the egg; refrigerate rest of egg. Spread herb mixture over dough to within 1/2 in. of edges. Roll up jelly-roll style, starting with a short side; pinch seams to seal and tuck ends under.

4. Place seam side down in two 9-in. x 5-in. x 3-in. loaf pans coated with cooking spray. Cover; let rise until doubled, about 45 minutes. Brush with reserved egg. Bake at 375° for 40-50 minutes or until bread sounds hollow when tapped. Remove from pans to wire racks. **Yield:** 2 loaves (12 slices each).

Nutrition Facts: 1 slice equals 134 calories, 2 g fat (1 g saturated fat), 11 mg cholesterol, 309 mg sodium, 25 g carbohydrate, 3 g fiber, 5 g protein. **Diabetic Exchange:** 1-1/2 starch.

⚜ ⚜ ⚜
Southwestern Savory Muffins

Prep/Total Time: 30 min.

Laura Parker, Los Alamos, New Mexico

I modified a muffin recipe I'd found and came up with this one. It's now a favorite breakfast treat for my husband and me.

10 bacon strips
  2 cups all-purpose flour
1/4 cup sugar
  1 tablespoon baking powder
3/4 cup milk
  1 egg
1-1/2 cups (6 ounces) shredded cheddar cheese
1/4 cup diced green chilies

1. In a skillet, cook the bacon until crisp; reserve 1/3 cup drippings. Crumble bacon and set aside. In a large bowl, combine flour, sugar and baking powder. In a mix-

ing bowl, beat milk, egg and drippings; stir into dry ingredients just until moistened.

2. Fold in the cheese, chilies and bacon. Fill greased or paper-lined muffin cups three-fourths full. Bake at 400° for 15-20 minutes or until golden brown. Serve warm. **Yield:** 14 servings.

1 package (10 ounces) fresh spinach, torn
4 ounces reduced-fat cream cheese
2 tablespoons reduced-fat mayonnaise
1 teaspoon salt-free lemon-pepper seasoning
3 tablespoons cornmeal

1. In a large mixing bowl, combine 2 cups flour, sugar, yeast, lemon peel and 1 teaspoon salt. In a saucepan, heat water, 3/4 cup milk, oil and 3 teaspoons lemon juice to 120°-130°. Add to dry ingredients; beat just until moistened. Stir in enough remaining flour to form a soft dough (dough will be sticky).

2. Turn onto a floured surface; knead until smooth and elastic, about 6-8 minutes. Place in a bowl coated with cooking spray, turning once to coat top. Cover and let rise until doubled, about 1 hour.

3. Place spinach in a steamer basket in a saucepan over 1 in. of water; bring to a boil. Cover and steam until wilted; drain. Combine the cream cheese, mayonnaise, lemon-pepper and remaining lemon juice and salt. Stir in spinach; cool.

4. Punch dough down. Roll into a 24-in. x 14-in. rectangle. Spread filling to within 1/2 in. of edges. Roll up jelly-roll style, starting with a long side; pinch seams to seal and tuck ends under. Cut into 20 slices.

5. Coat baking sheets with cooking spray and sprinkle with cornmeal. Place slices cut side up on pans. Cover and let rise until doubled, about 30 minutes. Brush remaining milk over rolls. Bake at 325° for 30-35 minutes or until golden brown. **Yield:** 20 rolls.

Nutrition Facts: 1 roll equals 130 calories, 3 g fat (1 g saturated fat), 4 mg cholesterol, 244 mg sodium, 22 g carbohydrate, 1 g fiber, 4 g protein. **Diabetic Exchange:** 1-1/2 starch.

🏵 🏵 🏵
Spinach Pinwheel Rolls

Prep: 30 min. **Bake:** 30 min.

Maryalice Wood, Langley, British Columbia

Whether warm or cold, these tender rolls with their tasty filling are always a hit. I like them with a Greek salad.

✓ Uses less fat, sugar or salt. Includes Nutrition Facts and Diabetic Exchange.

      4 to 5 cups all-purpose flour
      1 tablespoon sugar
      3 teaspoons active dry yeast
      1 teaspoon grated lemon peel
1-1/2 teaspoons salt, *divided*
   3/4 cup water
   3/4 cup plus 2 tablespoons fat-free milk, *divided*
      1 tablespoon canola oil
      4 teaspoons lemon juice, *divided*

🏵 🏵 🏵
Quick Caramel Rolls

Prep/Total Time: 30 min.

Jeannette Westphal, Gettysburg, South Dakota

Refrigerated crescent rolls and caramel ice cream topping make these yummy, gooey treats a snap to assemble.

   1/4 cup butter
   1/2 cup chopped pecans
      1 cup caramel ice cream topping
      2 tubes (8 ounces *each*) refrigerated crescent rolls

1. Place butter in a 13-in. x 9-in. x 2-in. baking pan; heat in a 375° oven until melted. Sprinkle with pecans. Add ice cream topping and mix well.

2. Remove dough from tubes (do not unroll); cut each section of dough into six rolls. Arrange rolls in prepared pan with cut side down. Bake at 375° for 20-25

minutes or until golden. Immediately invert onto a serving plate. Serve warm. **Yield:** 2 dozen.

Surprise Sausage Bundles

(Also pictured on page 154)

Prep: 45 min. + rising **Bake:** 20 min.

Barb Ruis, Grandville, Michigan

Kielbasa and sauerkraut star in the hearty stuffing for these rolls, which are great with a salad or soup.

- 6 **bacon strips, diced**
- 1 **cup chopped onion**
- 1 **can (16 ounces) sauerkraut, rinsed and well drained**
- 1/2 **pound fully cooked smoked kielbasa or Polish sausage, coarsely chopped**
- 2 **tablespoons brown sugar**
- 1/2 **teaspoon garlic salt**
- 1/4 **teaspoon caraway seeds**
- 1/8 **teaspoon pepper**
- 1 **package (16 ounces) hot roll mix**
- 2 **eggs**
- 1 **cup warm water (120° to 130°)**
- 2 **tablespoons butter, softened**

Poppy seeds

1. In a skillet, cook bacon until crisp; remove to paper towels. Reserve 2 tablespoons drippings. Saute onion in drippings until tender. Stir in sauerkraut, sausage, brown sugar, garlic salt, caraway seeds and pepper. Cook and stir for 5 minutes. Remove from the heat; add the bacon. Set aside to cool.

2. In a bowl, combine the contents of the hot roll mix. Stir in one egg, the water and the butter to form a soft dough. Turn onto a floured surface; knead until smooth and elastic, about 5 minutes. Cover the dough with a large bowl; let stand for 5 minutes.

3. Divide dough into 16 pieces. On a floured surface, roll out each piece into a 4-in. circle. Top each with 1/4 cup filling. Fold dough around filling, forming a ball; pinch edges to seal. Place seam side down on greased baking sheets. Cover loosely with plastic wrap coated with cooking spray. Let rise in a warm place for 15 minutes.

4. Beat remaining egg; brush over bundles. Sprinkle with poppy seeds. Bake at 350° for 16-17 minutes or until golden brown. Serve warm. **Yield:** 16 servings.

Grand Prize Winner

🏵 🏵 🏵

Golden Raisin Wheat Bread

Prep: 35 min. + rising **Bake:** 35 min.

Nilah Schenck, Beloit, Wisconsin

I freeze extra loaves of this moist bread in freezer bags. Then when I need a loaf, I just thaw it overnight. The golden raisins and honey add a wonderful touch of sweetness.

    3/4 cup golden raisins
    1/2 cup boiling water
      3 cups whole wheat flour
      2 packages (1/4 ounce *each*) active dry yeast
      1 tablespoon salt
      1 teaspoon baking soda
      1 carton (16 ounces) plain yogurt
      1 cup water
    1/3 cup honey
      5 tablespoons butter
  4-1/2 to 5 cups all-purpose flour

1. In a small bowl, combine raisins and water; let stand for 10 minutes. Drain well; set aside. In a large bowl, combine whole wheat flour, yeast, salt and baking soda. In a saucepan, heat yogurt, water, honey and butter to 120°-130°. Add to dry ingredients. Add raisins and enough all-purpose flour to form a soft dough.

2. Turn onto a floured surface; knead until smooth and elastic, about 6-8 minutes. Place in a greased bowl, turning once to grease top. Cover and let rise in a warm place until doubled, about 1 hour.

3. Punch dough down; divide into thirds. Shape into loaves. Place in three greased 9-in. x 5-in. x 3-in. loaf pans. Cover and let rise until doubled, about 30 minutes. Bake at 350° for 35-40 minutes or until golden brown. Remove from pans to cool on wire racks. **Yield:** 3 loaves.

⚜⚜⚜
Cinnamon Crisps
Prep: 30 min. + rising Bake: 10 min.

Sarah Bueckert, Austin, Manitoba

I first tried the recipe for these nut-topped rolls when I still lived at home with my parents. My dad especially loved them.

        4 cups all-purpose flour
        1 package (1/4 ounce) active dry yeast
1-1/4 cups warm milk (120° to 130°)
        1/4 cup shortening
        1/4 cup sugar
        1 teaspoon salt
        1 egg
FILLING:
        1/2 cup *each* sugar and packed brown sugar
        1/4 cup butter, melted
        1 teaspoon ground cinnamon
TOPPING:
        1 cup sugar
        1 teaspoon ground cinnamon
        1/2 cup chopped pecans
        1/4 cup butter, melted

1. In a mixing bowl, combine 2 cups flour and yeast. Add milk, shortening, sugar and salt to flour mixture; beat for 1 minute. Add egg; beat for 1 minute. Beat on medium for 3 minutes. Stir in enough remaining flour to form a soft dough.

2. Turn dough onto a floured surface; knead until smooth and elastic, about 6-8 minutes. Place in a greased bowl, turning once to grease top. Cover and let rise until doubled, about 1 hour.

3. Combine filling ingredients. Punch dough down; divide in half. On a floured surface, roll one portion into a 12-in. square. Spread with half the filling. Roll up tightly; pinch to seal. Cut into 1-in. slices; place four slices on three greased baking sheets. Cover with waxed paper; flatten slices into 3-in. circles. Repeat with remaining dough and filling. Cover and let rise until doubled, about 30 minutes.

4. Cover with waxed paper; flatten into 5-in. circles. Combine sugar, cinnamon and pecans. Brush rolls with butter; sprinkle with nut topping. Cover with waxed paper; flatten again. Bake, uncovered, at 400° for 10-12 minutes or until browned. **Yield:** 2 dozen.

⚜⚜⚜
Cinnamon Rhubarb Muffins
Prep/Total Time: 30 min.

Barbara Perry, Saginaw, Michigan

The tangy rhubarb center makes these fluffy muffins extra scrumptious and perfect for either breakfast or snacking.

1-1/2 cups all-purpose flour
        1/2 cup plus 1 tablespoon sugar, *divided*
        2 teaspoons baking powder
1-1/4 teaspoons ground cinnamon, *divided*
        1/4 teaspoon salt
        1 egg, beaten
        2/3 cup buttermilk
        1/4 cup butter, melted
        1/2 cup chopped fresh *or* frozen rhubarb, thawed
             and drained
        1/4 cup peach preserves

1. In a bowl, combine flour, 1/2 cup sugar, baking powder, 1 teaspoon cinnamon and salt. Combine egg, buttermilk and butter; stir into dry ingredients just until moistened.

2. Spoon 1 tablespoonful of batter into nine greased or paper-lined muffin cups. Combine rhubarb and preserves; place 1 tablespoonful in the center of each cup (do not spread). Top with remaining batter. Combine remaining sugar and cinnamon; sprinkle over batter. Bake at 400° for 20 minutes or until top of muffin springs back when lightly touched in the center. **Yield:** 9 muffins.

🎀🎀🎀
Applesauce Oat Muffins

Prep: 15 min. **Bake:** 20 min. + cooling

Hannah Barringer, Loudon, Tennessee

My grandmother passed this recipe down to me. The muffins are tender on the inside and have a crispy topping.

- 1-1/2 cups quick-cooking oats
- 1-1/4 cups all-purpose flour
- 1/2 cup packed brown sugar
- 1 teaspoon baking powder
- 3/4 teaspoon baking soda
- 3/4 teaspoon ground cinnamon
- 1/2 teaspoon salt
- 1 cup unsweetened applesauce
- 1/2 cup fat-free milk
- 3 tablespoons canola oil
- 1 egg white

TOPPING:
- 1/4 cup quick-cooking oats
- 1 tablespoon brown sugar
- 1/8 teaspoon ground cinnamon
- 1 tablespoon butter, melted

In a large mixing bowl, combine first seven ingredients. In another bowl, combine applesauce, milk, oil and egg white. Stir into dry ingredients just until moistened. Fill muffin cups coated with cooking spray three-fourths full. Combine topping ingredients; sprinkle over batter. Bake at 400° for 16-18 minutes or until a toothpick comes out clean. Cool for 10 minutes; remove to wire rack. **Yield:** 10 muffins.

🎀🎀🎀
Maple Oatmeal Bread

Prep: 20 min. + rising **Bake:** 40 min.

Marian Tobin, Underhill, Vermont

This is one of my favorite recipes—especially because it features maple syrup, which the state of Vermont is famous for.

- 1 cup hot brewed coffee
- 3/4 cup boiling water
- 1/2 cup maple syrup
- 1/3 cup vegetable oil
- 1 cup old-fashioned oats
- 1/2 cup sugar
- 2 teaspoons salt
- 2 packages (1/4 ounce *each*) active dry yeast
- 1/4 cup warm water (110° to 115°)
- 2 eggs, lightly beaten
- 5-1/2 to 6 cups bread flour

1. In a bowl, combine first seven ingredients. Cool to 110°-115°. In a large bowl, dissolve yeast in warm water. Add oat mixture, eggs and 2 cups flour; mix well. Stir in enough remaining flour to form a soft dough.

2. Turn onto a floured surface; knead until smooth and elastic, about 6-8 minutes. Place in a greased bowl, turning once to grease top. Cover and let rise in a warm place until doubled, about 1 hour.

3. Punch dough down. Turn onto a lightly floured surface; divide in half. Shape into loaves. Place in two greased 9-in. x 5-in. x 3-in. loaf pans. Cover and let rise until doubled, about 30 minutes. Bake at 350° for 40-45 minutes or until golden brown. Remove from pans to wire racks to cool. **Yield:** 2 loaves.

Pecan Pie Mini Muffins

Prep: 10 min.
Bake: 25 min.

Pat Schrand, Enterprise, Alabama

While these nutty bites are delicious year-round, you could easily turn them into an edible Christmas gift. The muffins look festive in a tin or on a decorative tray.

1 cup packed brown sugar
1/2 cup all-purpose flour
1 cup chopped pecans
2/3 cup butter, melted
2 eggs, beaten

1. In a bowl, combine the brown sugar, flour and pecans; set aside. Combine the butter and beaten eggs. Stir into the brown sugar mixture. Fill greased and floured miniature muffin cups two-thirds full.

2. Bake at 350° for 22-25 minutes or until a toothpick comes out clean. Immediately remove muffins from the pans to wire racks to cool. **Yield:** about 2-1/2 dozen.

🎀🎀🎀
Onion Sandwich Rolls

Prep: 25 min. + rising **Bake:** 20 min.

Josie-Lynn Belmont, Woodbine, Georgia

With mild onion flavor, these tempting rolls are great with Italian meals…or as sandwich rolls or hamburger buns.

✓ Uses less fat, sugar or salt. Includes Nutrition Facts and Diabetic Exchange.

1 envelope reduced-sodium onion soup mix
1/2 cup boiling water
1 tablespoon margarine
3-1/2 to 4 cups all-purpose flour, *divided*
2 packages (1/4 ounce *each*) quick-rise yeast
1 tablespoon sugar
1 cup warm water (120° to 130°)

1. In a bowl, combine soup mix, boiling water and margarine; cool to 120°-130°. In a mixing bowl, combine 1 cup flour, yeast and sugar. Add warm water; beat until smooth. Stir in 1 cup flour. Beat in soup mixture and enough remaining flour to form a soft dough.

2. Turn onto a floured surface; knead until smooth and elastic, about 6-8 minutes. Cover; let stand for 10 minutes. Divide into 12 portions; shape each into a ball. Place on greased baking sheets; flatten slightly.

3. Place two large shallow pans on the work surface; fill half-full with boiling water. Place baking pans with rolls over water-filled pans. Cover; let rise for 15 minutes. Bake at 375° for 16-19 minutes or until golden brown. Remove from pans to wire rack. **Yield:** 1 dozen.

Nutrition Facts: 1 roll equals 160 calories, 1 g fat (0 saturated fat), 0 cholesterol, 168 mg sodium, 32 g carbohydrate, 0 fiber, 5 g protein. **Diabetic Exchange:** 2 starch.

🎀🎀🎀
Handy Sausage Biscuits

Prep: 25 min. **Bake:** 10 min.

Nancy Parker, Seguin, Texas

Similar to old-fashioned biscuits made from scratch, these are even better thanks to the tasty sausage throughout.

3/4 pound bulk pork sausage
2-2/3 cups all-purpose flour
2 tablespoons sugar
1-1/2 teaspoons baking powder
1/2 teaspoon baking soda
1/2 teaspoon salt
1/2 cup shortening
1 package (1/4 ounce) active dry yeast
1/4 cup warm water (110° to 115°)
1 cup buttermilk
Melted butter

1. In a skillet, cook sausage over medium heat until no longer pink; drain well and set aside. In a bowl, combine flour, sugar, baking powder, baking soda and salt; cut in shortening until crumbly. Stir in the sausage.

2. In another bowl, dissolve yeast in water; let stand for 5 minutes. Add buttermilk. Stir into dry ingredients just until moistened.

3. On a lightly floured surface, gently knead dough 6-8 times. Roll out to 1/2-in. thickness; cut with a

2-in. biscuit cutter. Place on lightly greased baking sheets. Brush tops of biscuits with butter. Bake at 450° for 10-12 minutes or until golden brown. Serve warm. **Yield:** 2-3 dozen.

Editor's Note: No rising time is necessary before baking. The dough can be rerolled.

🎀 🎀 🎀

Pineapple Cheese Braid

(Also pictured on page 154)

Prep: 45 min. + rising **Bake:** 25 min. + cooling

Shirley Kensinger, Roaring Spring, Pennsylvania

Folks are always pleasantly surprised by this bread's pineapple filling. When in a hurry, I'll use canned pie filling.

>   2 packages (1/4 ounce *each*) active dry yeast
>   1 cup warm water (110° to 115°)
> 1/2 cup butter, softened
>   5 tablespoons sugar
>   2 eggs
> 1/4 teaspoon salt
> 4-1/4 to 4-1/2 cups all-purpose flour
> **PINEAPPLE FILLING:**
>   1 can (8 ounces) crushed pineapple, undrained
> 1/2 cup sugar
>   3 tablespoons cornstarch
> **CREAM CHEESE FILLING:**
>   2 packages (8 ounces *each*) cream cheese,
>   softened
> 1/3 cup sugar
>   1 tablespoon lemon juice
> 1/2 teaspoon vanilla extract
> **ICING (optional):**
>   1 cup confectioners' sugar
>   2 to 3 tablespoons milk

1. In a large mixing bowl, dissolve yeast in water. Add butter, sugar, eggs, salt and 2 cups flour; beat on low speed for 3 minutes. Stir in enough remaining flour to form a soft dough.

2. Turn the dough onto a floured surface; knead dough until smooth and elastic, about 6-8 minutes. Place in a greased bowl, turning once to grease top. Cover dough and let rise in a warm place until doubled, about 45 minutes.

3. For the filling, combine the pineapple, sugar and cornstarch in a saucepan. Bring to a boil; reduce heat. Cook and stir until thickened. Cool. In a mixing bowl, combine the cream cheese filling ingredients; mix well.

4. Punch dough down. Divide dough in half. On a floured surface, roll each portion of dough into a 15-in. x 9-in. rectangle. Place on greased baking sheets. Spread the cream cheese filling lengthwise down the center third of each rectangle. Spread the pineapple filling on top.

5. On each long side, cut 1-in.-wide strips 3 in. into center. Starting at one end, fold alternating strips at an angle across filling. Seal ends. Cover and let rise for 20 minutes.

6. Bake at 350° for 25-30 minutes or until golden brown. Cool. If desired, combine the icing ingredients and drizzle over the braids. Store braids in refrigerator. **Yield:** 2 loaves.

🎀 🎀 🎀

Bacon-Onion Crescent Buns

Prep: 40 min. + rising **Bake:** 15 min.

Helen Wilson, San Benito, Texas

These savory crescents are a hit with everyone who tastes them. I've served them for both dinner and brunch.

4-3/4 to 5-1/4 cups all-purpose flour
  1/2 cup sugar
    1 package (1/4 ounce) active dry yeast
  1/2 teaspoon salt
    1 cup milk
  1/2 cup butter, cubed
  1/2 teaspoon caraway seeds
    3 eggs
    1 pound sliced bacon, diced
    1 small onion, finely chopped
  1/8 teaspoon white pepper
    2 tablespoons water

1. In a mixing bowl, combine 2 cups flour, sugar, yeast and salt. In a saucepan, heat the milk and butter to 120°-130°. Add to dry ingredients; beat on medium speed for 2 minutes. Add caraway and 2 eggs; mix well. Stir in enough remaining flour to form a stiff dough. Turn onto a floured surface; knead until smooth and elastic, about 6-8 minutes. Place in a greased bowl, turning once to grease top. Cover and let rise in a warm place until doubled, about 1 hour.

2. Meanwhile, in a large skillet, cook bacon over medium heat until crisp. Remove with a slotted spoon to paper towels. Saute onion in the bacon drippings. Remove onion with a slotted spoon; set aside. When cool, combine the bacon, onion and white pepper; set aside.

3. Punch dough down. Turn onto a lightly floured surface; divide into four portions. Roll each into a 12-in. circle; cut into 12 wedges. Sprinkle a heaping teaspoonful of bacon mixture over each. Roll up from wide end. Place point end down 2 in. apart on greased baking sheets. Cover; let rise about 30 minutes.

4. In a small bowl, beat water and remaining egg; brush over rolls. Bake at 350° for 12-14 minutes or until golden brown. Refrigerate leftovers. **Yield:** 4 servings.

1 cup butter, softened
3 egg yolks, beaten
1 cup (8 ounces) sour cream
1/2 cup sugar
1/2 cup finely chopped pecans
3/4 teaspoon ground cinnamon
1 medium tart apple, peeled and finely chopped
ICING:
1 cup confectioners' sugar
4 teaspoons milk
1/4 teaspoon vanilla extract
Finely chopped pecans

1. In a large mixing bowl, combine the yeast and flour; add butter and mix well. Add egg yolks and sour cream; mix well. Shape into four balls. Place balls in separate resealable plastic bags or wrap in plastic wrap; refrigerate overnight.

2. Combine sugar, pecans and cinnamon; set aside. On a floured surface, roll each ball into a 9-in. circle. Sprinkle with sugar mixture and apple. Cut each into 16 wedges; roll up from wide edge. Pinch to seal. Place point side down on greased baking sheets.

3. Bake at 350° for 16-20 minutes or until lightly browned. Immediately remove to wire racks to cool. Combine sugar, milk and vanilla until smooth; drizzle over twists. Sprinkle with pecans. **Yield:** 64 twists.

Editor's Note: The yeast does not need to be dissolved in liquid, and no rising time is necessary before baking.

🎀 🎀 🎀

Austrian Apple Twists

Prep: 30 min. + chilling **Bake:** 20 min.

Kathy Bless, Fayetteville, Pennsylvania

This recipe has been a favorite for years. I like to bake the twists for special occasions because everyone enjoys them.

1 package (1/4 ounce) active dry yeast
3 cups all-purpose flour

🎀 🎀 🎀

Caraway Rye Rolls

Prep: 15 min. + rising **Bake:** 20 min.

Dot Christiansen, Bettendorf, Iowa

The caraway and rye flavors really come through in these tender yeast rolls, which have a crispy golden crust.

2 packages (1/4 ounce each) active dry yeast
1/2 cup warm water (110° to 115°)
2 cups warm 4% cottage cheese (110° to 115°)
1/2 cup sugar
2 eggs, beaten
2 tablespoons caraway seeds
2 teaspoons salt
1/2 teaspoon baking soda
1 cup rye flour
3 to 4 cups all-purpose flour

1. In a large mixing bowl, dissolve yeast in warm water. Add cottage cheese, sugar, eggs, caraway, salt, baking soda, rye flour and 1 cup all-purpose flour; mix well. Gradually stir in enough remaining all-purpose flour to form a sticky batter (do not knead). Cover; let rise in a warm place until doubled, about 1 hour.

2. Stir dough down. Turn onto a lightly floured surface; divide into 24 pieces. Place in well-greased muffin cups. Cover and let rise until doubled, about 35 minutes. Bake at 350° for 18-20 minutes or until golden brown. Cool for 1 minute before removing from pans to wire racks. **Yield:** 2 dozen.

🏅🏅🏅
Tomato Cheese Pinwheels

Prep: 30 min. + rising **Bake:** 10 min.

Maggie Gassett, Hillsborough, New Hampshire

These cheesy pinwheels get snatched up in a flash. The light cheddar tang complements the tomato flavor beautifully.

🏅🏅🏅
Apricot Cranberry Bread

(Also pictured on page 154)

Prep: 20 min. **Bake:** 65 min. + cooling

Diane Roth, Milwaukee, Wisconsin

I was making cranberry bread one day and wanted to try something new. I found some apricot jam—it was just the thing!

        2 cups all-purpose flour
        1 cup sugar
        1 to 2 teaspoons grated orange peel
1-1/2 teaspoons baking powder
    1/2 teaspoon baking soda
    1/2 teaspoon salt
        1 egg
    3/4 cup water
    1/4 cup vegetable oil
        1 cup fresh *or* frozen halved cranberries
    1/4 cup apricot preserves

1. In a large bowl, combine flour, sugar, peel, baking powder, baking soda and salt. In a small bowl, beat egg, water and oil; stir into dry ingredients just until moistened. Fold in berries.

2. Pour batter into a greased and floured 9-in. x 5-in.

        4 to 4-1/2 cups all-purpose flour, *divided*
        2 tablespoons sugar
        1 package (1/4 ounce) active dry yeast
1-1/4 teaspoons salt
    3/4 cup warm tomato juice (120° to 130°)
    1/2 cup warm water (120° to 130°)
    1/4 cup butter
        1 egg
        2 cups (8 ounces) finely shredded sharp cheddar cheese
        2 tablespoons minced chives

1. In a mixing bowl, combine 1 cup flour, sugar, yeast and salt. Add tomato juice, water and butter; beat for 2 minutes on medium speed. Add egg and enough remaining flour to form a soft dough. Place in a greased bowl, turning once to grease top. Cover and refrigerate for 2 hours or until doubled.

2. Punch dough down. Divide in half; roll each half into a 15-in. x 12-in. rectangle approximately 1/8 in. thick. Cut into 3-in. squares. Place 2 in. apart on greased baking sheets. Make 1-in. slits in each corner of each square.

3. Combine cheese and chives; place 1 heaping teaspoon in the center of each square. Bring every other corner up to center, overlapping slightly to form a pinwheel; press firmly. Bake at 400° for 8-10 minutes. Remove to a wire rack to cool. **Yield:** 40 pinwheels.

x 3-in. loaf pan. Cut apricots in the preserves into small pieces; spoon preserves over batter. Cut through batter with a knife to swirl. Bake at 350° for 65-70 minutes or until a toothpick inserted near the center comes out clean. Cool for 10 minutes; remove from pan to a wire rack. **Yield:** 1 loaf.

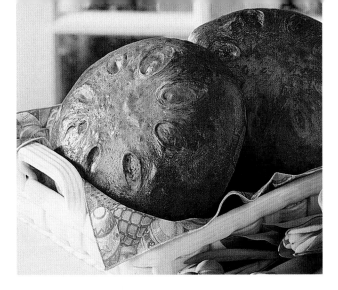

⚜⚜⚜
Banana Yeast Bread

Prep: 25 min. + rising **Bake:** 30 min.

Maralee Meyer, Milford, Nebraska

Our two children dislike plain bananas—but they've always enjoyed this bread. The recipe is from my grandmother.

3/4 cup milk
1/2 cup butter

1/2 cup sugar
5-1/4 to 6 cups all-purpose flour
2 packages (1/4 ounce *each*) active dry yeast
1 teaspoon salt
3 eggs
3 medium ripe bananas, mashed
1 teaspoon water

1. In a saucepan, cook and stir milk, butter and sugar over medium heat until butter is melted; cool to 120°-130°. In a mixing bowl, combine 2 cups of flour, yeast, salt, 2 eggs, bananas and milk mixture; beat on low speed until combined. Beat on medium for 3 minutes. Stir in enough of the remaining flour to form a firm dough.

2. Turn onto a floured surface; knead until smooth and elastic, about 4-6 minutes. Place in a greased bowl, turning once to grease top. Cover and let rise in a warm place until doubled, about 45 minutes.

3. Divide dough in half; shape each into a round loaf. Place on a greased baking sheet; cut slits in tops. Cover and let rise until doubled, about 45 minutes. Beat remaining egg with water; brush over the loaves. Bake at 375° for 30-35 minutes or until golden brown. **Yield:** 2 loaves.

⚜⚜⚜
Amish Onion Cake

Prep: 25 min. **Bake:** 35 min.

Mitzi Sentiff, Alexandria, Virginia

This rich, moist bread with an onion-poppy seed topping is a wonderful break from your everyday bread routine.

3 to 4 medium onions, chopped
2 cups cold butter, *divided*
1 tablespoon poppy seeds
1-1/2 teaspoons salt
1-1/2 teaspoons paprika
1 teaspoon coarsely ground pepper
4 cups all-purpose flour
1/2 cup cornstarch
1 tablespoon baking powder
1 tablespoon sugar
1 tablespoon brown sugar
5 eggs
3/4 cup milk
3/4 cup sour cream

1. In a large skillet, cook onions in 1/2 cup butter over low heat for 10 minutes. Stir in the poppy seeds, salt, paprika and pepper; cook until golden brown, stirring occasionally. Remove from the heat; set aside.

2. In a bowl, combine the flour, cornstarch, baking powder and sugars. Cut in 1-1/4 cups butter until

mixture resembles coarse crumbs. Melt the remaining butter. In a bowl, whisk the eggs, milk, sour cream and melted butter. Make a well in dry ingredients; stir in egg mixture just until moistened.

3. Spread into a greased 10-in. springform pan. Spoon onion mixture over the dough. Place pan on a baking sheet. Bake at 350° for 35-40 minutes or until a toothpick inserted near the center comes out clean. Serve warm. **Yield:** 10-12 servings.

Cream Cheese Swirl Brownies, p. 179

Dipped Peanut Butter Cookies, p. 185

S'more Clusters, p. 181

Cookies, Bars & Candy

Grab a rich chocolate brownie, frosted cutout, refreshing peppermint patty or any of the other tempting treats featured in this chapter. After just one taste, you'll likely want to whip up another batch!

Brownie Ice Cream Cones, p. 177

2/3 cup butter, cubed
3/4 cup baking cocoa
1/4 cup vegetable oil
2 cups sugar
4 eggs
2 teaspoons vanilla extract
1-1/2 cups all-purpose flour
1 teaspoon baking powder
1 teaspoon salt
2/3 cup semisweet chocolate chips
1/2 cup milk chocolate chips
1 cup coarsely chopped pecans
Confectioners' sugar
Pecan halves, toasted, optional

1. Melt butter in a large saucepan. Whisk in cocoa and oil until smooth. Cook and stir over low heat until cocoa is blended. Transfer to a large bowl; stir in sugar. Add eggs, one at a time, stirring well after each addition. Stir in vanilla. Combine flour, baking powder and salt; gradually add to cocoa mixture. Stir in chocolate chips and nuts.

2. Spread into a greased 13-in. x 9-in. x 2-in. baking pan. Bake at 350° for 25-30 minutes or until a toothpick inserted near the center comes out clean. Cool in pan on a wire rack. Dust with confectioners' sugar. Garnish with pecan halves if desired. **Yield:** 2 dozen.

✿ ✿ ✿
Moist Cake Brownies

Prep: 15 min. **Bake:** 25 min.

Louise Stacey, Dane, Wisconsin

These brownies have been in my recipe collection since I was 9 years old. I've altered the recipe over the years, and now I think it has the perfect amount of everything.

✿ ✿ ✿
White Velvet Cutouts

Prep: 25 min. + chilling **Bake:** 10 min.

Kim Hinkle, Wauseon, Ohio

We make these cutouts every Christmas and give lots of them as gifts. The rich cookies absolutely melt in your mouth!

2 cups butter, softened
1 package (8 ounces) cream cheese, softened
2 cups sugar
2 egg yolks
1 teaspoon vanilla extract
4-1/2 cups all-purpose flour
BUTTER CREAM FROSTING:
3-1/2 cups confectioners' sugar, *divided*
3 tablespoons butter, softened
1 tablespoon shortening
1/2 teaspoon vanilla extract
3 to 4 tablespoons milk, *divided*
Red and/or green food coloring, optional

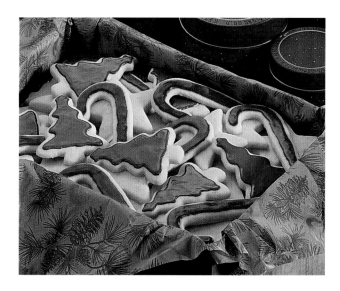

1. In a mixing bowl, cream butter and cream cheese until light and fluffy. Add sugar, egg yolks and vanilla; mix well. Gradually add flour. Cover and chill 2 hours or until firm.

2. Roll out on a floured surface to 1/4-in. thickness. Cut into 3-in. shapes; place 1 in. apart on greased bak-

ing sheets. Bake at 350° for 10-12 minutes or until set (not browned). Cool 5 minutes; remove to wire racks to cool.

3. For frosting, combine 1-1/2 cups sugar, butter, shortening, vanilla and 3 tablespoons milk in a mixing bowl; beat until smooth. Gradually add remaining sugar; beat until light and fluffy, about 3 minutes. Add enough remaining milk and food coloring if desired until frosting reaches desired consistency. Frost cookies. **Yield:** about 7 dozen.

Chunky Peanut Brittle

Prep: 10 min.
Cook: 20 min. + cooling

Janet Gonola, East McKeesport, Pennsylvania

As a farm girl, I often made Christmas goodies with my mother for our family of eight candy-loving kids. Now, my own children and grandkids say the season wouldn't be the same without this chocolaty brittle.

1-1/2 teaspoons plus 1-1/2 cups butter, *divided*
    2 cups peanut butter chips, *divided*
1-3/4 cups sugar
    3 tablespoons light corn syrup
    3 tablespoons water
1-1/2 cups salted peanuts, coarsely chopped
    1/2 cup semisweet chocolate chips

1. Butter the bottom and sides of a 15-in. x 10-in. x 1-in. baking pan with 1-1/2 teaspoons of butter. Sprinkle with 1 cup peanut butter chips; set aside.

2. In a heavy saucepan, bring the sugar, corn syrup, water and remaining butter to a boil over medium heat, stirring constantly. Cook and stir until the butter is melted. Cook, without stirring, until a candy thermometer reads 300° (hard-crack stage).

3. Remove from the heat; stir in peanuts. Quickly pour onto prepared baking pan; sprinkle with chocolate chips and remaining peanut butter chips. With a knife, gently swirl softened chips over top of brittle. Cool before breaking into pieces. Store brittle in an airtight container. **Yield:** 2-1/2 pounds.

Editor's Note: We recommend that you test your candy thermometer before each use by bringing water to a boil; the thermometer should read 212°. Adjust your recipe temperature up or down based on your test.

🎗🎗🎗
Christmas Shortbread Wreaths

Prep: 30 min. + chilling **Bake:** 20 min. + cooling

Donna Gendre, Stettler, Alberta

When I needed something festive for a cookie exchange, I adapted this recipe from plain shortbread. The wreaths are so quick and easy to prepare, I'm happy to share them at the holidays with teachers, friends and neighbors.

> 1 cup all-purpose flour
> 1/2 cup cornstarch
> 1/2 cup confectioners' sugar
> 3/4 cup butter, softened

Red and green sprinkles

1. In a bowl, combine flour, cornstarch and sugar. Blend in butter with a wooden spoon until the dough is smooth. Form into two balls. Chill for 30 minutes or until firm.

2. On a floured surface, roll one ball into a 9-in. circle; transfer to a greased baking sheet. Cut out center with a small round cookie cutter. If desired, scallop the outside and inner edges of the wreath with the edge of a cookie cutter or a knife. Cut the wreath into 12 wedges. Separate the wedges, leaving 1/8 in. between. Decorate outer and inner edges with sprinkles. Repeat for remaining dough.

3. Bake at 300° for 18-22 minutes or until golden brown. Cool on pan for 5 minutes. Recut wreath into wedges. Remove to a wire rack to cool completely. To serve, arrange as a wreath on a large flat serving plate. **Yield:** 2 dozen (2 wreaths).

🎗🎗🎗
Southern Pralines

Prep: 30 min. + cooling

Bernice Eberhart, Fort Payne, Alabama

This recipe is truly Southern, and it's been a family favorite for years. I've packed many a Christmas tin with this candy.

> 3 cups packed brown sugar
> 1 cup heavy whipping cream
> 2 tablespoons light corn syrup
> 1/4 teaspoon salt
> 1/4 cup butter
> 2 cups chopped pecans
> 1-1/4 teaspoons vanilla extract

1. In a large heavy saucepan over medium heat, bring the brown sugar, whipping cream, corn syrup and salt to a boil, stirring constantly. Cook until a candy thermometer reads 234° (soft-ball stage), stirring occasionally. Remove from the heat; add butter (do not stir). Cool until candy thermometer reads 150°, about 35 minutes.

2. Stir in the pecans and vanilla. Stir with a wooden spoon until candy just begins to thicken but is still glossy, about 5-7 minutes. Quickly drop by heaping teaspoonfuls onto waxed paper; spread to form 2-in.

patties. Let stand until set. Store in an airtight container. **Yield:** about 3-1/2 dozen.

Editor's Note: We recommend that you test your candy thermometer before each use by bringing water to a boil; the thermometer should read 212°. Adjust your recipe temperature up or down based on your test.

🎗🎗🎗
Apricot Cheese Crescents

Prep: 1 hour + chilling **Bake:** 15 min./batch

Ruth Gilhousen, Knoxdale, Pennsylvania

Traditionally, I bake these for Christmas. A cross between sweet breads and cookies, the pretty crescents are also something that I've been asked to make for weddings.

- 2 cups all-purpose flour
- 1/2 teaspoon salt
- 1 cup cold butter
- 1 cup (8 ounces) 4% cottage cheese

FILLING:
- 1 package (6 ounces) dried apricots
- 1/2 cup water
- 1/2 cup sugar

TOPPING:
- 3/4 cup finely chopped almonds
- 1/2 cup sugar
- 1 egg white, lightly beaten

1. In a large bowl, combine flour and salt; cut in butter until crumbly. Add cottage cheese; mix well. Shape into 1-in. balls. Cover and refrigerate several hours or overnight.

2. For the filling, combine apricots and water in a saucepan. Cover and simmer for 20 minutes. Cool for 10 minutes. Pour into a blender; cover and process on high speed until smooth. Transfer to a bowl; stir in sugar. Cover and chill.

3. For topping, combine almonds and sugar; set aside. On a floured surface, roll the balls into 2-1/2-in. circles. Spoon about 1 teaspoon of filling onto each. Fold dough over filling and pinch edges to seal.

4. Place crescents on greased baking sheets. Brush tops with egg white; sprinkle with almond mixture. Bake at 375° for 12-15 minutes or until lightly browned. **Yield:** 4-1/2 dozen.

🎗🎗🎗
Brownie Ice Cream Cones

(Also pictured on page 173)

Prep: 20 min. **Bake:** 20 min. + cooling

Marlene Rhodes, Panama City, Florida

Often, I'll find a recipe that sounds interesting and put my own twist on it. That's what I did with these fun treats.

- 1 package (4 ounces) German sweet chocolate
- 1/4 cup butter, cubed
- 3/4 cup sugar
- 2 eggs
- 1/2 cup all-purpose flour
- 1/2 cup chopped walnuts, optional
- 1 teaspoon vanilla extract
- 24 ice cream cake cones (about 3 inches tall)
- 24 scoops ice cream

Colored *or* chocolate sprinkles

1. In a microwave, melt the chocolate and butter; stir until smooth. Cool slightly; pour into a large bowl. Add sugar and eggs until well blended. Stir in the flour, walnuts if desired and vanilla.

2. Place cones in muffin cups; fill half full with batter. Bake at 350° for 20-22 minutes or until brownies are set on top and a toothpick inserted near center comes out with moist crumbs (do not overbake). Cool completely. Just before serving, top with a scoop of ice cream; garnish with sprinkles. **Yield:** 2 dozen.

🎀🎀🎀
Chocolate Caramel Candy

Prep: 45 min. + chilling

Jane Meek, Pahrump, Nevada

This dazzling treat tastes like a Snickers bar but has home-made flavor beyond compare. When I entered the candy in a recipe contest at our harvest festival, it won five ribbons, including grand prize and the judges' special award.

      2 teaspoons butter
      1 cup milk chocolate chips
  1/4 cup butterscotch chips
  1/4 cup creamy peanut butter
FILLING:
  1/4 cup butter
      1 cup sugar
  1/4 cup evaporated milk
1-1/2 cups marshmallow creme
  1/4 cup creamy peanut butter
      1 teaspoon vanilla extract
1-1/2 cups chopped salted peanuts
CARAMEL LAYER:
      1 package (14 ounces) caramels
  1/4 cup heavy whipping cream
ICING:
      1 cup (6 ounces) milk chocolate chips

  1/4 cup butterscotch chips
  1/4 cup creamy peanut butter

1. Line a 13-in. x 9-in. x 2-in. pan with foil; butter the foil with 2 teaspoons butter and set aside. In a small saucepan, combine the milk chocolate chips, butterscotch chips and peanut butter; stir over low heat until melted and smooth. Spread into prepared pan. Refrigerate until set.

2. For filling, in a small heavy saucepan, melt butter over medium heat. Add sugar and milk; bring to a gentle boil. Reduce heat to medium-low; boil and stir for 5 minutes. Remove from the heat; stir in the marshmallow creme, peanut butter and vanilla. Add peanuts. Spread over first layer. Refrigerate until set.

3. For caramel layer, in a small heavy saucepan, combine the caramels and cream; stir over low heat until melted and smooth. Cook and stir 4 minutes longer. Spread over the filling. Refrigerate until set.

4. For icing, in another saucepan, combine chips and peanut butter; stir over low heat until melted and smooth. Pour over the caramel layer. Refrigerate for at least 4 hours or overnight.

5. Remove from the refrigerator 20 minutes before cutting. Remove from pan and cut into 1-in. squares. Store in an airtight container. **Yield:** about 8 dozen.

Cream Cheese Swirl Brownies

(Also pictured on page 172)

Prep: 20 min. **Bake:** 25 min.

Heidi Johnson, Worland, Wyoming

I'm a chocolate lover, and this treat has satisfied my cravings many times. No one guesses the brownies are light.

> ✓ Uses less fat, sugar or salt. Includes Nutrition Facts and Diabetic Exchanges.

- 3 eggs
- 6 tablespoons reduced-fat stick margarine
- 1 cup sugar, *divided*
- 3 teaspoons vanilla extract
- 1/2 cup all-purpose flour
- 1/4 cup baking cocoa
- 1 package (8 ounces) reduced-fat cream cheese

1. Separate two eggs, putting each white in a separate bowl (discard yolks or save for another use); set aside. In a small mixing bowl, beat margarine and 3/4 cup sugar until crumbly. Add the whole egg, one egg white and vanilla; mix well. Combine flour and cocoa; add to egg mixture and beat until blended. Pour into a 9-in. square baking pan coated with cooking spray; set aside.

2. In a mixing bowl, beat cream cheese and remaining sugar until smooth. Beat in the second egg white.

Drop by rounded tablespoonfuls over the batter; cut through batter with a knife to swirl. Bake at 350° for 25-30 minutes or until set and edges pull away from sides of pan. Cool on a wire rack. **Yield:** 1 dozen.

Nutrition Facts: 1 brownie equals 167 calories, 7 g fat (3 g saturated fat), 28 mg cholesterol, 108 mg sodium, 23 g carbohydrate, trace fiber, 4 g protein. **Diabetic Exchanges:** 1-1/2 starch, 1 fat.

Editor's Note: This recipe was tested with Parkay Light stick margarine.

Nutmeg Sugar Crisps

Prep/Total Time: 25 min.

Kristi Thorpe, Portland, Oregon

My grandma shared her recipe for these old-fashioned sugar cookies that have the unexpected taste of nutmeg. They are light, crunchy and so delicious. That's why they're always a part of our Christmas holiday celebration.

- 1 cup butter, softened
- 3/4 cup sugar
- 1/2 cup confectioners' sugar
- 1 egg
- 1 teaspoon vanilla extract
- 2-1/2 cups all-purpose flour
- 1/2 teaspoon baking soda
- 1/2 teaspoon cream of tartar
- 1/4 to 1/2 teaspoon ground nutmeg
- 1/8 teaspoon salt

1. In a mixing bowl, cream the butter and sugars. Beat in the egg and vanilla extract; mix well. Combine the flour, baking soda, cream of tartar, nutmeg and salt; add to the creamed mixture and mix well. Refrigerate for 1 hour.

2. Shape the dough into 3/4-in. balls; place 2 in. apart on greased baking sheets. Flatten balls with a glass dipped in sugar. Bake at 350° for 10-12 minutes or until lightly browned. Cool on wire racks. **Yield:** about 6 dozen.

🎗🎗🎗 Oat Pecan Cookie Mix

Prep/Total Time: 15 min.

Bev Woodcock, Kingston, Ontario

This present will be welcomed by anyone who enjoys home-made cookies. The mix is simple to prepare, and the results are yummy. I decorate the jar lids with fabric and tie on a tag with baking instructions as a finishing touch.

- 1 cup all-purpose flour
- 1/2 cup sugar
- 1/2 teaspoon baking soda
- 1/2 teaspoon baking powder
- 1/2 cup packed brown sugar
- 3/4 cup old-fashioned oats
- 1/2 cup chopped pecans
- 1 cup crisp rice cereal

ADDITIONAL INGREDIENTS:
- 1/2 cup butter, softened
- 1 egg
- 1 teaspoon vanilla extract

1. In a small bowl, combine the flour, sugar, baking soda and baking powder. In a 1-qt. glass jar, layer the flour mixture, brown sugar, oats, pecans and rice cereal, packing well between each layer. Cover and store in a cool dry place for up to 6 months. **Yield:** 1 batch (about 4 cups total).

2. To make cookies: In a large mixing bowl, cream butter until light and fluffy. Beat in egg and vanilla. Gradually add cookie mix. Drop by rounded teaspoonfuls 2 in. apart onto greased baking sheets. Bake at 350° for 8-10 minutes or until golden brown. Cool for 2 minutes before removing from pans to wire racks. **Yield:** about 3 dozen.

🎗🎗🎗 Snow Flurry Brownies

Prep: 10 min. **Bake:** 25 min.

Sherry Olson, Boulder, Colorado

These brownies are the best dessert in my recipe box. I've even prepared them on the spur of the moment while company was over for dinner. They take just minutes to mix up, are out of the oven in half an hour and get rave reviews.

- 1 cup sugar
- 1/2 cup butter, melted
- 2 eggs
- 1/2 teaspoon vanilla extract
- 2/3 cup all-purpose flour
- 1/2 cup baking cocoa
- 1/2 teaspoon baking powder
- 1/2 teaspoon salt
- 1/2 cup vanilla *or* white chips
- 1/2 cup chopped macadamia nuts *or* almonds

1. In a large bowl, whisk together the sugar, butter, eggs and vanilla. Combine the flour, cocoa, baking powder and salt; add to sugar mixture until well blended. Stir in vanilla chips and nuts.

2. Spread into a greased 8-in. square baking pan. Bake at 350° for 25-30 minutes or until a toothpick inserted near the center comes out with moist crumbs (do not overbake). Cool on a wire rack. Cut into diamond shapes if desired. **Yield:** 16 brownies.

S'more Clusters

(Also pictured on page 172)
Prep/Total Time: 15 min.

Kathy Schmittler, Sterling Heights, Michigan

Our two sons love to help me break up the chocolate and graham crackers for these sweet treats. That way, the boys can tell their friends they made them! The chocolaty clusters taste just like s'mores, but without the gooey mess.

- **6 milk chocolate candy bars (1.55 ounces *each*), broken into pieces**
- **1-1/2 teaspoons vegetable oil**
- **2 cups miniature marshmallows**
- **8 whole graham crackers, broken into bite-size pieces**

In a large microwave-safe bowl, toss chocolate and oil. Microwave, uncovered, at 50% power for 1 to 1-1/2 minutes or until chocolate is melted, stirring once. Stir in marshmallows and graham crackers. Spoon into paper-lined muffin cups (about 1/3 cup each). Refrigerate for 1 hour or until firm. **Yield:** 1 dozen.

Editor's Note: This recipe was tested in a 1,100-watt microwave.

Banana Nut Bars

Prep: 15 min. **Bake:** 20 min.

Susan Huckaby, Smiths, Alabama

My sister gave me this recipe, which is always in demand with family, friends and co-workers. It's amazing how fast the tempting bars vanish when I serve them! The homemade cream cheese frosting is a heavenly way to top them off.

- **1 cup butter, cubed**
- **1/2 cup water**

- **1-1/2 cups sugar**
- **1/2 cup packed brown sugar**
- **1 cup mashed ripe bananas (about 2 medium)**
- **1/2 cup buttermilk**
- **2 eggs**
- **1 teaspoon vanilla extract**
- **2 cups all-purpose flour**
- **1 teaspoon baking soda**
- **1/2 cup chopped pecans *or* walnuts**

FROSTING:
- **1 package (8 ounces) cream cheese, softened**
- **1/2 cup butter, softened**
- **1 teaspoon vanilla extract**
- **3-1/2 cups confectioners' sugar**

1. In a small saucepan, bring butter and water to a boil. Remove from the heat; set aside. In a large mixing bowl, beat the sugars, bananas, buttermilk, eggs and vanilla until blended. Combine flour and baking soda; gradually add to sugar mixture. Carefully beat in butter mixture until blended. Stir in nuts.

2. Pour into a greased 15-in. x 10-in. x 1-in. baking pan. Bake at 350° for 18-22 minutes or until a toothpick inserted near the center comes out clean. Cool on a wire rack.

3. For the frosting, in a large mixing bowl, beat the cream cheese and butter until light and fluffy. Beat in the vanilla. Gradually add the confectioners' sugar until smooth. Spread over bars. Store in the refrigerator. **Yield:** 3 dozen.

1/4 teaspoon baking powder
1/8 teaspoon salt
Red and green gel food coloring
1/3 cup raisins
1 teaspoon sesame seeds

1. In a large mixing bowl, cream butter and sugar. Beat in egg and extract. Combine the flour, baking powder and salt; gradually add to creamed mixture. Set aside 1 cup of dough.

2. Tint the remaining dough red; shape into a 3-1/2-in.-long log. Wrap in plastic wrap. Tint 1/3 cup of the reserved dough green; wrap in plastic wrap. Wrap the remaining plain dough. Refrigerate for 2 hours or until firm.

3. On a lightly floured surface, roll the plain dough into an 8-1/2-in. x 3-1/2-in. rectangle. Place the red dough log on the end of a short side of the rectangle; roll up. Roll the green dough into a 10-in. x 3-1/2-in. rectangle. Place the red and white log on the end of a short side on the green dough; roll up. Wrap in plastic wrap; refrigerate overnight.

4. Unwrap and cut into 3/16-in. slices (just less than 1/4 in.). Place 2 in. apart on ungreased baking sheets. Cut raisins into small pieces. Lightly press raisin bits and sesame seeds into red dough to resemble watermelon seeds. Bake at 350° for 9-11 minutes or until firm. Immediately cut cookies in half. Remove to wire racks to cool. **Yield:** about 3 dozen.

🎗🎗🎗

Watermelon Slice Cookies

Prep: 25 min. + chilling **Bake:** 10 min./batch

Sue Ann Benham, Valparaiso, Indiana

When I baked these rich butter cookies for a neighborhood event, one neighbor thought they were so attractive that she kept one in her freezer for the longest time—just so she could show it to her friends and relatives!

3/4 cup butter, softened
3/4 cup sugar
1 egg
1/2 teaspoon almond extract
2 cups all-purpose flour

🎗🎗🎗

Creamy Peppermint Patties

Prep: 40 min. + chilling

Donna Gonda, North Canton, Ohio

These smooth chocolate candies are ideal for folks who like a little sweetness after a meal but don't want a big serving.

1 package (8 ounces) cream cheese, softened
1 teaspoon peppermint extract
9 cups confectioners' sugar
3/4 cup milk chocolate chips
3/4 cup semisweet chocolate chips
3 tablespoons shortening

1. In a large mixing bowl, beat the cream cheese and peppermint extract until smooth. Gradually add the confectioners' sugar, beating well. Shape into 1-in. balls. Place on waxed paper-lined baking sheets. Flatten balls into patties. Cover and refrigerate for 1 hour or until chilled.

2. In a microwave, melt chips and shortening; stir until smooth. Cool slightly. Dip patties in melted chocolate; place on waxed paper until firm. Store in the refrigerator. **Yield:** about 4 dozen.

🎀🎀🎀
Four-Nut Brittle

Prep: 20 min. + cooling

Kelly-Ann Gibbons, Prince George, British Columbia

This recipe's one I created myself. I enjoy various kinds of nuts and wanted a candy that has a different crunch in every bite.

   1 tablespoon plus 1/4 cup butter, *divided*
   2 cups sugar
   1 cup light corn syrup
   1/2 cup water
   1/2 cup salted peanuts
   1/2 cup *each* coarsely chopped almonds, pecans and walnuts
   2 teaspoons baking soda
1-1/2 teaspoons vanilla extract

1. Butter the sides of a large heavy saucepan with 1 tablespoon butter. Add the sugar, corn syrup and water; bring to a boil, stirring constantly. Cook and stir over medium-low heat until a candy thermometer reads 238° (soft-ball stage). Stir in all of the nuts and the remaining butter. Cook over medium heat to 300° (hard-crack stage).

2. Remove from heat; vigorously stir in baking soda and vanilla until blended. Quickly pour onto two greased baking sheets, spreading as thinly as possible with a metal spatula. Cool completely; break into pieces. Store in an airtight container with waxed paper between layers. **Yield:** 1-3/4 pounds.

Editor's Note: We recommend that you test your candy thermometer before each use by bringing water to a boil; the thermometer should read 212°. Adjust your recipe temperature up or down based on your test.

🎀🎀🎀
Dark Chocolate Mocha Brownies

Prep: 20 min. **Bake:** 25 min. + cooling

Linda McCoy, Oostburg, Wisconsin

Dark chocolate is a favorite around our house. I came up with this recipe by reworking one I've used for a long time.

   1 cup butter, melted
   2 cups packed brown sugar
   3 eggs
   1 tablespoon instant coffee granules
   2 teaspoons vanilla extract
   1 cup all-purpose flour
   1 cup baking cocoa
   1/2 teaspoon baking powder
   1/2 teaspoon salt
   6 ounces bittersweet chocolate, coarsely chopped
FROSTING:
   1/4 butter, melted
   3 tablespoons sour cream
   2 teaspoons vanilla extract
2-3/4 to 3 cups confectioners' sugar
   2 ounces grated bittersweet chocolate

1. In a large mixing bowl, cream butter and brown sugar until light and fluffy. Beat in eggs, one at a time. Beat in coffee and vanilla. Combine the flour, cocoa,

baking powder and salt; gradually add to creamed mixture. Stir in chocolate.

2. Spread into a greased 13-in. x 9-in. x 2-in. baking pan. Bake at 350° for 25-30 minutes or until a toothpick inserted near the center comes out clean. Cool on a wire rack.

3. For frosting, in a small mixing bowl, beat the butter, sour cream and vanilla until smooth. Gradually stir in sugar until smooth and reaches desired consistency. Frost brownies. Sprinkle with grated chocolate. **Yield:** 5 dozen.

🎀 🎀 🎀
Chocolate-Covered Cherries
Prep: 30 min. + chilling

Janice Pehrson, Omaha, Nebraska

Kids will have fun helping to prepare this yummy recipe, but they'll have to wait a week or two for the filling to set before enjoying the fruits of their labors!

- 60 maraschino cherries with stems
- 2 cups confectioners' sugar
- 3 tablespoons butter, softened
- 3 tablespoons light corn syrup
- 1/4 teaspoon salt
- 2 cups (12 ounces) semisweet chocolate chips
- 2 tablespoons shortening

1. Pat cherries dry with paper towels; set aside. In a small mixing bowl, combine the sugar, butter, corn syrup and salt; mix well. Knead until smooth. Cover and refrigerate for 1 hour.

2. Roll into 1/2-in. balls; flatten each into a 2-in. circle. Wrap each circle around a cherry and lightly roll in hands. Place cherries with stems up on waxed paper-lined baking sheets. Cover loosely and refrigerate for 1 hour.

3. In a microwave or heavy saucepan, melt chocolate chips and shortening; stir until smooth. Holding onto the stem, dip each cherry into chocolate; set on waxed paper. Refrigerate until hardened. Store in a covered container. Refrigerate for 1-2 weeks before serving. **Yield:** 5 dozen.

🎀 🎀 🎀
Volcano Brownie Cups
Prep: 20 min. **Bake:** 30 min.

Kellie Durazo, Merced, California

I just love recipes like this. Without a lot of fuss or extra time, I can turn out an elegant, irresistible dessert that looks like I've been cooking all day. I enjoy entertaining, and these treats always elicit oohs and aahs from guests.

- 1 cup butter, softened
- 1/2 cup sugar
- 3 eggs
- 3 egg yolks
- 1 teaspoon vanilla extract
- 2 cups (12 ounces) semisweet chocolate chips, melted
- 1 cup all-purpose flour
- 1/4 teaspoon salt
- 1 cup ground toasted pecans
- 6 squares (1 ounce *each*) white baking chocolate
- Confectioners' sugar, optional

1. In a large mixing bowl, cream butter and sugar until light and fluffy. Beat in the eggs, yolks and vanilla. Beat in melted chocolate. Combine flour and salt; gradually add to creamed mixture. Stir in nuts.

2. Spoon into six greased 10-oz. custard cups; place on

a baking sheet. Bake at 350° for 10 minutes or until a toothpick inserted near the center comes out clean. Remove from the oven. Push one square of chocolate into center of each brownie; let stand for 5 minutes.

3. Run a knife around edge of custard cups; invert onto serving plates. Dust with confectioners' sugar if desired. Serve warm. **Yield:** 6 servings.

Dipped Peanut Butter Cookies

(Also pictured on page 172)

Prep: 30 min. + chilling
Bake: 15 min.

Stephanie DeLoach, Magnolia, Arkansas

Baking mix makes these soft, moist cookies a snap to stir up, yet they're pretty enough to serve at parties.

- 1 **cup peanut butter**
- 1 **can (14 ounces) sweetened condensed milk**
- 1 **egg**
- 1 **teaspoon vanilla extract**
- 2 **cups biscuit/baking mix**
- 3/4 **to 1 pound milk chocolate candy coating**
- 1 **tablespoon shortening**

1. In a mixing bowl, combine peanut butter, milk, egg and vanilla; beat until smooth. Stir in baking mix; mix well. Cover and refrigerate for 1 hour. Shape into 1-in. balls; place 1 in. apart on ungreased baking sheets. Flatten each with the bottom of a glass. Bake at 350° for 8-10 minutes or until golden brown. Cool on wire racks.

2. In a small saucepan over low heat, melt candy coating and shortening. Dip each cookie halfway into chocolate; shake off excess. Place on waxed paper-lined baking sheets to harden. **Yield:** about 5 dozen.

Candy Coating Clue

Candy coating is commonly sold in bulk in large individual blocks, in bags of flat discs and in packages of individual 1-ounce squares. It is available in dark, milk and white chocolate varieties. Feel free to try white or dark chocolate for Dipped Peanut Butter Cookies.

🎀🎀🎀
Scandinavian Almond Bars

Prep: 20 min. **Bake:** 20 min.

Melva Baumer, Millmont, Pennsylvania

Delicate and crisp with a rich butter and almond flavor, these cookies are irresistible, and they look lovely on a cookie tray.

- 1/2 cup butter, softened
- 1 cup sugar
- 1 egg
- 1/2 teaspoon almond extract
- 1-3/4 cups all-purpose flour
- 2 teaspoons baking powder
- 1/4 teaspoon salt
- 1 tablespoon milk
- 1/2 cup sliced almonds, chopped

ICING:
- 1 cup confectioners' sugar
- 1/4 teaspoon almond extract
- 1 to 2 tablespoons milk

1. In a mixing bowl, cream butter and sugar; beat in egg and extract. Combine dry ingredients; add to creamed mixture and mix well. Divide dough into fourths; form into 12-in. x 3-in. rectangles. Place 5 in. apart on greased baking sheets. Brush with milk; sprinkle with almonds.

2. Bake at 325° for 18-20 minutes or until firm to the touch and edges are lightly browned. Cool on pans for 5 minutes, then cut diagonally into 1-in. slices. Remove to wire racks to cool completely. Combine icing ingredients; drizzle over bars. **Yield:** about 4 dozen.

🎀🎀🎀
Caramel Heavenlies

Prep: 20 min. **Bake:** 15 min.

Dawn Burns, Troy, Ohio

My mom made these treats for cookie exchanges when I was a little girl, letting me sprinkle on the almonds and coconut.

- 12 whole graham crackers
- 2 cups miniature marshmallows
- 3/4 cup butter
- 3/4 cup packed brown sugar
- 1 teaspoon ground cinnamon
- 1 teaspoon vanilla extract
- 1 cup sliced almonds
- 1 cup flaked coconut

1. Line a 15-in. x 10-in. x 1-in. baking pan with foil. Place graham crackers in pan; cover with marshmallows. In a saucepan over medium heat, cook and stir butter, brown sugar and cinnamon until the butter is melted and sugar is dissolved. Remove from the heat; stir in vanilla. Spoon over the marshmallows. Sprinkle with almonds and coconut.

2. Bake at 350° for 14-16 minutes or until browned. Cool completely. Cut into 2-in. square pieces, then cut each square piece in half to form two triangles. **Yield:** about 6 dozen.

✿✿✿ Chocolate Truffle Cookies

Prep: 25 min. + chilling **Bake:** 10 min./batch

Delaine Fortenberry, McComb, Mississippi

Here's a snack for "serious" chocolate lovers. The enticing cookies are somewhat bittersweet and very chocolaty.

- 4 squares (1 ounce *each*) unsweetened chocolate
- 2 cups (12 ounces) semisweet chocolate chips, **divided**
- 1/3 cup butter
- 1 cup sugar
- 3 eggs
- 1-1/2 teaspoons vanilla extract
- 1/2 cup all-purpose flour
- 2 tablespoons baking cocoa
- 1/4 teaspoon baking powder
- 1/4 teaspoon salt
- Confectioners' sugar

1. In a microwave or double boiler, melt unsweetened chocolate, 1 cup of chocolate chips and butter; cool for 10 minutes. In a mixing bowl, beat sugar and eggs for 2 minutes. Beat in vanilla and the chocolate mixture. Combine flour, cocoa, baking powder and salt; beat into chocolate mixture. Stir in remaining chocolate chips. Cover and chill for at least 3 hours.

2. Remove about 1 cup of dough. With lightly floured hands, roll into 1-in. balls. Place on ungreased baking sheets. Bake at 350° for 10-12 minutes or until lightly puffed and set. Cool on pan 3-4 minutes before removing to a wire rack to cool completely. Repeat with remaining dough. Dust with confectioners' sugar. **Yield:** about 4 dozen.

✿✿✿ Giant Cherry Oatmeal Cookies

Prep: 15 min. **Bake:** 10 min./batch

Irene McDade, Cumberland, Rhode Island

These colossal cookies are moist and chewy on the inside and are fun to eat. With a glass of cold milk, they're polished off in no time by my grandchildren.

- 1/2 cup shortening
- 1/2 cup butter, softened
- 3/4 cup packed brown sugar
- 1/2 cup sugar
- 2 eggs
- 1 teaspoon vanilla extract
- 2-1/2 cups old-fashioned oats
- 1-1/3 cups all-purpose flour
- 2 teaspoons apple pie spice
- 1/2 teaspoon baking powder
- 1/4 teaspoon baking soda
- 1/4 teaspoon salt
- 1-1/2 cups dried cherries, chopped
- 1/2 to 1 teaspoon grated orange peel

1. In a large mixing bowl, cream shortening, butter and sugars. Beat in the eggs and vanilla. Combine the oats, flour, apple pie spice, baking powder, baking soda and salt; gradually add to the creamed mixture. Stir in cherries and orange peel.

2. Drop by 1/3 cupfuls onto an ungreased baking sheet. Press to form a 4-in. circle. Bake at 375° for 9-12 minutes or until golden brown. Let stand for 1 minute before removing to wire racks to cool. **Yield:** 1 dozen.

Ice Cream Party Roll, p. 195

Coconut Peach Pie, p. 196

Triple-Layer Banana Cake, p. 203

Cakes & Pies

For a memorable dessert guaranteed to please everyone at the table, turn to the home-style delights here. From Grandma's Chocolate Cake to Strawberry Banana Pie, these treats just can't miss!

Chocolate-Cherry Mousse Delight, p. 202

🎗️🎗️🎗️
Orange Tea Cake

Prep: 20 min. **Bake:** 30 min. + cooling

Beth Duerr, North Tonawanda, New York

This from-scratch sponge cake has a hint of orange in every bite and is wonderful served with a cup of hot tea or coffee.

✓ Uses less fat, sugar or salt. Includes Nutrition Facts and Diabetic Exchange.

    7 eggs, *separated*
1-1/2 cups sugar, *divided*

    6 tablespoons orange juice
4-1/2 teaspoons grated orange peel
1-3/4 cups all-purpose flour
    1/2 teaspoon salt
    3/4 teaspoon confectioners' sugar

1. In a large mixing bowl, beat egg yolks until slightly thickened. Gradually add 1/2 cup sugar, beating until thick and lemon-colored. Beat in orange juice and peel. Sift together flour and salt; add to egg mixture. Beat until smooth.

2. In another mixing bowl, beat egg whites until soft peaks form. Add remaining granulated sugar, 1 tablespoon at a time, beating until stiff peaks form. Fold a fourth of the egg whites into batter; fold in remaining whites. Gently spoon into an ungreased 10-in. tube pan. Cut through batter with a knife to remove air pockets.

3. Bake on the lowest oven rack at 350° for 30-35 minutes or until cake springs back when lightly touched. Immediately invert pan onto a wire rack; cool completely, about 1 hour. Run a knife around sides of cake and remove to a serving plate. Dust with confectioners' sugar. **Yield:** 12 servings.

Nutrition Facts: 1 slice equals 211 calories, 3 g fat (1 g saturated fat), 124 mg cholesterol, 135 mg sodium, 40 g carbohydrate, 1 g fiber, 6 g protein. **Diabetic Exchange:** 2-1/2 starch.

🎗️🎗️🎗️
Orange Applesauce Cupcakes

Prep: 20 min. **Bake:** 20 min. + cooling

Janis Plourde, Smooth Rock Falls, Ontario

Kids of all ages rave about these fruity cupcakes. For a tasty variation, substitute crushed pineapple for the applesauce.

    6 tablespoons butter, softened
    1 cup packed brown sugar
    1 egg
1/2 cup unsweetened applesauce
    1 teaspoon vanilla extract
    1 teaspoon grated orange peel
    1 cup all-purpose flour
    1 teaspoon baking powder
1/2 teaspoon salt
1/4 teaspoon baking soda
1/2 cup chopped pecans
FROSTING:
1/4 cup butter, softened
    2 cups confectioners' sugar
1-1/2 teaspoons grated orange peel
    2 to 4 teaspoons orange juice

1. In a mixing bowl, cream the butter and brown sugar. Add egg; beat well. Beat in applesauce, vanilla and

orange peel. Combine the flour, baking powder, salt and baking soda; add to creamed mixture. Stir in pecans.

2. Fill paper-lined muffin cups half-full. Bake at 350° for 20-25 minutes or until a toothpick comes out clean. Cool for 10 minutes before removing from pan to a wire rack to cool completely.

3. For frosting, in a small mixing bowl, cream butter and confectioners' sugar. Add orange peel and enough orange juice to achieve spreading consistency. Frost cupcakes. **Yield:** 1 dozen.

Strawberry Cheesecake Torte

Prep: 30 min. + chilling
Bake: 25 min. + cooling

Kathy Martinez, Enid, Oklahoma

After I sampled this dessert at a party, a friend shared the recipe. It originally called for pound cake, and I decided to lighten it up by substituting angel food.

 Uses less fat, sugar or salt. Includes Nutrition Facts.

- 1 package (16 ounces) angel food cake mix
- 1 tablespoon confectioners' sugar
- 1 package (.3 ounce) sugar-free strawberry gelatin
- 1/2 cup boiling water
- 1/4 cup seedless strawberry jam
- 1 package (8 ounces) reduced-fat cream cheese, cubed
- 1/3 cup fat-free milk
- 2 tablespoons lemon juice
- 3 cups reduced-fat whipped topping
- 1 package (3.4 ounces) instant cheesecake or vanilla pudding mix
- 1 cup sliced fresh strawberries
- 1 kiwifruit, peeled, halved and sliced
- 1-1/2 teaspoons grated lemon peel

1. Line a 15-in. x 10-in. x 1-in. baking pan with ungreased parchment paper. Prepare cake mix according to package directions. Spread batter evenly in prepared pan. Bake at 350° for 24-26 minutes or until top is lightly browned. Sprinkle sugar over a waxed paper-lined baking sheet. Immediately invert cake onto baking sheet. Gently peel off parchment paper; cool completely.

2. Dissolve gelatin in boiling water. Stir in jam until melted. With a fork, poke cake at 1/2-in. intervals. Brush with gelatin mixture; chill for 10 minutes.

3. In a bowl, beat the cream cheese, milk and lemon juice. Add the whipped topping and cheesecake pudding mix; whisk well. Reserve 1 cup. Place the remaining pudding mixture in a pastry bag with a large star tip.

4. Trim edges of cake. Cut widthwise into three equal rectangles; place one on serving plate. Spread 1/2 cup reserved pudding mixture in center. Pipe pudding mixture around top edge of cake. Repeat with second cake layer. Top with remaining cake layer. Pipe pudding mixture along top edges. Fill center with fruit. Sprinkle with lemon peel. Store in refrigerator. **Yield:** 12 servings.

Nutrition Facts: 1 piece equals 284 calories, 6 g fat (4 g saturated fat), 11 mg cholesterol, 427 mg sodium, 51 g carbohydrate, 1 g fiber, 6 g protein.

Grandma's Chocolate Cake

Prep: 30 min. + cooling **Bake:** 40 min. + cooling

Dorothy Eagen, Allentown, Pennsylvania

My grandmother made this delicious treat for me every year on my birthday. The from-scratch cake has the perfect topping—a fudgy homemade frosting. It's wonderful for chocolate lovers!

    1/2 **cup shortening**
1-1/2 **cups sugar**
    2 **eggs**
    2 **cups all-purpose flour**
    1/2 **cup baking cocoa**
    1 **teaspoon baking soda**
    1 **teaspoon baking powder**
    1/2 **teaspoon salt**
    1 **cup buttermilk**
    1/2 **cup hot water**
CHOCOLATE FUDGE FROSTING:
    2 **squares (1 ounce *each*) unsweetened chocolate**
    1 **tablespoon butter**
1-1/2 **cups sugar**
    1/2 **cup water**
    1/4 **teaspoon cream of tartar**
    1 **teaspoon vanilla extract**
    1 **to 2 tablespoons half-and-half cream**

1. In a mixing bowl, cream shortening and sugar. Add eggs, one at a time, beating well after each addition. Combine the flour, cocoa, baking soda, baking powder and salt. Add to creamed mixture alternately with buttermilk and hot water; mix well. Pour into a greased 13-in. x 9-in. x 2-in. baking pan. Bake at 350° for 40-45 minutes or until a toothpick inserted near the center comes out clean. Cool on a wire rack.

2. For frosting, melt chocolate and butter in a saucepan. Add the sugar, water and cream of tartar. Bring to a boil, stirring constantly. Cook and stir until a candy thermometer reads 240° (soft-ball stage). Remove from the heat. Cool completely, without stirring, about 1 hour. Add vanilla; beat until thickened. Add cream; beat until smooth. Frost cake. **Yield:** 12-16 servings.

Editor's Note: We recommend that you test your candy thermometer before each use by bringing water to a boil; the thermometer should read 212°. Adjust your recipe temperature up or down based on your test.

Apple Pie a la Mode

Prep: 20 min. + freezing

Trisha Kruse, Eagle, Idaho

Here is a family favorite that combines apple pie filling, butter pecan ice cream, caramel topping and chopped nuts. It's a five-ingredient dessert that tastes like one from a restaurant.

    1 **can (21 ounces) apple pie filling**
    1 **graham cracker crust (9 inches)**
    2 **cups butter pecan ice cream, softened**
    1 **jar (12 ounces) caramel ice cream topping**
    1/4 **cup chopped pecans, toasted**

1. Spread half the apple pie filling over crust. Top with half the ice cream; cover and freeze for 30 minutes. Drizzle with half the caramel topping; cover and freeze for 30 minutes.

2. Top the pie with the remaining apple pie filling; cover and freeze for 30 minutes. Top with the re-

maining ice cream; cover and freeze until firm. Pie may be frozen for up to 2 months.

3. Remove pie from the freezer about 30 minutes before serving. Warm remaining caramel topping; drizzle some on serving plates. Top with a slice of pie; drizzle remaining caramel topping over pie and sprinkle with pecans. **Yield:** 6-8 servings.

These moist, old-fashioned molasses cupcakes were my grandmother's specialty. To keep them from disappearing too quickly, she used to store them out of sight. Somehow, we always figured out her hiding places!

🎀 🎀 🎀
Shoofly Cupcakes
Prep: 15 min. **Bake:** 20 min. + cooling

Beth Adams, Jacksonville, Florida

    4 cups all-purpose flour
    2 cups packed brown sugar
1/4 teaspoon salt
    1 cup cold butter, cubed
    2 teaspoons baking soda
    2 cups boiling water
    1 cup molasses

1. In a large bowl, combine the flour, brown sugar and salt. Cut in the butter until crumbly. Set aside 1 cup of the crumb mixture for the cupcake topping. Add the baking soda to the remaining crumb mixture. Stir in the boiling water and molasses.

2. Fill paper-lined muffin cups two-thirds full. Sprinkle with reserved crumb mixture. Bake at 350° for 20-25 minutes or until a toothpick comes out clean. Cool for 10 minutes before removing from pans to wire racks. **Yield:** 2 dozen.

Editor's Note: This recipe does not use eggs.

🎀 🎀 🎀
Raspberry Mocha Torte
Prep: 1 hour **Bake:** 15 min. + chilling

Adrene Schmidt, Waldersee, Manitoba

I combined three of my favorite things to make this wonderful layered dessert—raspberries, chocolate and coffee.

    6 eggs, *separated*
3/4 cup sugar, *divided*
    1 cup all-purpose flour
FILLING:
1/3 cup sugar
    3 eggs
    2 egg yolks
    1 teaspoon instant coffee granules
    2 squares (1 ounce *each*) semisweet chocolate, melted
    1 teaspoon vanilla extract
    1 cup butter, softened
1/2 cup raspberry jam
Fresh raspberries and mint, optional

1. In a large mixing bowl, beat egg yolks and 1/2 cup sugar until thick and lemon-colored. In a small mixing bowl, beat the egg whites on medium speed until soft peak form. Gradually beat in remaining sugar, 1 tablespoon at a time, on high until stiff peaks form. Gently fold into egg yolk mixture along with the flour.

2. Divide batter between three waxed paper-lined ungreased 9-in. round baking pans. Bake at 350° for 15-20 minutes or until golden brown. Cool for 10 minutes before removing from pans to wire racks.

3. In a small saucepan, whisk the sugar, eggs, egg yolks and coffee granules. Add chocolate. Cook over medium heat, stirring constantly, until mixture reaches 160° and coats the back of a metal spoon. Remove from the heat; stir in vanilla. Cool. In a small mixing bowl, cream butter. Gradually beat in cooled chocolate mixture until smooth.

4. To assemble, place one cake layer on a serving plate; spread with half of the mocha filling. Top with another cake layer; spread with raspberry jam. Place remaining cake on top; spread with the remaining mocha filling. Refrigerate for 3 hours. Garnish with raspberries and mint if desired. **Yield:** 8-10 servings.

🎀🎀🎀
Rhubarb-Orange
Angel Food Torte

Prep: 30 min. **Bake:** 25 min.

Sheila Long, Elmwood, Ontario

This eye-catching torte is the perfect dessert for guests. And it's so simple. Just spread a fruit sauce between layers of a prepared angel food cake, then frost it and garnish with berries.

> ✓ Uses less fat, sugar or salt. Includes Nutrition Facts.

  1 package (16 ounces) angel food cake mix
  1-1/2 cups sliced fresh or frozen rhubarb
  3/4 cup frozen unsweetened raspberries, thawed
  6 tablespoons sugar
  5 tablespoons orange juice, *divided*
  1/2 teaspoon grated orange peel
  1 teaspoon minced fresh gingerroot
  2 teaspoons cornstarch
  1 carton (8 ounces) frozen reduced-fat whipped topping, thawed
Fresh raspberries, optional

1. Prepare cake mix according to package directions. Gently spoon batter into an ungreased 10-in. tube pan. Cut through batter with a knife to remove air pockets. Bake according to package directions. Immediately invert pan onto a wire rack; cool completely, about 1 hour. Run a knife around sides of cake and remove from pan.

2. In a saucepan, combine the rhubarb, berries, sugar, 4 tablespoons juice, peel and ginger. Cook, uncovered, over medium heat until rhubarb is tender, about 7 minutes. In a small bowl, combine cornstarch and remaining juice until smooth; stir into fruit mixture. Bring to a boil; cook and stir for 2 minutes or until thickened. Remove from the heat; cool completely.

3. Split cake into three horizontal layers. Place the bottom layer on a serving plate; spread half of the rhubarb mixture evenly to within 1/2 in. of edges. Top with second cake layer; spread remaining rhubarb mixture to within 1/2 in. of edges. Replace cake top. Frost top and sides with whipped topping. Garnish with raspberries if desired. Refrigerate leftovers. **Yield:** 12 servings.

Nutrition Facts: 1 slice equals 215 calories, 2 g fat (2 g saturated fat), 0 cholesterol, 224 mg sodium, 44 g carbohydrate, trace fiber, 4 g protein.

Just Gingerroot

Fresh gingerroot is available in your grocer's produce section. The root should have a smooth skin that is not wrinkled or cracked. Stored in a heavy-duty resealable plastic bag, unpeeled gingerroot may be frozen for up to 1 year.

Ice Cream Party Roll

(Also pictured on page 188)
Prep: 45 min. **Bake:** 10 min. + freezing

Laura Andrews, Mantee, Mississippi

Here's a tempting take on the popular cake roll. It features a from-scratch chocolate cake, vanilla ice cream and berry jam.

- **4 eggs, *separated***
- **3/4 cup sugar, *divided***
- **1/2 cup cake flour**
- **1/3 cup baking cocoa**
- **1 teaspoon baking powder**
- **1/4 teaspoon salt**
- **1/2 cup strawberry or raspberry jam**
- **2 cups vanilla ice cream, softened**
- **Confectioners' sugar**
- **Hot fudge topping and whipped topping**

1. In a mixing bowl, beat egg whites until soft peaks form. Gradually add 1/4 cup sugar, beating until stiff peaks form. In another bowl, beat egg yolks and remaining sugar until thick and lemon-colored, 5 minutes. Combine flour, cocoa, baking powder and salt; add to yolk mixture. Mix well. Fold in egg white mixture.

2. Line a greased 15-in. x 10-in. x 1-in. baking pan with waxed paper; grease the paper. Spread batter evenly in pan. Bake at 375° for 10-12 minutes or until cake springs back when lightly touched. Cool for 5 minutes. Invert cake onto a kitchen towel dusted with confectioners' sugar. Gently peel off paper. Roll up cake in towel jelly-roll style, starting with a short side. Cool on a wire rack.

3. Unroll cake; spread jam to within 1/2 in. of edges. Top with ice cream. Roll up without towel. Place seam side down on a platter. Cover and freeze for at least 4 hours before slicing. May be frozen for up to 2 months. Sprinkle with confectioners' sugar; serve with hot fudge topping and whipped topping. **Yield:** 12 servings.

Cream Cheese Chocolate Cupcakes

Prep: 20 min. **Bake:** 25 min. + cooling

Shirley Dunbar, Mojave, California

Cream cheese inside these cakes makes them so rich. Plus, they have the classic combination of peanut butter and chocolate.

- **1 package (8 ounces) cream cheese, softened**
- **1/3 cup sugar**
- **1 egg**
- **1/8 teaspoon salt**
- **1 cup semisweet chocolate chips**
- **1 cup peanut butter chips**

CUPCAKES:
- **1-1/2 cups all-purpose flour**
- **1 cup sugar**
- **1/4 cup baking cocoa**
- **1 teaspoon baking soda**
- **1/2 teaspoon salt**
- **1 cup water**
- **1/3 cup vegetable oil**
- **1 tablespoon white vinegar**
- **1 teaspoon vanilla extract**

1. In a bowl, beat the cream cheese until smooth. Add the sugar, egg and salt; mix well. Fold in chocolate and peanut butter chips; set aside. For cupcakes, in a bowl, combine the flour, sugar, cocoa, baking soda and salt. Add water, oil, vinegar and vanilla; mix well.

2. Fill paper-lined muffin cups half-full with batter. Top each with about 2 tablespoons of the cream cheese mixture. Bake at 350° for 25-30 minutes or until a toothpick inserted into cupcake comes out clean. Cool for 10 minutes before removing from pans to wire racks to cool completely. **Yield:** 1-1/2 dozen.

Chocolate Banana Split Cupcakes

Prep: 20 min. **Bake:** 20 min. + cooling

Lorelie Miller, Benito, Manitoba

My mom made these goodies when I was young. They go over just as well now when I bake them for my own children.

- 1-1/4 cups all-purpose flour
- 1/2 cup sugar
- 1/4 teaspoon baking soda
- 1/4 teaspoon salt
- 1/2 cup mashed banana (about 1 medium)
- 1/2 cup butter, melted
- 1/4 cup buttermilk
- 1 egg, lightly beaten
- 1/2 teaspoon vanilla extract
- 1/2 cup chopped walnuts
- 2 milk chocolate bars (1.55 ounces *each*) broken into squares, *divided*

FROSTING:
- 1-1/2 cups confectioners' sugar
- 1 tablespoon butter, melted
- 1/2 teaspoon vanilla extract
- 1 to 2 tablespoons milk
- 12 maraschino cherries with stems

1. In a bowl, combine the flour, sugar, baking soda and salt. In another bowl, combine the banana, butter, buttermilk, egg and vanilla. Add to the dry ingredients; stir just until combined. Fold in the nuts. Spoon 1 tablespoon of batter into each paper-lined muffin cup. Top each with one candy bar square. Fill the remainder of the cup two-thirds full with batter.

2. Bake at 350° for 20-25 minutes or until a toothpick inserted in the cupcake comes out clean. Cool for 10 minutes before removing from pan to a wire rack to cool completely.

3. In a bowl, combine the confectioners' sugar, butter, vanilla and enough milk to achieve spreading consistency. Frost cupcakes. In a microwave, melt the remaining candy bar squares; drizzle over frosting. Top each with a cherry. **Yield:** 1 dozen.

Coconut Peach Pie

(Also pictured on page 188)

Prep: 20 min. + chilling **Bake:** 30 min. + cooling

Beatrice Crutchfield, Norcross, Georgia

A relative shared this recipe with me. I love peaches, and the wonderful meringue crust is tender and crispy. It's one of my favorite summertime desserts.

- 3 egg whites
- Dash salt
- 3/4 cup plus 2 tablespoons sugar, *divided*
- 1-1/4 cups flaked coconut, toasted, *divided*
- 1/3 cup chopped almonds, toasted
- 3-1/2 cups sliced peeled peaches (about 6 medium)
- 1 cup heavy whipping cream

1. In a mixing bowl, beat egg whites and salt on medium speed until foamy. Gradually add 3/4 cup sugar, 1 tablespoon at a time, beating on high until stiff peaks form. Fold in 1 cup coconut and almonds. Spread onto the bottom and up the sides of a greased 9-in. pie plate. Bake at 350° for 30 minutes or until light golden brown. Cool completely on a wire rack.

2. Arrange peaches in crust. In a chilled mixing bowl, beat whipping cream with remaining sugar until stiff peaks form. Spread over peaches; sprinkle with remaining coconut. Refrigerate for 1 hour before slicing. **Yield:** 6-8 servings.

🎗🎗🎗
Cookie Ice Cream Cake

Prep: 35 min. + freezing

Heather McKillip, Aurora, Illinois

I discovered this recipe online and changed it a little to suit my family's tastes. It gets lots of compliments because people like the hot fudge topping and unique cookie crust.

- 44 **miniature chocolate chip cookies**
- 1/4 **cup butter, melted**
- 1 **cup hot fudge topping,** *divided*
- 1 **quart vanilla ice cream, softened**
- 1 **quart chocolate ice cream, softened**

1. Crush 25 cookies; set remaining cookies aside. In a bowl, combine cookie crumbs and butter. Press onto the bottom of a greased 10-in. springform pan. Freeze for 15 minutes.

2. In a microwave-safe bowl, heat 3/4 cup hot fudge topping on high for 15-20 seconds or until pourable; spread over crust. Arrange reserved cookies around the edge of pan. Freeze for 15 minutes. Spread vanilla ice cream over fudge topping; freeze for 30 minutes. Spread with chocolate ice cream. Cover and freeze until firm. May be frozen for up to 2 months.

3. Remove from the freezer 10 minutes before serving. Remove sides of pan. Warm remaining hot fudge topping; drizzle over top. **Yield:** 10-12 servings.

🎗🎗🎗
Peanut Butter Layer Cake

Prep: 25 min. **Bake:** 30 min. + cooling

Carolyn Hylton, Covington, Virginia

My husband is a big fan of peanut butter, so this cake always puts a smile on his face. Sometimes I switch frosting recipes and use a chocolate frosting garnished with peanuts.

- 1/2 **cup butter, softened**
- 1-1/4 **cups sugar**
- 1/2 **cup peanut butter chips, melted**
- 2 **eggs**
- 1 **teaspoon vanilla extract**
- 2 **cups all-purpose flour**
- 1 **teaspoon baking soda**
- 1/2 **teaspoon baking powder**
- 1/4 **teaspoon salt**
- 1-1/2 **cups milk**

PEANUT BUTTER FROSTING:
- 1 **cup peanut butter chips, melted**
- 1 **package (8 ounces) cream cheese, softened**
- 1 **teaspoon vanilla extract**
- 1/8 **teaspoon salt**
- 3 **cups confectioners' sugar**
- 2 to 3 **tablespoons milk**

1. In a large mixing bowl, cream butter and sugar until light and fluffy. Add melted peanut butter chips; mix well. Add eggs, one at a time, beating well after each addition. Beat in vanilla. Combine the flour, baking soda, baking powder and salt; add to creamed mixture alternately with milk.

2. Pour into two greased and floured 9-in. round baking pans. Bake at 350° for 30-35 minutes or until a toothpick inserted near the center comes out clean. Cool for 10 minutes before removing from pans to wire racks to cool completely.

3. For frosting, in a small mixing bowl, beat the melted chips, cream cheese, vanilla and salt until light and fluffy. Add confectioners' sugar alternately with enough milk to achieve spreading consistency. Spread frosting between layers and over top and sides of cake. **Yield:** 12-14 servings.

★ ★ ★
Eggnog Cake

Prep: 30 min. + cooling **Bake:** 30 min. + cooling

Debra Frappolli, Wayne, New Jersey

This wonderful cake is full of eggnog flavor. I especially like to serve it to family and friends at Christmastime.

   1/2 **cup butter, softened**
1-1/4 **cups sugar**
     3 **eggs**
   1/2 **teaspoon** *each* **vanilla and rum extract**
     2 **cups all-purpose flour**
     2 **teaspoons baking powder**
     1 **teaspoon salt**
     1 **cup eggnog**

FROSTING:
   1/4 **cup all-purpose flour**
   1/4 **teaspoon salt**
1-1/2 **cups eggnog**
     1 **cup butter, softened**
1-1/2 **cups sugar**
1-1/2 **teaspoons vanilla extract**
Red and green gel food coloring, optional

1. In a large mixing bowl, cream butter and sugar until light and fluffy. Add eggs, one at a time, beating well after each addition. Add extracts. Combine the flour, baking powder and salt; add to creamed mixture alternately with eggnog. Pour into two 9-in. round baking pans coated with cooking spray.

2. Bake at 350° for 30-35 minutes or until a toothpick inserted near center comes out clean. Cool 10 minutes before removing to wire racks to cool completely.

3. For frosting, in a small saucepan, combine flour and salt. Gradually stir in eggnog until smooth. Bring to a boil over medium heat; cook and stir for 2 minutes or until thickened. Cool to room temperature.

4. In a large mixing bowl, cream butter and sugar until light and fluffy. Beat in eggnog mixture and vanilla until fluffy. Remove 1/4 cup frosting for decorating if desired; tint 3 tablespoons green and 1 tablespoon red. Spread plain frosting between layers and over top and sides of cake. Use green and red frosting to pipe leaves and berries on cake. Store in the refrigerator. **Yield:** 12 servings.

Editor's Note: This recipe was tested with commercially prepared eggnog.

★ ★ ★
Chocolate Chipper Pie Mix

Prep/Total Time: 20 min.

Carole Martin, Coffeeville, Mississippi

A batch of this mix makes a great holiday gift…and yields a mouth-watering chocolate pecan pie.

     1 **cup sugar**
   1/2 **cup all-purpose flour**
     1 **cup (6 ounces) semisweet chocolate chips**
   1/2 **cup** *each* **flaked coconut and chopped pecans**
ADDITIONAL INGREDIENTS:
     2 **eggs, lightly beaten**
   1/4 **cup butter, melted**
     1 **unbaked pastry shell (9 inches)**

In a bowl, combine sugar and flour; place in a resealable plastic bag and label "Dry Ingredients." Place chips, coconut and pecans in another resealable plastic bag and label "Chocolate Filling Ingredients." Place both bags in a gift basket along with directions for

preparing Chocolate Chipper Pie. Store in a cool dry place for up to 3 months. **Yield:** 1 batch.

To prepare pie: In large bowl, combine the eggs, butter and contents of "Dry Ingredients" packet; mix well. Stir in the contents of the "Chocolate Filling Ingredients" packet. Spoon into pie shell. Bake at 350° for 30-35 minutes or until filling is set and crust is golden. Cool on a wire rack. **Yield:** 1 pie (6-8 servings).

🎀🎀🎀
Coconut Cupcakes

Prep: 20 min. Bake: 20 min. + cooling

Judy Wilson, Sun City West, Arizona

When I took these treats to a picnic for our computer club, they went like hotcakes! Now I often double the recipe.

1-1/2 cups butter, softened
2 cups sugar
5 eggs
1 to 1-1/2 teaspoons vanilla extract
1 to 1-1/2 teaspoons almond extract

3 cups all-purpose flour
1 teaspoon baking powder
1/2 teaspoon baking soda
1/2 teaspoon salt
1 cup buttermilk
1-1/4 cups flaked coconut
CREAM CHEESE FROSTING:
1 package (8 ounces) cream cheese, softened
3/4 cup butter, softened
1/2 teaspoon vanilla extract
1/2 teaspoon almond extract
2-3/4 cups confectioners' sugar
Additional flaked coconut, toasted

1. In a large mixing bowl, cream butter and sugar until light and fluffy. Add eggs, one at a time, beating well after each addition. Beat in extracts. Combine the flour, baking powder, baking soda and salt; add to creamed mixture alternately with buttermilk. Fold in coconut.

2. Fill paper-lined muffin cups two-thirds full. Bake at 350° for 18-20 minutes or until a toothpick comes out clean. Cool for 10 minutes before removing from pans to wire racks to cool completely.

3. For frosting, in a mixing bowl, beat cream cheese, butter and extracts until smooth. Gradually beat in confectioners' sugar. Frost the cupcakes; sprinkle with toasted coconut. **Yield:** 2-1/2 dozen.

🎀🎀🎀
Walnut Glory Cake

Prep: 15 min. Bake: 45 min.

Marjorie Yoder, Epworth, Georgia

I've served this attractive, drizzled sponge cake at church dinners, reunions and other events for over 40 years.

9 eggs, *separated*
1-1/2 cups sugar, *divided*
2 teaspoons vanilla extract
3/4 cup all-purpose flour
2 teaspoons ground cinnamon
1 teaspoon salt
2 cups finely chopped walnuts
2 cups confectioners' sugar
2 to 3 tablespoons milk

1. In a mixing bowl, beat egg yolks until slightly thickened. Gradually add 3/4 cup sugar, beating until thick and lemon-colored. Beat in vanilla. Combine the flour, cinnamon and salt; add to batter and beat until smooth.

2. In another mixing bowl, beat egg whites on medium speed until soft peaks form. Add the remaining sugar, 1 tablespoon at a time, beating on high until stiff peaks form. Fold a fourth of the egg whites into batter; fold in remaining egg whites. Fold in walnuts.

3. Spoon into an ungreased 10-in. tube pan (pan will be full). Bake at 350° for 45-50 minutes or until cake springs back when lightly touched. Immediately invert pan; cool completely. Run a knife around side of cake and remove from pan. In a small bowl, combine confectioners' sugar and enough milk to achieve drizzling consistency; drizzle over cake. **Yield:** 10-12 servings.

Mocha Dream Cake

Prep: 30 min. + cooking **Bake:** 20 min.

Shirley Seltzer, Nanaimo, British Columbia

Baking cocoa gives this angel food cake a chocolaty boost without adding lots of fat, and the mocha frosting is yummy!

✓ Uses less fat, sugar or salt. Includes Nutrition Facts.

- 3/4 cup baking cocoa
- 1/2 cup boiling water
- 1/4 cup sugar
- 1 package (16 ounces) angel food cake mix
- 1-1/4 cups cold water
- 1 tablespoon instant coffee granules
- 1-1/2 cups cold fat-free milk
- 1 envelope whipped topping mix
- 1 package (1.4 ounces) sugar-free instant chocolate pudding mix

1. Line a 15-in. x 10-in. x 1-in. baking pan with parchment paper; set aside. In a bowl, stir the cocoa, boiling water and sugar until cocoa and sugar are dissolved. Cool. In a mixing bowl, beat cake mix, cold water and cocoa mixture on low speed until moistened. Beat on medium for 1 minute. Gently spoon batter into prepared pan. Cut through batter with a knife to remove air pockets.

2. Bake at 350° for 18-20 minutes or until cake springs back when lightly touched. Immediately invert pan onto a wire rack. Remove cake pan and gently peel off parchment paper. Cool.

3. In a small mixing bowl, dissolve coffee granules in milk; add whipped topping and pudding mix. Beat on low speed until moistened; beat on high until smooth and soft peaks form. Refrigerate for 5 minutes.

4. Cut cake widthwise into three equal rectangles. Place one cake piece on a serving plate; spread with a third of the pudding mixture. Repeat layers twice. **Yield:** 12 servings.

Nutrition Facts: 1 piece equals 210 calories, 2 g fat (1 g saturated fat), 1 mg cholesterol, 392 mg sodium, 46 g carbohydrate, 2 g fiber, 6 g protein.

Lemon Sparkle Cupcakes

Prep: 15 min. **Bake:** 20 min. + cooling

Janice Porter, Platte, South Dakota

Bursting with lemony zing, these cupcakes don't require frosting. My family prefers the crunchy sugar-and-spice topping.

- 2/3 cup shortening
- 1 cup sugar
- 3 eggs
- 1-2/3 cups all-purpose flour
- 2-1/2 teaspoons baking powder
- 1/2 teaspoon salt
- 2/3 cup milk
- 1 tablespoon grated lemon peel

TOPPING:
- 1/4 cup sugar
- 1 tablespoon grated lemon peel
- 1/8 teaspoon ground nutmeg

1. In a mixing bowl, cream shortening and sugar. Add eggs, one at a time, beating well after each addition. Combine flour, baking powder and salt; add to creamed mixture alternately with milk. Stir in peel.

2. Fill paper-lined muffin cups two-thirds full. Combine the topping ingredients; sprinkle a rounded 1/2 teaspoonful over each cupcake. Bake at 350° for 20-24 minutes or until a toothpick comes out clean. Cool for 10 minutes before removing from pans to wire racks to cool completely. **Yield:** about 1-1/4 dozen.

Chocolate Chip Banana Cream Pie

Prep: 25 min. **Bake:** 10 min. + chilling

Taylor Carroll, Parkesburg, Pennsylvania

This rich treat is a hit every time I serve it. The chilled filling, brimming with bananas, is refreshing, and the cookie crust provides a chocolaty crunch.

- 1 tube (16-1/2 ounces) refrigerated chocolate chip cookie dough
- 1/3 cup sugar
- 1/4 cup cornstarch
- 1/8 teaspoon salt
- 2-1/3 cups milk
- 5 egg yolks, lightly beaten
- 2 tablespoons butter
- 2 teaspoons vanilla extract, *divided*
- 3 medium firm bananas
- 1-1/2 cups heavy whipping cream
- 3 tablespoons confectioners' sugar

1. Cut cookie dough in half widthwise. Let one portion stand at room temperature for 5-10 minutes to soften (return the other half to the refrigerator for another use).

2. Press dough onto the bottom and up the sides of an ungreased 9-in. pie plate. Bake at 375° for 11-12 minutes or until lightly browned. Cool on a wire rack.

3. In a large saucepan, combine the sugar, cornstarch and salt. Stir in milk until smooth. Cook and stir over medium-high heat until thickened and bubbly. Reduce heat; cook and stir 2 minutes longer. Remove from the heat. Stir a small amount of hot filling into egg yolks; return all to the pan, stirring constantly. Bring to a gentle boil; cook and stir 2 minutes longer. Remove from the heat; stir in butter and 1 teaspoon vanilla.

4. Spread 1 cup filling into the prepared cookie crust. Slice bananas; arrange over filling. Pour remaining filling over bananas. Refrigerate for 2 hours or until set.

5. In a chilled large mixing bowl, beat cream until it begins to thicken. Add confectioners' sugar and remaining vanilla; beat until stiff peaks form. Spread over pie. Refrigerate for 1 hour or until chilled. Refrigerate leftovers. **Yield:** 6-8 servings.

Chocolate-Cherry Mousse Delight

(Also pictured on page 189)

Prep: 25 min. + standing **Bake:** 40 min. + cooling

Teresa Gilbreth, Columbia, Missouri

I concocted this for a ladies' get-together. The cherry cake is served with mousse and chocolate-covered cherries.

 Uses less fat, sugar or salt. Includes Nutrition Facts.

- 1 jar (10 ounces) maraschino cherries with stems
- 1 package (16 ounces) angel food cake mix
- 2/3 cup semisweet chocolate chips
- 1-1/2 cups cold fat-free milk
- 1 package (1.4 ounces) sugar-free instant chocolate pudding mix
- 1 carton (8 ounces) frozen reduced-fat whipped topping, thawed

1. Drain cherries, reserving juice; set cherries aside. Add enough cold water to juice to measure 1-1/4 cups. In a mixing bowl, beat cake mix and juice on low speed until moistened. Beat on medium for 1 minute. Gently spoon into an ungreased 10-in. tube pan. Cut through batter with a knife to remove air pockets.

2. Bake on the lowest oven rack at 350° for 40-50 minutes or until dark golden brown and cracks feel very dry. Immediately invert pan onto a wire rack; cool completely, about 1 hour. Run a knife around sides of cake and remove from pan.

3. In a microwave or heavy saucepan, melt chocolate chips; stir until smooth. Pat cherries dry with paper towels. Holding cherries by the stem, dip in chocolate and place on waxed paper. Refrigerate until set.

4. In a bowl, whisk milk and pudding mix until thickened, about 2 minutes. Let stand for 15 minutes; whisk for 1 minute or until smooth. Fold in whipped topping. Slice cake; serve with mousse and dipped cherries. **Yield:** 12 servings.

Nutrition Facts: 1 slice equals 280 calories, 5 g fat (4 g saturated fat), 1 mg cholesterol, 392 mg sodium, 54 g carbohydrate, 1 g fiber, 5 g protein.

Chocolate Orange Cupcakes

Prep: 15 min. **Bake:** 20 min. + cooling

Shirley Brazel, Coos Bay, Oregon

Chocolate and orange are perfect together in these cakes. To give them a moist brownie-like texture, I add mayonnaise.

- 1-1/2 cups all-purpose flour
- 1/2 cup sugar
- 1/4 cup baking cocoa
- 1 teaspoon baking soda
- 1/4 teaspoon salt
- 1/2 cup mayonnaise
- 1 teaspoon grated orange peel
- 1 teaspoon vanilla extract
- 1/2 cup orange juice
- 1/2 cup semisweet chocolate chips
- Confectioners' sugar

1. In a bowl, combine the flour, sugar, cocoa, baking soda and salt. In another bowl, combine the mayonnaise, orange peel and vanilla; gradually add orange juice until blended. Stir into dry ingredients just until combined. Stir in chocolate chips (batter will be thick).

2. Fill paper-lined muffin cups two-thirds full. Bake at 350° for 18-23 minutes or until a toothpick comes out clean. Cool for 10 minutes before removing from pan to a wire rack to cool completely. Dust with confectioners' sugar. **Yield:** 9 cupcakes.

Editor's Note: Reduced-fat or fat-free mayonnaise may not be substituted for regular mayonnaise in this recipe.

🎀🎀🎀
Triple-Layer Banana Cake

(Also pictured on page 188)

Prep: 20 min. **Bake:** 25 min. + cooling

Patty Roberts, Athens, Ohio

A family favorite, the recipe for this memorable cake was passed on to me by my mom. I like to add a crunchy peanut garnish.

        3/4 cup butter, softened
          2 cups sugar
          3 eggs
    1-1/2 cups mashed ripe bananas (about 3 medium)
    1-1/2 teaspoons vanilla extract
          3 cups all-purpose flour
    1-1/2 teaspoons baking powder
    1-1/2 teaspoons baking soda
        3/4 teaspoon salt
          1 cup buttermilk
FROSTING:
          6 tablespoons peanut butter
          3 tablespoons butter, softened
    5-1/4 cups confectioners' sugar
          8 to 10 tablespoons milk
Peanut halves, optional

1. In a large mixing bowl, cream butter and sugar until light and fluffy. Add eggs, one at a time, beating well after each addition. Beat in bananas and vanilla. Combine the flour, baking powder, baking soda and salt; add to creamed mixture alternately with buttermilk.

2. Pour into three greased and floured 9-in. round baking pans. Bake at 350° for 25-30 minutes or until a toothpick inserted near the center comes out clean. Cool for 10 minutes before removing from pans to wire racks to cool completely.

3. For frosting, in a large mixing bowl, beat the peanut butter and butter until smooth. Beat in confectioners' sugar and enough milk to achieve spreading consistency. Frost between layers and over top and sides of cake. Garnish with peanuts if desired. **Yield:** 14 servings.

🎀🎀🎀
Pumpkin Angel Food Cake

Prep: 15 min. **Bake:** 40 min. + cooling

Pamela Overton, Charleston, Illinois

Here's an easy way to dress up an angel food cake mix using canned pumpkin, nutmeg and other spices.

✓ Uses less fat, sugar or salt. Includes Nutrition Facts and Diabetic Exchanges.

          1 cup canned pumpkin
          1 teaspoon vanilla extract
        1/2 teaspoon ground cinnamon
        1/2 teaspoon ground nutmeg
        1/4 teaspoon ground cloves
        1/8 teaspoon ground ginger
          1 package (16 ounces) angel food cake mix
         14 tablespoons reduced-fat whipped topping
Additional ground cinnamon, optional

1. In a large bowl, combine pumpkin, vanilla, cinnamon, nutmeg, cloves and ginger. Prepare cake mix according to package directions. Fold a fourth of the batter into pumpkin mixture; gently fold in remaining batter. Gently spoon into an ungreased 10-in. tube pan. Cut through batter with a knife to remove air pockets.

2. Bake on the lowest oven rack at 350° for 38-44 minutes or until top is golden brown and cake springs back when lightly touched. Immediately invert pan; cool completely, about 1 hour. Run a knife around side and center tube of pan. Remove cake to a serving plate. Garnish each slice of cake with 1 tablespoon whipped topping; sprinkle with cinnamon if desired. **Yield:** 14 servings.

Nutrition Facts: 1 slice equals 151 calories, 1 g fat (1 g saturated fat), 0 cholesterol, 264 mg sodium, 33 g carbohydrate, 1 g fiber, 3 g protein. **Diabetic Exchange:** 2 starch.

🎀🎀🎀 Hawaiian Cream Pie

Prep: 20 min. **Bake:** 15 min.

Jane Wilsdorf, Holliday, Missouri

When it comes to pie, my favorite is coconut cream, but my husband prefers banana cream. This recipe pleases us both!

- 2/3 cup sugar
- 1/4 cup cornstarch
- 1/2 teaspoon salt
- 2 cups milk
- 3 egg yolks, lightly beaten
- 2 tablespoons butter
- 1 teaspoon vanilla extract
- 1/2 cup crushed pineapple, drained
- 1/4 cup flaked coconut
- 1 to 2 large firm bananas, sliced
- 1 pastry shell (9 inches), baked

MERINGUE:

- 3 egg whites
- 1/4 teaspoon cream of tartar
- 6 tablespoons sugar
- 1/4 cup flaked coconut

1. In a saucepan, combine the sugar, cornstarch and salt. Stir in milk until smooth. Cook and stir over medium-high heat for 2 minutes or until thickened and bubbly. Reduce heat; cook and stir 2 minutes longer. Remove from the heat. Stir a small amount of hot filling into egg yolks; return all to pan, stirring constantly. Bring to a gentle boil; cook and stir 2 minutes more. Remove from the heat; stir in butter and vanilla. Fold in pineapple and coconut. Place sliced bananas into pastry shell; set aside.

2. In a mixing bowl, beat egg whites and cream of tartar on medium speed until soft peaks form. Gradually beat in sugar, 1 tablespoon at a time, on high until stiff glossy peaks form and sugar is dissolved. Pour hot filling over bananas. Spread meringue evenly over hot filling, sealing edges to crust. Sprinkle with coconut.

3. Bake at 350° for 15 minutes or until the meringue is golden. Cool on a wire rack for 1 hour. Refrigerate for at least 3 hours before serving. Store leftovers in the refrigerator. **Yield:** 6-8 servings.

🎀🎀🎀 Strawberry Banana Pie

Prep: 45 min. + freezing

Bernice Janowski, Stevens Point, Wisconsin

With its sugar-cone crust and layers of bananas and strawberry ice cream, this is a winner—especially in summer.

- 1 package (5-1/4 ounces) ice cream sugar cones, crushed
- 1/4 cup ground pecans
- 1/3 cup butter, melted
- 2 cups vanilla ice cream, softened
- 2 medium ripe bananas, mashed
- 2 large firm bananas, cut into 1/4-inch slices
- 2 cups strawberry ice cream, softened
- 1 pint fresh strawberries
- 1 carton (8 ounces) frozen whipped topping, thawed

1. In a bowl, combine crushed ice cream cones, pecans and butter. Press onto bottom and up sides of a greased 10-in. pie plate. Refrigerate 30 minutes.

2. In a bowl, combine vanilla ice cream and mashed bananas. Spread over the crust; cover and freeze for 30 minutes. Arrange sliced bananas over ice cream; cover and freeze for 30 minutes. Top with strawberry ice cream; cover and freeze for about 45 minutes.

3. Hull and halve strawberries; place around edge of pie. Mound or pipe whipped topping in center of pie. Cover and freeze for up to 1 month. Remove from freezer 30 minutes before serving. **Yield:** 8-10 servings.

Cream-Filled Pumpkin Cupcakes

Prep: 35 min. **Bake:** 20 min. + cooling

Ali Johnson, Petersburg, Pennsylvania

Here's a deliciously different use for pumpkin. Bursting with flavor, these sweet and spicy cupcakes are bound to dazzle your family in fall or any time of year.

- 4 eggs
- 2 cups sugar
- 3/4 cup vegetable oil
- 1 can (15 ounces) solid-pack pumpkin
- 2 cups all-purpose flour
- 2 teaspoons baking soda
- 1 teaspoon salt
- 1 teaspoon baking powder
- 1 teaspoon ground cinnamon

FILLING:
- 1 tablespoon cornstarch
- 1 cup milk
- 1/2 cup shortening
- 1/4 cup butter, softened
- 2 cups confectioners' sugar
- 1/2 teaspoon vanilla extract, optional

1. In a mixing bowl, combine the eggs, sugar, oil and pumpkin. Combine the flour, baking soda, salt, baking powder and cinnamon; add to pumpkin mixture and beat until well mixed.

2. Fill paper-lined muffin cups two-thirds full. Bake at 350° for 18-22 minutes or until a toothpick comes out clean. Cool cupcakes for 10 minutes before removing from pans to wire racks to cool completely.

3. For filling, combine cornstarch and milk in a small saucepan until smooth. Bring to a boil, stirring constantly. Remove from the heat; cool to room temperature.

4. In a mixing bowl, cream shortening, butter and confectioners' sugar. Beat in vanilla if desired. Gradually add the cornstarch mixture, beating until light and fluffy.

5. Using a sharp knife, cut a 1-in. circle 1 in. deep in the top of each cupcake. Carefully remove tops and set aside. Spoon or pipe filling into cupcakes. Replace tops. **Yield:** about 1-3/4 dozen.

1-1/2 cups all-purpose flour
1/2 cup baking cocoa
1-1/4 teaspoons baking soda
1 teaspoon salt
FROSTING:
2/3 cup butter-flavored shortening
2/3 cup butter, softened
1 cup sugar
1 can (5 ounces) evaporated milk
1 tablespoon water
1/2 teaspoon vanilla extract
2 cups confectioners' sugar

1. In a mixing bowl, beat eggs, sugar, buttermilk, oil and vanilla until blended. Combine the flour, cocoa, baking soda and salt; gradually add to egg mixture.

2. Fill paper-lined muffin cups two-thirds full. Bake at 350° for 20-22 minutes or until a toothpick comes out clean. Cool for 10 minutes before removing from pans to wire racks to cool completely.

3. For frosting, in a large mixing bowl, cream the shortening, butter and sugar. Stir in the milk, water and vanilla. Gradually beat in confectioners' sugar.

4. Cut a small hole in the corner of a pastry or resealable plastic bag; insert a small star tip. Fill bag with frosting. Push tip 1 in. into center of cupcake and fill with frosting just until tip of cake begins to crack. Pipe frosting in a spiral pattern over the top, beginning near the edge of the cupcake. **Yield:** 1-1/2 dozen.

Heavenly Surprise Cupcakes

Prep: 20 min. Bake: 20 min. + cooling

Judie Heiderscheit, Holy Cross, Iowa

The recipe for these filled and frosted cupcakes was handed down by my mother-in-law. They truly are heavenly!

2 eggs
1-1/4 cups sugar
1 cup buttermilk
2/3 cup vegetable oil
1 teaspoon vanilla extract

Walnut Carrot Cake

Prep: 15 min. Bake: 50 min. + cooling

Darlene Brenden, Salem, Oregon

This carrot cake is wonderfully moist and flavorful. It also has a nice texture and cuts beautifully for serving to guests.

1 cup butter, softened
1-2/3 cups sugar
4 eggs
1 teaspoon vanilla extract
1 teaspoon grated lemon peel
2-1/2 cups all-purpose flour
1 package (3.4 ounces) instant lemon pudding mix
1-1/2 teaspoons baking powder
1 teaspoon *each* baking soda and ground cinnamon
1/2 teaspoon salt
1 cup (8 ounces) plain yogurt
2-1/2 cups grated carrots
3/4 cup chopped walnuts
1 can (16 ounces) cream cheese frosting

1. In a large mixing bowl, cream butter and sugar. Add eggs, one at a time, beating well after each addition. Beat in the vanilla and lemon peel. Combine the flour,

pudding mix, baking powder, baking soda, cinnamon and salt; add to creamed mixture alternately with yogurt. Stir in carrots and nuts.

2. Transfer to a greased and floured 10-in. fluted tube pan. Bake at 350° for 50-55 minutes or until a toothpick inserted near the center comes out clean. Cool for 10 minutes before removing from pan to a wire rack. Cool completely before frosting. Store in the refrigerator. **Yield:** 12-16 servings.

Lemon Cherry Cake

Prep: 20 min. **Bake:** 30 min. + cooling

Janice Greenhalgh, Florence, Kentucky

Our family loves cherries, so this is always a hit. The cherries and lemon peel give the yellow cake distinctive flavor.

- 1-1/2 cups coarsely chopped fresh *or* frozen pitted sweet cherries
- 3/4 cup butter, softened
- 1-3/4 cups sugar
- 3 eggs
- 2 teaspoons grated lemon peel
- 1-1/2 teaspoons vanilla extract
- 2-1/2 cups all-purpose flour
- 2-1/2 teaspoons baking powder
- 1/2 teaspoon salt
- 1-1/4 cups milk

TOPPING:
- 1 package (8 ounces) cream cheese, softened
- 2 tablespoons lemon juice
- 2 teaspoons grated lemon peel
- 3-1/2 to 4 cups confectioners' sugar

1. Pat cherries dry with paper towels; set aside. In a large mixing bowl, cream butter and sugar until light and fluffy. Add eggs, one at a time, beating well after each addition. Beat in lemon peel and vanilla. Combine the flour, baking powder and salt; add to creamed mixture alternately with milk.

2. Pour into a greased 13-in. x 9-in. x 2-in. baking pan. Sprinkle with cherries. Bake at 375° for 30-35 minutes or until a toothpick inserted near the center comes out clean. Cool on a wire rack.

3. For topping, in a mixing bowl, beat cream cheese, lemon juice and peel until smooth. Beat in enough confectioners' sugar until mixture achieves desired consistency. Cut cake; top each piece with a dollop of topping. **Yield:** 12-15 servings.

Chocolate-Coconut Angel Cupcakes

Prep: 20 min. + standing **Bake:** 30 min. + cooling

Bernice Janowski, Stevens Point, Wisconsin

These lower-in-fat cupcakes don't taste light at all, and the meringue-like tops make them delightfully different.

☑ Uses less fat, sugar or salt. Includes Nutrition Facts and Diabetic Exchanges.

- 6 egg whites
- 1-1/3 cups sugar, *divided*
- 2/3 cup all-purpose flour
- 1/4 cup baking cocoa
- 1/2 teaspoon baking powder
- 1 teaspoon almond extract
- 1/2 teaspoon cream of tartar
- 1/4 teaspoon salt
- 1 cup flaked coconut

1. Place egg whites in a large mixing bowl; let stand at room temperature for 30 minutes. Combine 1 cup sugar, flour, cocoa and baking powder. Sift together twice; set aside.

2. Add the almond extract, cream of tartar and salt to egg whites; beat on medium speed until soft peaks form. Gradually add the remaining sugar, about 2 ta-

blespoons at a time, beating on high until stiff glossy peaks form. Gradually fold in cocoa mixture, about 1/2 cup at a time. Gently fold in coconut.

3. Fill paper-lined muffin cups two-thirds full. Bake at 350° for 30-35 minutes or until golden brown and top appears dry. Cool for 10 minutes before removing from pans to wire racks. **Yield:** 1-1/2 dozen.

Nutrition Facts: 1 cupcake equals 103 calories, 2 g fat (1 g saturated fat), 0 cholesterol, 68 mg sodium, 21 g carbohydrate, 1 g fiber, 2 g protein. **Diabetic Exchange:** 1-1/2 starch.

Chocolate Berry Parfaits, p. 210

Sweet Potato Cobbler, p. 224

Rich Truffle Wedges, p. 219

Just Desserts

Just try to resist delectable delights such as Apple Dumpling Dessert, White Chocolate Mousse and Homemade Ice Cream Sandwiches. You'll want to prepare these taste-tempting treats again and again!

Strawberry Cheesecake Ice Cream, p. 221

This creamy dessert is easy to make for weekday dinners, yet pretty enough for company. Instant chocolate pudding is layered with a mixture of pureed strawberries and whipped cream to create the yummy parfaits.

- 2 cups cold milk
- 1 package (3.9 ounces) instant chocolate pudding mix
- 1 package (10 ounces) frozen sweetened strawberries, thawed
- 1 cup heavy whipping cream
- 1/4 cup confectioners' sugar
- Sliced fresh strawberries, optional

1. In a mixing bowl, beat milk and pudding mix until thick and smooth, about 2 minutes; set aside. Drain strawberries (discard the juice or save for another use); place berries in a blender. Cover and process until smooth; set aside.

2. In a mixing bowl, beat the heavy whipping cream and sugar until stiff peaks form. Gently fold in the strawberry puree. Divide half of the chocolate pudding among four or six parfait glasses or bowls. Top with half of the strawberry mixture. Repeat the layers. Garnish each parfait with a fresh strawberry slice if desired. **Yield:** 4-6 servings.

🎗 🎗 🎗
Chocolate Berry Parfaits

(Also pictured on page 208)
Prep/Total Time: 15 min.

Lynn McAllister, Mt. Ulla, North Carolina

🎗 🎗 🎗
Warm Apple Topping

Prep/Total Time: 30 min.

Sharon Manton, Harrisburg, Pennsylvania

My husband and I love preparing entire meals on the grill, to the surprise and delight of our guests. We created this unique grilled dessert for my mother, who can't eat most grain products. She was thrilled with the sweet and nutty apple topping spooned over vanilla ice cream.

- 3 medium tart apples, peeled
- 1/3 cup raisins
- 1 tablespoon lemon juice
- 1/3 cup packed brown sugar
- 1/4 teaspoon ground cinnamon
- 1/4 teaspoon ground cloves
- 1/8 teaspoon salt
- 1/8 teaspoon ground nutmeg
- 2 tablespoons cold butter
- 1/3 cup finely chopped walnuts
- Vanilla ice cream

1. Cut each apple into 16 wedges; place all on an 18-in. square piece of heavy-duty foil. Sprinkle with raisins; drizzle with lemon juice. In a bowl, combine the brown sugar, cinnamon, cloves, salt and nutmeg; cut in the butter. Stir in the walnuts. Sprinkle over apples and raisins.

2. Fold foil around apple mixture and seal tightly. Grill over indirect medium heat for 18-22 minutes or until apples are tender. Serve over ice cream. **Yield:** 3 cups.

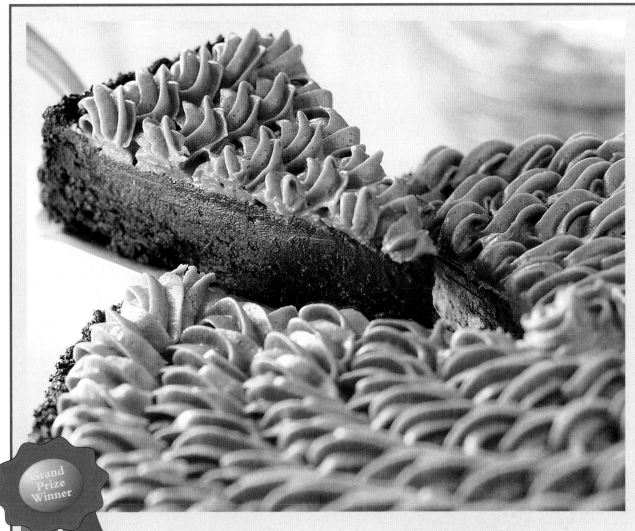

Chocolate Velvet Dessert

(Also pictured on front cover)

Prep: 20 min. + chilling
Bake: 45 min. + cooling

Molly Seidel, Edgewood, New Mexico

This creamy concoction is the result of several attempts to duplicate a dessert I enjoyed on vacation.

1-1/2 cups chocolate wafer crumbs
   2 tablespoons sugar
  1/4 cup butter, melted
   2 cups (12 ounces) semisweet chocolate
     chips
   6 egg yolks
1-3/4 cups heavy whipping cream
   1 teaspoon vanilla extract
CHOCOLATE BUTTERCREAM FROSTING:
  1/2 cup butter, softened
   3 cups confectioners' sugar
   3 tablespoons baking cocoa
   3 to 4 tablespoons milk

1. In a small bowl, combine wafer crumbs and sugar; stir in butter. Press onto the bottom and 1-1/2 in. up the sides of a greased 9-in. springform pan. Place on a baking sheet. Bake at 350° for 10 minutes. Cool on a wire rack.

2. In a microwave, melt chocolate chips; stir until smooth. Cool. In a small mixing bowl, combine egg yolks, cream and vanilla. Gradually stir a third of the cream mixture into melted chocolate until blended. Fold in remaining cream mixture just until blended. Pour into crust.

3. Place pan on a baking sheet. Bake at 350° for 45-50 minutes or until center is almost set. Cool on a wire rack for 10 minutes. Carefully run a knife around edge of pan to loosen; cool 1 hour longer. Refrigerate overnight.

4. In a small mixing bowl, combine frosting ingredients. Using a large star tip, pipe frosting on dessert. Refrigerate leftovers. **Yield:** 12-16 servings.

🎀🎀🎀
Apple Dumpling Dessert

Prep: 30 min. **Bake:** 35 min.

Janet Weaver, Wooster, Ohio

My husband loves apple dumplings, but they take so long to prepare. So one of our daughters created a quick-to-fix variation with a nice bonus—no bites of dry crust without filling because it's all mixed throughout!

PASTRY:
- 4 **cups all-purpose flour**
- 2 **teaspoons salt**

- 1-1/3 **cups shortening**
- 8 to 9 **tablespoons cold water**

FILLING:
- 8 **cups chopped peeled tart apples**
- 1/4 **cup sugar**
- 3/4 **teaspoon ground cinnamon**

SYRUP:
- 2 **cups water**
- 1 **cup packed brown sugar**

Whipped topping *or* **vanilla ice cream, optional**
Mint leaves, optional

1. In a bowl, combine flour and salt; cut in shortening until the mixture resembles coarse crumbs. Sprinkle with water, 1 tablespoon at a time, and toss with a fork until dough can be formed into a ball. Divide dough into four parts.

2. On a lightly floured surface, roll one part to fit the bottom of an ungreased 13-in. x 9-in. x 2-in. baking dish. Place in dish; top with a third of the apples. Combine sugar and cinnamon; sprinkle a third over apples.

3. Repeat layers of pastry, apples and cinnamon-sugar twice. Roll out remaining dough to fit top of dish and place on top. Using a sharp knife, cut 2-in. slits through all layers at once.

4. For syrup, bring water and sugar to a boil. Cook and stir until sugar is dissolved. Pour over top crust. Bake at 400° for 35-40 minutes or until browned and bubbly. Serve warm with whipped topping or ice cream if desired. Garnish with mint if desired. **Yield:** 12 servings.

🎀🎀🎀
White Chocolate Mousse

Prep/Total Time: 30 min.

Susan Herbert, Aurora, Illinois

This elegant, fluffy dessert is a feast for both the eyes and the palate. Almost any fresh fruit may be used, so the mousse can grace special meals throughout the year. Plus, the recipe is easy to double if you're hosting a larger group.

- 1 **cup heavy whipping cream**
- 2 **tablespoons sugar**
- 1 **package (3 ounces) cream cheese, softened**
- 3 **squares (1 ounce** *each***) white baking chocolate, melted and cooled**
- 2 **cups blueberries, raspberries** *or* **strawberries**

Additional berries, optional

1. In a mixing bowl, beat cream until it begins to thicken. Gradually add sugar, beating until stiff peaks form; set aside.

2. In another mixing bowl, beat cream cheese until fluffy. Add chocolate and beat until smooth. Fold in whipped cream. Alternate layers of mousse and berries in parfait glasses, ending with mousse. Garnish with additional berries if desired. Serve immediately or refrigerate for up to 3 hours. **Yield:** 4-6 servings.

❧❧❧
Chocolate Mint Torte

Prep: 35 min. + freezing

Joni Mehl, Grand Rapids, Michigan

For this frozen treat, I melt chocolate mint candies and mix them into the filling. A sprinkling of extra candies adds fun.

27 cream-filled chocolate sandwich cookies, crushed
1/3 cup butter, melted
 4 ounces chocolate-covered peppermint candies
1/4 cup milk
 1 jar (7 ounces) marshmallow creme
 2 cups heavy whipping cream, whipped
Additional whipped cream and chocolate-covered peppermint patties

1. In a small bowl, combine cookie crumbs and butter. Press onto the bottom and 1-1/2 in. up the sides of a greased 9-in. springform pan. Chill for at least 30 minutes.

2. In a small saucepan, heat candies and milk over low heat until candy is melted; stir until smooth. Cool for 10-15 minutes. Place marshmallow creme in a large mixing bowl; gradually beat in mint mixture. Fold in whipped cream. Transfer to prepared crust. Cover and freeze until firm. May be frozen for up to 2 months.

3. Remove from the freezer about 30 minutes before serving. Remove sides of pan. Garnish with additional whipped cream and candies. **Yield:** 12 servings.

❧❧❧
Lemon Lime Dessert

Prep: 20 min. **Cook:** 10 min. + freezing

Marsha Schindler, Fort Wayne, Indiana

Topped with a smooth lemon sauce, this make-ahead delight offers a wonderfully refreshing blend of citrus flavors.

1-1/2 cups graham cracker crumbs
  14 tablespoons butter, melted, *divided*
1-1/4 cups sugar, *divided*
 1/2 gallon vanilla ice cream, softened
   1 quart lime sherbet, softened
   2 eggs, lightly beaten
 1/4 cup lemon juice

1. In a large bowl, combine the cracker crumbs, 7 tablespoons butter and 1/4 cup sugar. Press into an ungreased 13-in. x 9-in. x 2-in. dish; freeze until firm. In a large mixing bowl, combine ice cream and sherbet; pour over the crust. Freeze until firm.

2. In a heavy saucepan, combine eggs and remaining sugar. Stir in lemon juice and remaining butter. Cook and stir until mixture reaches 160° and coats the back of a metal spoon. Cover and refrigerate until cool.

3. Spread over ice cream mixture. Cover and freeze for 3 hours or overnight. May be frozen for up to 2 months. Just before serving, remove from the freezer and cut into squares. **Yield:** 12-15 servings.

A Light Touch

Lemon Lime Dessert and other recipes in this book call for eggs that are lightly beaten. To lightly beat eggs, simply beat them using a fork until the yolks and whites are combined.

🎗🎗🎗

Honey Pecan Cheesecake

Prep: 20 min. + chilling **Bake:** 40 min. + chilling

Tish Frish, Hampden, Maine

Birthdays and holidays are great times for cheesecake, and Thanksgiving's the perfect occasion for this particular one. In our annual church bake-off, it won first place.

      1 cup crushed vanilla wafers (about 22 wafers)
  1/4 cup ground pecans
      2 tablespoons sugar
      5 tablespoons butter, melted
FILLING:
      3 packages (8 ounces *each*) cream cheese, softened
  3/4 cup packed dark brown sugar
      3 eggs, lightly beaten
      2 tablespoons all-purpose flour
      1 tablespoon maple flavoring
      1 teaspoon vanilla extract
  1/2 cup chopped pecans
TOPPING:
  1/4 cup honey
      1 tablespoon butter

      1 tablespoon water
  1/2 cup chopped pecans

1. In a small bowl, combine the wafer crumbs, pecans and sugar; stir in butter. Press onto the bottom of a greased 9-in. springform pan. Refrigerate.

2. In a large mixing bowl, beat the cream cheese and sugar until smooth. Add the eggs; beat on low speed just until combined. Add the flour, maple flavoring and vanilla extract; beat until blended. Stir in the pecans. Pour into the crust. Place the pan on a double-thickness of heavy-duty foil (about 16 in. x 16 in.). Securely wrap the foil around the pan.

3. Place in a large baking pan. Fill larger pan with hot water to a depth of 1 in. Bake at 350° for 40-45 minutes or until center is just set. Cool on a wire rack for 10 minutes. Remove foil. Carefully run a knife around edge of pan to loosen; cool 1 hour longer. Refrigerate overnight.

4. For topping, combine the honey, butter and water in a small saucepan; cook and stir over medium heat for 2 minutes. Add nuts; cook 2 minutes longer (mixture will be thin). Spoon over cheesecake. Carefully remove sides of pan before serving. Refrigerate leftovers. **Yield:** 12 servings.

⚜ ⚜ ⚜
Strawberry Swirls

Prep: 20 min. **Bake:** 40 min.

Paula Steele, Obion, Tennessee

My mother-in-law's apple cobbler was the inspiration for my strawberry variation. We consider it our special spring treat.

2 cups sugar
2 cups water
1/2 cup butter, melted
1/2 cup shortening
1-1/2 cups self-rising flour
1/2 cup milk
2 cups finely chopped fresh strawberries, drained
Whipped cream, optional

1. In a saucepan, combine sugar and water; cook and stir over medium heat until sugar is dissolved. Remove from the heat; allow to cool. Pour butter into a 13-in. x 9-in. x 2-in. baking dish; set aside.

2. In a bowl, cut shortening into flour until mixture resembles coarse crumbs. Stir in milk until moistened. Turn onto a lightly floured surface; knead until smooth, about 8-10 times. Roll into a 12-in. x 8-in. rectangle; sprinkle with the strawberries. Roll up jelly-roll style, starting with a long side; seal the seam. Cut into 12 slices. Place with cut side down over butter. Carefully pour syrup around rolls.

3. Bake at 350° for 40-45 minutes or until golden brown and edges are bubbly. Serve warm with whipped cream if desired. **Yield:** 12 servings.

Editor's Note: As a substitute for 1-1/2 cups self-rising flour, place 2-1/4 teaspoons baking powder and 3/4 teaspoon salt in a measuring cup. Add all-purpose flour to measure 1 cup. Combine with an additional 1/2 cup all-purpose flour.

⚜ ⚜ ⚜
Apricot Cheese Kugel

Prep: 15 min. **Bake:** 45 min.

Florence Palermo, Melrose Park, Illinois

This sweet noodle kugel is a fun dessert and a super addition to any brunch buffet. My family and friends scrape the pan clean. I got the recipe from my sister years ago.

1 package (16 ounces) wide egg noodles
1 package (8 ounces) cream cheese, softened
1 cup butter, softened
1-1/2 cups sugar
1/2 cup lemon juice
12 eggs
1 jar (18 ounces) apricot preserves
1/2 teaspoon ground cinnamon, *divided*

1. Cook noodles according to package directions. Meanwhile, in a mixing bowl, beat cream cheese, butter and sugar until smooth; add lemon juice and mix well. Beat in eggs, one at a time. Drain and rinse noodles; add to egg mixture.

2. Spoon half into an ungreased 13-in. x 9-in. x 2-in.

baking dish. Top with half of the preserves; sprinkle with half of the cinnamon. Repeat layers.

3. Bake, uncovered, at 325° for 45 minutes or until golden brown and a knife inserted near the center comes out clean. Serve warm. **Yield:** 12-16 servings.

✿✿✿
Cherry Crunch Ice Cream
Prep: 25 min. + chilling **Freeze:** 4 hours

Dorothy Koshinski, Decatur, Illinois

I received this wonderful recipe many years ago from a friend. The custard-style ice cream has a mild cherry flavor with a fun oat crunch. You're sure to crave a second scoop!

> 6 eggs
> 2 cups sugar
> 2 cups milk
> 1 package (3.4 ounces) instant vanilla pudding mix
> 4 cups heavy whipping cream
> 1 teaspoon vanilla extract

Dash salt

> 1 cup old-fashioned oats
> 1/2 cup all-purpose flour
> 1/2 cup packed brown sugar
> 1/2 teaspoon ground cinnamon
> 1/3 cup cold butter
> 1 can (21 ounces) cherry pie filling

1. In a large saucepan, whisk eggs, sugar and milk until combined. Cook and stir over low heat until mixture reaches 160° and coats the back of a metal spoon. Remove from the heat; cool. Beat in the pudding mix, cream, vanilla and salt. Cover and refrigerate for 8 hours or overnight.

2. In a bowl, combine the oats, flour, brown sugar and cinnamon. Cut in butter until the mixture resembles coarse crumbs. Spread in an ungreased 15-in. x 10-in. x 1-in. baking pan. Bake at 350° for 10-15 minutes or until golden brown. Cool on a wire rack.

3. Stir pie filling into cream mixture. Fill cylinder of ice cream freezer two-thirds full; freeze according to manufacturer's directions. Refrigerate remaining mixture until ready to freeze.

4. After removing from ice cream freezer, stir a portion of oat mixture into each batch. Transfer to a freezer container. Cover and freeze for at least 4 hours before serving. **Yield:** 2-1/2 quarts.

✿✿✿
Banana Sundae Sauce
Prep/Total Time: 10 min.

Kathy Rairigh, Milford, Indiana

This luscious banana-based topping makes vanilla ice cream extra special. Both kids and adults enjoy it.

> 1/2 cup butter
> 1-1/2 cups confectioners' sugar
> 1 tablespoon water
> 1 teaspoon lemon juice
> 1 teaspoon vanilla extract
> 1/4 teaspoon ground cinnamon
> 2 cups sliced firm bananas (about 2 large)

Vanilla ice cream

1. In a small saucepan, melt the butter. Whisk in the confectioners' sugar, water and lemon juice until smooth. Cook over medium-low heat for 3-5 minutes, stirring occasionally.

2. Remove the sauce from the heat; stir in the vanilla and cinnamon. Fold in the bananas. Serve the sauce warm over ice cream. **Yield:** 2 cups.

✿✿✿
Very Berry Melba

Prep: 20 min. + chilling **Cook:** 10 min. + cooling

Gloria Woudenberg, Atlanta, Michigan

My sister gave me this yummy dessert recipe when we lived in southern Michigan, which has many blueberry farms.

  1/2 gallon vanilla ice cream, softened
  1/4 cup orange juice concentrate
1-1/2 to 2 teaspoons ground cinnamon
    3 cups fresh *or* frozen blueberries
    2 cups fresh *or* frozen raspberries
    1 tablespoon lemon juice
  1/2 cup sugar
    2 tablespoons cornstarch

1. In a bowl, combine ice cream, orange juice concentrate and cinnamon. Cover and freeze for 2-3 hours or until firm.

2. Meanwhile, combine berries and lemon juice in a saucepan; cover and cook over low heat for 10 minutes, stirring occasionally. Combine sugar and cornstarch; stir into pan. Bring to a boil over medium heat; boil for 2 minutes, stirring constantly. Remove from the heat. Cool; cover and refrigerate.

3. To serve, spoon ice cream into a bowl or parfait glass; top with the berry sauce. **Yield:** 8-10 servings.

✿✿✿
Rhubarb Crumble

Prep: 45 min. **Bake:** 30 min.

Amy Freeman, Cave Creek, Arizona

When I first made this crumble, my husband enjoyed it but thought it needed a custard sauce. We found a terrific sauce recipe from England, and the two are perfect together.

    8 cups chopped fresh *or* frozen rhubarb
1-1/4 cups sugar, *divided*
2-1/2 cups all-purpose flour
  1/4 cup packed brown sugar
  1/4 cup quick-cooking oats
    1 cup cold butter
CUSTARD SAUCE:
    6 egg yolks
  1/2 cup sugar
    2 cups heavy whipping cream
1-1/4 teaspoons vanilla extract

1. In a saucepan, combine rhubarb and 3/4 cup sugar. Cover and cook over medium heat, stirring occasionally, until the rhubarb is tender, about 10 minutes. Pour into a greased 13-in. x 9-in. x 2-in. baking dish. In a bowl, combine flour, brown sugar, oats and remaining sugar. Cut in butter until crumbly; sprinkle over rhubarb. Bake at 400° for 30 minutes.

2. Meanwhile, in a saucepan, whisk the egg yolks and sugar; stir in cream. Cook and stir over low heat until a thermometer reads 160° and mixture thickens, about 15-20 minutes. Remove from the heat; stir in vanilla. Serve warm over rhubarb crumble. **Yield:** 12 servings (2-1/2 cups sauce).

Editor's Note: If using frozen rhubarb, measure rhubarb while still frozen, then thaw completely. Drain in a colander, but do not press liquid out.

🎀🎀🎀
Angel Berry Trifle

Prep/Total Time: 15 min.

Brenda Paine, Clinton Township, Michigan

I usually fix this with fresh berries, but I've also made it with frozen cherries and light cherry pie filling.

☑ Uses less fat, sugar or salt. Includes Nutrition Facts and Diabetic Exchanges.

1-1/2 cups cold fat-free milk
    1 package (1 ounce) sugar-free instant vanilla pudding mix
    1 cup (8 ounces) fat-free vanilla yogurt
    6 ounces reduced-fat cream cheese, cubed
1/2 cup reduced-fat sour cream
    2 teaspoons vanilla extract
    1 carton (12 ounces) frozen reduced-fat whipped topping, thawed, *divided*
    1 prepared angel food cake (18 inches), cut into 1-inch cubes
    1 pint *each* blackberries, raspberries and blueberries

1. In a small bowl, whisk the milk and pudding mix for 2 minutes or until thickened. In a mixing bowl, beat the yogurt, cream cheese, sour cream and vanilla until smooth. Fold in pudding mixture and 1 cup whipped topping.

2. Place a third of cake cubes in a 4-qt. trifle bowl. Top with a third of pudding mixture, a third of berries and half of remaining whipped topping. Repeat layers once. Top with remaining cake, pudding and berries. Serve immediately or refrigerate. **Yield:** 14 servings.

Nutrition Facts: 3/4 cup equals 209 calories, 6 g fat (5 g saturated fat), 10 mg cholesterol, 330 mg sodium, 32 g carbohydrate, 3 g fiber, 5 g protein. **Diabetic Exchanges:** 1 starch, 1 fat, 1/2 fruit, 1/2 reduced-fat milk.

🎀🎀🎀
Strawberry Ice Cream

Prep: 20 min. + chilling **Freeze:** 30 min.

Leone Mayne, Frostproof, Florida

Our state produces a lot of strawberries, and they are so good in recipes such as this pretty homemade ice cream.

    2 eggs
    2 cups milk
1-1/4 cups sugar
    1 cup miniature marshmallows
    2 cups pureed unsweetened strawberries
    1 cup half-and-half cream
1/2 cup heavy whipping cream
    1 teaspoon vanilla extract

1. In a large heavy saucepan, combine eggs and milk; stir in sugar. Cook and stir over medium-low heat until mixture is thick enough to coat a metal spoon and a thermometer reads at least 160°, about 14 minutes. Remove from the heat; stir in the marshmallows until melted.

2. Set saucepan in ice and stir the mixture for 5-10 minutes or until cool. Stir in the remaining ingredients. Cover and refrigerate overnight. When ready to freeze, pour into the cylinder of an ice cream freezer and freeze according to manufacturer's directions. **Yield:** about 2 quarts.

Rich Truffle Wedges

(Also pictured on page 208)

Prep: 30 min. + cooling

Bake: 25 min. + cooling

Patricia Vatta, Norwood, Ontario

I've served this decadent dessert numerous times, to the delight of guests and family members. It has a fudgy consistency and big chocolate taste. The tart raspberry sauce looks beautiful spooned over each slice.

- 1/2 cup butter
- 6 squares (1 ounce *each*) semisweet chocolate, chopped
- 3 eggs
- 2/3 cup sugar
- 1 teaspoon vanilla extract
- 1/4 teaspoon salt
- 2/3 cup all-purpose flour

GLAZE:
- 1/4 cup butter
- 2 squares (1 ounce *each*) semisweet chocolate
- 2 squares (1 ounce *each*) unsweetened chocolate
- 2 teaspoons honey

SAUCE:
- 2 cups fresh *or* frozen unsweetened raspberries
- 2 tablespoons sugar

Whipped cream, fresh raspberries and mint, optional

1. In a microwave or double boiler, melt butter and chocolate; stir until smooth. Cool for 10 minutes. In a mixing bowl, beat eggs, sugar, vanilla and salt until thickened, about 4 minutes. Blend in chocolate mixture. Stir in flour; mix well.

2. Pour into a greased and floured 9-in. springform pan. Bake at 350° for 25-30 minutes or until a toothpick inserted near the center comes out clean. Cool completely on a wire rack.

3. Combine the glaze ingredients in a small saucepan; cook and stir over low heat until melted and smooth. Cool slightly. Run a knife around the edge of springform pan to loosen; remove cake to serving plate. Spread glaze over the top and sides; set aside.

4. Puree berries in a blender or food processor. Press through a sieve if desired; discard seeds. Stir in sugar; chill until serving. Spoon sauce over individual servings. Garnish with whipped cream, berries and mint if desired. **Yield:** 12 servings.

🎗🎗🎗
Lemon Icebox Dessert

Prep: 40 min. + chilling **Bake:** 20 min. + cooling

Corene Thorsen, Oconomowoc, Wisconsin

This dessert has a light lemon flavor with a tender, flaky crust. It's perfect for serving during the warm summer months.

- 1-1/2 cups all-purpose flour
- 4-1/2 teaspoons sugar
- 3/4 cup cold butter

FILLING:

- 8 eggs, *separated*
- 2 cups sugar, *divided*
- 2/3 cup lemon juice
- 3 tablespoons grated lemon peel
- 1 tablespoon unflavored gelatin
- 1/2 cup plus 2 tablespoons cold water, *divided*
- 1/2 teaspoon cream of tartar

TOPPING:

- 1 cup heavy whipping cream
- 1 tablespoon confectioners' sugar
- 1 cup flaked coconut
- 1 tablespoon grated orange peel

1. In a small bowl, combine the flour and sugar. Cut in butter until crumbly. Press into a greased 13-in. x 9-in. x 2-in. baking dish. Bake at 350° for 18-22 minutes or until lightly browned. Cool on a wire rack.

2. For the filling, in a large heavy saucepan, combine the egg yolks, 1 cup sugar, lemon juice and peel. Sprinkle the gelatin over 1/2 cup cold water; let stand for 1 minute. Add to the egg yolk mixture. Cook and stir over medium heat until the mixture reaches 160° and coats the back of a metal spoon. Remove from the heat; cool completely.

3. In another large saucepan, combine egg whites, cream of tartar, and remaining sugar and water. Cook over low heat, beating with a hand mixer on low speed until mixture reaches 160°. Pour into a large mixing bowl; beat on high until soft peaks form. Gently fold into yolk mixture. Spread over crust.

4. For topping, in a small mixing bowl, beat the cream and confectioners' sugar until soft peaks form; spread over filling. Combine coconut and orange peel; sprinkle over top. Cover and chill for 4 hours or overnight. Refrigerate leftovers. **Yield:** 12-16 servings.

🎗🎗🎗
Grape Ice

Prep: 15 min. + freezing

Sharron Kemp, High Point, North Carolina

When I was growing up, this slushy dessert was a popular request at our house. Mom stirred it up in no time with grape juice concentrate and just three other basic ingredients.

- 3-1/2 cups water
- 3/4 cup sugar
- 1 can (12 ounces) frozen grape juice concentrate, thawed
- 1 tablespoon lemon juice

1. In a microwave-safe bowl, combine water and sugar. Cover and microwave on high for 30-90 seconds; stir until sugar is dissolved.

2. Stir in the grape juice concentrate and lemon juice. Pour the mixture into a 1-1/2-qt. freezer container. Cover and freeze for at least 12 hours, stirring several times. May be frozen for up to 3 months. Just before serving, break apart with a large spoon. **Yield:** 6 servings.

Editor's Note: This recipe was tested in a 1,100-watt microwave.

🎀🎀🎀
Cran-Orange Ribbon Dessert

Prep: 30 min. **Bake:** 10 min. + freezing

Deborah Bills, Paducah, Kentucky

I dress up vanilla ice cream with cream cheese and orange juice concentrate before spreading it over a quick homemade crust. The ribbon of cranberry sauce adds a touch of elegance.

- **1-2/3 cups graham cracker crumbs**
- **1/4 cup ground pecans**
- **3 tablespoons sugar**
- **6 tablespoons butter, melted**
- **1 package (8 ounces) cream cheese, softened**
- **1/2 gallon vanilla ice cream**
- **1 can (12 ounces) frozen orange juice concentrate, thawed**
- **1 can (16 ounces) whole-berry cranberry sauce**
- **1/2 teaspoon almond extract**

1. In a bowl, combine the cracker crumbs, pecans and sugar. Add butter; mix well. Press into a greased 13-in. x 9-in. x 2-in. baking dish. Bake at 350° for 8-10 minutes or until set. Cool on a wire rack.

2. In a large mixing bowl, beat cream cheese until smooth. Add ice cream; mix well. Gradually beat in orange juice concentrate; spread half over crust. Cover and freeze for 1 hour. Refrigerate remaining ice cream mixture.

3. In a food processor or blender, process the cranberry sauce and almond extract until blended; spread half over ice cream layer. Cover and freeze for at least 30 minutes. Spread with the remaining ice cream mixture and cranberry mixture. Cover and freeze until firm. May be frozen for up to 2 months. Remove from the freezer about 30 minutes before serving. **Yield:** 12-15 servings.

🎀🎀🎀
Strawberry Cheesecake Ice Cream

(Also pictured on page 209)

Prep: 10 min. **Freeze:** 30 min.

Karen Maubach, Fairbury, Illinois

Paging through an old cookbook, I found the recipe for this refreshing dessert. Made with reduced-fat and fat-free ingredients, it's lighter than other ice creams but still satisfies.

✓ Uses less fat, sugar or salt. Includes Nutrition Facts and Diabetic Exchanges.

- **3 cups sliced fresh strawberries**
- **6 ounces reduced-fat cream cheese**
- **2 cans (12 ounces *each*) fat-free evaporated milk**
- **1 can (14 ounces) fat-free sweetened condensed milk**
- **1 teaspoon vanilla extract**
- **1 cup reduced-fat whipped topping**

1. Place strawberries in a blender or food processor; cover and process until smooth. In a large mixing bowl, beat cream cheese until smooth. Add evaporated milk and condensed milk, vanilla and pureed strawberries; mix well. Fold in whipped topping.

2. Fill cylinder of ice cream freezer two-thirds full; freeze according to manufacturer's directions. Refrigerate remaining mixture until ready to freeze. Allow to ripen in ice cream freezer or firm up in your refrigerator freezer for 2-4 hours before serving. **Yield:** 2 quarts.

Nutrition Facts: 3/4 cup equals 234 calories, 4 g fat (3 g saturated fat), 15 mg cholesterol, 171 mg sodium, 38 g carbohydrate, 1 g fiber, 11 g protein. **Diabetic Exchanges:** 1-1/2 fruit, 1 fat-free milk, 1 fat.

❀ ❀ ❀
White Chocolate
Cherry Parfaits

Prep: 40 min. + chilling

Rita Sherman, Coleville, California

Layers of silky white chocolate mousse and sweet cherry sauce with a hint of orange alternate in this delectable dessert. I use a pastry bag to pipe the mousse into pretty dishes handed down from my husband's grandmother.

❀ ❀ ❀
Tropical Bananas

Prep/Total Time: 10 min.

Kathleen Jones, Chicago, Illinois

Lime juice and lime peel give a refreshing twist to this exotic-tasting dessert that's quick, nutritious and delicious. I like to serve it as a midday snack, too.

- 2 medium firm bananas, sliced
- 1 tablespoon lime juice
- 2 tablespoons salted peanuts
- 1 tablespoon honey
- 1 tablespoon flaked coconut
- 1-1/2 teaspoons grated lime peel

In a small bowl, toss bananas with lime juice. Add peanuts and honey; mix well. Spoon into individual dishes. Sprinkle with coconut and lime peel. Serve immediately. **Yield:** 2 servings.

- 1/2 cup sugar
- 2 tablespoons cornstarch
- 1/2 cup water
- 2 cups fresh *or* frozen pitted tart cherries
- 1/2 teaspoon orange extract

WHITE CHOCOLATE MOUSSE:
- 3 tablespoons sugar
- 1 teaspoon cornstarch
- 1/2 cup milk
- 2 egg yolks, lightly beaten
- 4 squares (1 ounce *each*) white baking chocolate, chopped
- 1/2 teaspoon vanilla extract
- 1-1/2 cups heavy whipping cream, whipped

1. In a small saucepan, combine sugar and cornstarch; stir in water until smooth. Add cherries. Bring to a boil over medium heat; cook and stir for 2 minutes or until thickened. Remove from the heat; stir in extract. Refrigerate until chilled.

2. In another saucepan, combine the sugar and cornstarch; stir in milk until smooth. Bring to a boil over medium heat. Reduce heat; cook and stir for 2 minutes. Remove from heat. Whisk a small amount of hot filling into egg yolks; return all to the pan, whisking constantly. Bring to a gentle boil; cook and stir for 2 minutes.

3. Remove from the heat. Stir in chocolate and vanilla until chocolate is melted. Cool to room temperature. Fold in whipped cream.

4. Spoon 1/4 cup mousse into each parfait glass. Top with a rounded 1/4 cup of cherry mixture. Repeat layers. Refrigerate until chilled. **Yield:** 6 servings.

Macadamia Berry Dessert

Prep: 30 min. + freezing

Louise Watkins, Sparta, Wisconsin

My family and friends just love this dessert. The crunchy nut crust and colorful filling make it special enough for guests. During the holidays, I substitute a can of whole-berry cranberry sauce for the raspberries.

1 cup crushed vanilla wafers (about 32 wafers)
1/2 cup finely chopped macadamia nuts
1/4 cup butter, melted
1 can (14 ounces) sweetened condensed milk
3 tablespoons orange juice
3 tablespoons lemon juice
1 package (10 ounces) frozen sweetened raspberries, thawed
1 carton (8 ounces) frozen whipped topping, thawed
Fresh raspberries and additional whipped topping, optional

1. Combine the wafer crumbs, nuts and butter. Press onto the bottom of a greased 9-in. springform pan. Bake at 375° for 8-10 minutes or until golden brown. Cool completely.

2. In a mixing bowl, beat the milk, orange juice and lemon juice on low speed until well blended. Add raspberries; beat on low until blended. Fold in whipped topping. Pour over crust. Cover and freeze for 3 hours or until firm. May be frozen for up to 3 months.

3. Remove from the freezer 15 minutes before serving. Carefully run a knife around edge of pan to loosen. Remove sides of pan. Garnish with raspberries and whipped topping if desired. **Yield:** 12 servings.

🎗🎗🎗
Sweet Potato Cobbler

(Also pictured on page 208)

Prep: 30 min. **Bake:** 30 min.

Sherry Parker, Jacksonville, Alabama

My grandmother used to make sweet potato cobbler but didn't use a recipe. I tried many before I discovered this one.

        2 pounds sweet potatoes, peeled and sliced
          1/4 inch thick
  3-1/2 cups water
  1-1/2 cups sugar
        3 tablespoons all-purpose flour
      1/2 teaspoon ground cinnamon
      1/4 teaspoon ground nutmeg
      1/4 teaspoon salt
      3/4 cup butter, cubed
PASTRY:
        2 cups all-purpose flour
      1/2 teaspoon salt
      2/3 cup shortening
        5 to 6 tablespoons cold water
        2 tablespoons butter, melted
        4 teaspoons sugar
Whipped cream, optional

1. In a saucepan, cook the sweet potatoes in water until crisp-tender, about 10 minutes. Drain, reserving 1-1/2 cups cooking liquid. Layer potatoes in a greased 13-in. x 9-in. x 2-in. baking dish; add reserved liquid. Combine sugar, flour, cinnamon, nutmeg and salt; sprinkle over potatoes. Dot with butter.

2. For pastry, combine flour and salt; cut in shortening until mixture resembles coarse crumbs. Gradually add water, tossing with a fork until a ball forms. On a floured surface, roll pastry into a 13-in. x 9-in. rectangle. Place over filling; cut slits in top. Brush with butter; sprinkle with sugar.

3. Bake at 400° for 30-35 minutes or until top is golden brown. Spoon into dishes; top with whipped cream if desired. **Yield:** 10-12 servings.

🎗🎗🎗
Peanut Butter Banana Pudding

Prep/Total Time: 20 min.

Laura McGinnis, Colorado Springs, Colorado

If there's anything I like better than bananas, it's bananas paired with peanut butter. With that favorite combination in mind, I came up with this extra-special pudding. The graham cracker crumbs add a pleasant crunch.

        4 cups milk
        1 package (3 ounces) vanilla cook-and-serve
          pudding mix
        1 package (3-1/2 ounces) butterscotch
          cook-and-serve pudding mix
  1-1/2 cups peanut butter, *divided*
        1 cup graham cracker crumbs
        1 cup confectioners' sugar
        4 medium firm bananas, sliced

1. In a large saucepan, combine milk and pudding mixes until blended. Bring to a boil over medium heat, stirring constantly. Remove from the heat; stir in 1/2 cup peanut butter until blended. Cover and refrigerate until chilled.

2. Meanwhile, in a small bowl, combine the graham cracker crumbs and confectioners' sugar; cut in the remaining peanut butter until crumbly. In individual dessert bowls, layer half of the pudding, half of the crumb mixture and half of the bananas. Repeat layers. **Yield:** 12 servings.

Three-Fruit Frozen Yogurt

Prep: 15 min. + freezing

Wendy Hilton, Laurel, Mississippi

I received this super-easy recipe for frozen yogurt from a friend. It takes just minutes to combine the bananas, strawberries and pineapple with a few other ingredients before popping everything into the freezer. I love being able to enjoy a big scoop of this homemade treat whenever I want.

    2 medium ripe bananas
    1 package (10 ounces) frozen sweetened sliced
      strawberries, thawed and drained
    1 can (8 ounces) crushed pineapple, drained
    1 carton (6 ounces) strawberry yogurt
1/2 cup sugar
    1 carton (8 ounces) frozen whipped topping,
      thawed

In a large bowl, mash the bananas and strawberries. Stir in the drained pineapple, strawberry yogurt and sugar. Fold in the whipped topping. Cover and freezer until firm. Yogurt may be frozen for up to 1 month. **Yield:** 1-1/2 quarts.

Strawberry Rhubarb Sauce

Prep/Total Time: 30 min.

Mary Pittman, Shawnee, Kansas

This tongue-tingling, versatile sauce can bring a sunny new taste to everything from plain pound cake to ice cream and bread pudding. As a busy mom, I don't have time for long, complicated recipes, and this one fits my lifestyle.

2-1/2 cups chopped fresh *or* frozen rhubarb
         (1-inch pieces)
    1 cup water
    1/2 cup sugar
      2 tablespoons grated lemon peel
    1/4 teaspoon salt
      1 cup sliced fresh *or* frozen unsweetened
        strawberries
      2 tablespoons lemon juice
    1/4 teaspoon ground cinnamon
      3 to 4 drops red food coloring, optional
Pound *or* angel food cake

1. In a saucepan, combine rhubarb, water, sugar, lemon peel and salt; bring to a boil. Reduce heat. Cook, uncovered, over medium heat until rhubarb is soft, about 10-15 minutes.

2. Remove from the heat and let stand for 5 minutes. Stir in the strawberries, lemon juice and cinnamon. Add the food coloring if desired. Cool. Serve over cake. **Yield:** 3 cups.

Editor's Note: If using frozen rhubarb, measure rhubarb while still frozen, then thaw completely. Drain in a colander, but do not press liquid out.

🎀🎀🎀
Tart Cherry Meringue Dessert
Prep: 25 min. **Bake:** 25 min. + chilling

Kathryn Dawley, Gray, Maine

I've been whipping up this sweet-tart cherry dessert for years to serve at baby showers, birthday parties and other special events. People really enjoy the tender crust, ruby-red cherry filling and melt-in-your-mouth meringue.

> 2 cups all-purpose flour
> 1 teaspoon salt
> 1 cup shortening
> 1 egg

FILLING:
> 1 can (14-1/2 ounces) pitted tart cherries
> 3 eggs, *separated*
> 1-1/2 cups sugar, *divided*
> 3 tablespoons quick-cooking tapioca
> 2 teaspoons lemon juice
> 6 to 8 drops red food coloring, optional
> 1 teaspoon vanilla extract
> 1/4 teaspoon cream of tartar
> 3/4 cup finely chopped almonds

1. In a small bowl, combine the flour and salt. Cut in the shortening until the mixture resembles coarse crumbs. Add the egg; mix well. Press onto the bottom and up the sides of a greased 11-in. x 7-in. x 2-in. baking dish. Bake at 375° for 20-22 minutes or until lightly browned.

2. Drain cherries, reserving juice; set cherries aside. Add enough water to juice to measure 1 cup. In a saucepan, combine egg yolks, 3/4 cup sugar, tapioca and cherry juice mixture. Let stand for 5 minutes. Bring to a boil over medium heat, stirring constantly; cook and stir for 2 minutes or until thickened. Stir in the cherries, lemon juice and food coloring if desired. Pour into crust.

3. In a small mixing bowl, beat egg whites, vanilla and cream of tartar on medium speed until soft peaks form. Gradually add remaining sugar, beating on high until stiff peaks form. Fold in nuts. Spread evenly over hot filling, sealing edges to crust.

4. Bake at 350° for 22-25 minutes or until meringue is golden brown. Cool on a wire rack for 1 hour; refrigerate for at least 3 hours before serving. Store in the refrigerator. **Yield:** 9 servings.

1 package (18-1/4 ounces) chocolate cake mix
1/4 cup shortening
1/4 cup butter, softened
1 egg
1 tablespoon water
1 teaspoon vanilla extract
1/2 gallon ice cream

1. In a mixing bowl, combine the chocolate cake mix, shortening, butter, egg, water and vanilla extract; beat until well blended. Divide into four equal parts. Between waxed paper, roll one part into a 10-in. x 6-in. rectangle.

2. Remove one piece of waxed paper and flip the dough onto an ungreased baking sheet. Score the dough into eight pieces, each 3-in. x 2-1/2-in. Repeat with the remaining dough. Bake at 350° for 8-10 minutes or until puffed. Immediately cut along the scored lines and prick holes in each piece with a fork; cool on baking sheets.

3. Cut the ice cream into 16 slices, each 3-in. x 2-1/2-in. x 1-in. Place the ice cream between two chocolate cookies; wrap in plastic wrap. Freeze on a baking sheet overnight. Store in an airtight container. **Yield:** 16 servings.

Editor's Note: Purchase a rectangle-shaped package of ice cream in the flavor of your choice for the easiest cutting.

🎖 🎖 🎖
Homemade Ice Cream Sandwiches

Prep: 25 min. + freezing **Bake:** 10 min. + cooling

Kea Fisher, Bridger, Montana

I inherited my love of cooking from my mother. She's a former home economics teacher and gave me this great recipe.

🎖 🎖 🎖
Coffee Ice Cream Torte

Prep: 20 min. + freezing

Janet Hutts, Gainesville, Georgia

Not only does this make-ahead dessert go over big with company, it calls for only four ingredients. But your guests will never guess that fact when they see the fancy-looking toffee garnish and the pretty ladyfingers along the sides.

2 packages (3 ounces *each*) ladyfingers
1 cup chocolate-covered English toffee bits or 4 Heath candy bars (1.4 ounces *each*), crushed, *divided*
1/2 gallon coffee ice cream, softened
1 carton (8 ounces) frozen whipped topping, thawed

1. Place ladyfingers around the edge of a 9-in. springform pan. Line the bottom of the pan with remaining ladyfingers. Stir 1/2 cup toffee bits into the ice cream; spoon into prepared pan. Cover with plastic wrap; freeze overnight or until firm. May be frozen for up to 2 months.

2. Just before serving, remove sides of pan. Garnish with the whipped topping and remaining toffee bits. **Yield:** 16 servings.

Simple Substitution

If you'd like to make Coffee Ice Cream Torte but can't find the coffee-flavored ice cream at your store, just dissolve instant coffee granules in warm water and stir it into vanilla ice cream.

General Recipe Index

This handy index lists every recipe by food category, major ingredient and/or cooking method, so you can easily locate recipes to suit your needs.

✓ Recipe includes Nutrition Facts and Diabetic Exchanges

Alphabetical Index

*This handy index lists every recipe in alphabetical order,
so you can easily find your favorite recipes.*

✓ Recipe includes Nutrition Facts and Diabetic Exchanges